People Who Shaped History

ISBN 1 84084 448 5

First published in 1999 by
Dempsey Parr
Queen Street House
4 Queen Street
Bath
BA1 1HE

Produced for Dempsey Parr by
Foundry Design & Production a part of
The Foundry Creative Media Company Ltd
Crabtree Hall, Crabtree Lane
Fulham, London, SW6 6TY

A copy of the CIP data for this book is available from the British Library.

People Who Shaped History

A • Dempsey • Parr
MICROPEDIA

Introduction

SINCE THE BEGINNING OF HISTORY mankind has affected the shape and direction of civilisation in a thousand different ways. Sometimes this has been a struggle against nature, adapting outside elements to improve quality of life; sometimes it has been a struggle against other groups of individuals that has given rise to such change. Individuals and groups of people have formulated ideas – some that have proved beneficial, some that have been ultimately destructive. Nearly all these ideas have had a profound effect on the world in which we live today, proving that smallest idea from a single person can cause a tidal wave of consequence. The world has been shaped, and often irrevocably changed, by one person, from the Prophet Muhammad to Christopher Columbus. It seems strange, now, for example, that for many centuries mankind believed the Earth was flat. It was not until the fifteenth century, when explorers struck out to discover new lands and wealth, that this theory was disproved.

While the great leaders – kings, queens, emperors,

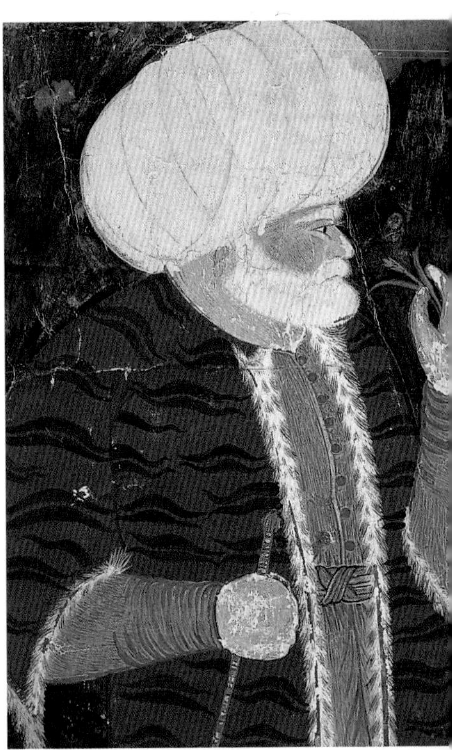

Suleiman the Magnificent. ▶

generals – should not be omitted from a book such as this, it is also important to investigate the contribution made by people from other areas of society and culture; it is not only the rich and powerful who have shaped the world. Characters from all walks of life have made an impact: musicians, artists, entertainers, scientists, philosophers, sportsmen – the list is endless.

Some people have had their five minutes of glory and then passed into the obscurity that comes with progress, overshadowed by new discoveries, greater inventions. Their contribution – good or bad – should not be overlooked; sometimes the seeds of one idea form the roots of another, and so on. In the field of science, in particular, this holds true. Occasionally people have stumbled across fame accidentally, expressing a thought, or making a discovery that has proved fundamental to future development. More frequently fame is the result of years of patient experimentation, great self-belief and determination. Many of these people have become icons in their own fields – from Julius Caesar and Joan of Arc to Isambard Brunel, Marilyn Monroe, Andy

Julius Caesar. ▲

Warhol and Neil Armstrong.

The twentieth century, in particular, has seen incredible advances in many areas of life, culture and society. The two World Wars alone proved to be catalysts for scientific and technological discovery and invention, as the need for new methods of surgery, improved medicines, more powerful weapons, became paramount. Culturally, the two wars saw inexorable changes the world over. The position of women in society was never to be the same after the First World War, when they were forced to take on the roles of men far from home, and the rise of suffragism and campaigns for women's rights saw women taking centre stage. As well as this, the wars created the inevitable heroes of their respective generations: great military leaders, strategists, writers and poets all have these events to thank for their place in the annals of history. On the flipside, the wars also brought to the fore some of the most notorious figures in history, guilty of many transgressions of basic human rights: Hitler and his 'Final Solution', Stalin's Fascist regime in Russia, Mussolini's Evil Empire in Italy or Pol Pot's Khmer Rouge regime.

Malcolm Little.▶

On the edge of a new millennium, we take for granted the product of the ideas of many individuals. But where would we be without electricity, airtravel, anaesthetics, computers? What would the world be like if Elvis Presley had never sung or if the genius of Shakespeare had never been discovered? Shaping the world, however, is not just an arena in which the well-intentioned play their parts. Fame comes in many forms, including notoriety. Here, then, is a history of people from every corner of the globe, who have truly shaped our world: the good, the great, the infamous; those who had a fleeting glimpse of fame, and those whose effect still echoes through the centuries.

Leon Trotsky. ▲

How To Use This Book

The entries in this Micropedia are organised alphabetically by surname for ease of reference. Names in **bold** indicate that a person has their own entry in the book for cross-referencing. Each entry is marked with a thematic icon that categorises the person, allowing easy access to people who have gained fame in similar fields. A number of people who have had a particularly significant impact in their fields have been selected as key figures and are marked.

ARCHITECTURE
ARMY
ART
BUSINESS
CAUSE
ENTERTAINMENT
LEADER
MEDIA
MUSIC
POLITICS
RELIGION
SCIENCE
SPORT
PHILOSOPHY
TRAVEL
LITERATURE

ABRAHAM

The great prophet Abraham was born in the ancient city of Ur in Mesopotamia, one of the earliest cities in the world. His original name was Abram. God appeared to him on several occasions, promising him and his people the land of Canaan. According to tradition, when he and his wife Sarah were 100, she gave birth to Isaac. Abraham was later called by God to sacrifice Isaac and was preparing to do so when angels intervened. Muslims believe that he built the Kaabah in Mecca for the worship of the One God.

ADAM, JOHN

Federalist John Adams (1735–1826) was the second president of the USA, holding office 1796–1800.

ADAMS, JOHN QUINCY

John Quincy Adams (1767–1848) was the sixth president of the USA, holding office 1824–28.

ADLER, ALFRED

A student of **Sigmund Freud**, and part of his inner circle in Vienna, Adler (1870–1937) rejected Freud's exclusive emphasis upon sexuality as our unconscious motivator, and stressed instead the will to power and the inferiority complexes that occurred when this was obstructed. These are explored in *The Neurotic Constitution* (1912).

ADLER, FELIX

Felix Adler (1851–1933) was a German-born American educator and founder of the ethical culture movement. He pioneered in education, advocating progressive education, free kindergartens and vocational training.

Sigmund Freud, teacher to Alfred Adler. ◀

ADRIAN IV

Adrian IV (1154–59) was the only Englishman to hold the office of Pope. The granting of sovereignty over Ireland to Henry II is attributed to him.

AESCHYLUS

Aeschylus (*c.* 525–465 BC), the founder of Greek tragedy with Euripides and Sophocles, wrote some 90 plays (499–458 BC) of which seven survive, including the *Orestia* trilogy (485 BC).

AGAMEMNON

The city of Mycenae was the home of King Agamemnon, the commander-in-chief of the Greek expedition against Troy, as described in **Homer**'s *Iliad*.

AHMOSE I

When King Ahmose I (r. 1539–14 BC) established the New Kingdom in Egypt, he realised that he needed a large standing army to ensure that the country would be adequately protected at all times. He created two vast armies, one to protect the Delta and one to garrison the south of the country. For the first time, strategy and tactics became an established part of warfare.

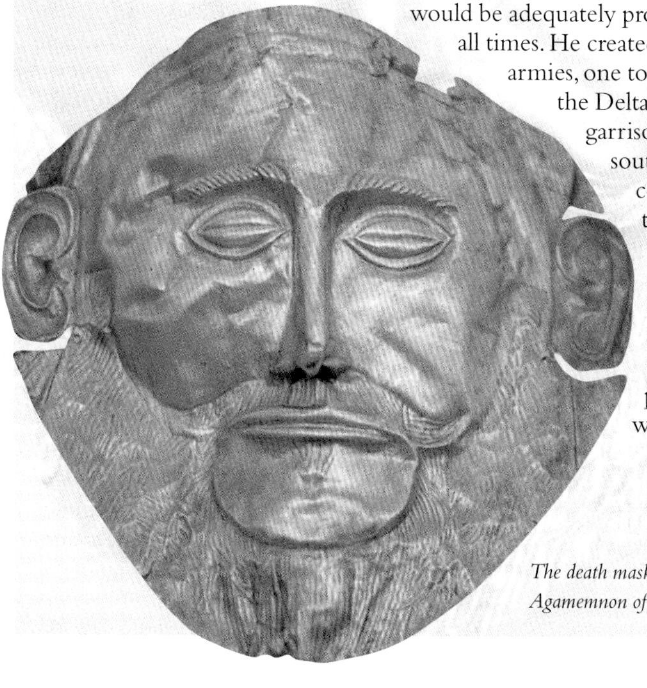

The death mask of King Agamemnon of Mycenae. ◀

The Lindisfarne Gospels, from Aiden's Holy Island. ▲

AIDEN

Aidan came from Iona and set up a monastery on the island of Lindisfarne in northern England. He travelled widely, often with King Oswald, who was happy to act as his interpreter. Fervent and enthusiastic, he was rarely in his monastery, but this fusion of church and state ceased when Oswald was killed in battle in AD 642. Aidan died in 651 and his monastery continued under Cuthbert (AD 634–687).

AKBAR

Akbar (1542–1605) was the greatest Mogul emperor, who ruled from 1556. His firm and wise leadership led to his being given the title 'Guardian of Mankind'.

AKHENATEN

Akhenaten was king of Egypt in the middle of the fourteenth century BC. He was entirely absorbed in religion and changed his court from the worship of Amen to that of Aten. He even changed his own name from Amenhotep. The changes were opposed by the entire priesthood of Amen. Akhenaten was so preoccupied with his religious changes that he took no action to defend the empire. As a result all the provinces conquered in Asia over the previous 200 years were lost.

ALBERT, PRINCE

Albert (1819–61), a German cousin of **Queen Victoria**, was a big influence on British political life. At first he was resented among the political establishment, but he proved to be a profound influence on Victoria. He rid the queen of her anti-Tory feelings and was also influential in the formulation of British foreign policy. His death from typhoid in 1861 provoked a distraught Queen Victoria to mourning and seclusion for a period of 10 years.

Prince Albert. ▼

ALCOCK, J. W.

The English aviator, J. W. Alcock (1892–1919), was the pilot of the first non-stop flight across the Atlantic Ocean. Alcock had already gained fame as a First World War flying ace. In June 1919 he and his navigator, Lt Arthur Whidden Brown, made their historic Newfoundland-to-Ireland transatlantic flight – a crossing of 16 hours 27 minutes – in a Vickers-Vimy biplane bomber. The plane landed nose-down in Ireland, but both men were unhurt and were later knighted for their accomplishment.

ALCUIN

Alcuin (*c.* AD 735–796) travelled widely and especially impressed Emperor **Charlemagne**, who appointed him to run his Palace School in Aachen. Later Alcuin became Abbot of Tours. His influence on the development of Christian liturgy has been enormous. He was the dominant intellectual of late eighth-century Europe. 'My name was Alcuin, and wisdom was always dear to me' is his epitaph.

ALEN, WILLIAM VAN

In complete contrast to contemporary socialist projects being built in Europe, the Chrysler

Building, designed by William van Alen (1888–1954), stands as a monument to capitalism. Very much a product of pre-Depression America, it was a celebration of the success of its client and of the free market. Until the early 1930s, the Chrysler Building was the tallest in the world at 259 m (850 ft).

ALEXANDER THE GREAT

Alexander the Great (356–323 BC) was the son of King **Philip II of Macedon** and succeeded his father in 336 BC. Alexander immediately took up Philip's war of aggression against Persia. He defeated the Persian army under Darius III at Issus. He occupied Syria and Phoenicia, then entered Egypt, where he founded Alexandria. In 331 BC he defeated Darius's grand army at Gaugamela and occupied Babylon, then marched to Susa and Persepolis. Alexander invaded the Punjab in 327 BC. After conquering most of it, he was stopped from pressing on to the Ganges by a mutiny of his soldiers. Alexander died in June 323 BC.

ALEXANDER VI (RODRIGO BORGIA)

Alexander VI (1431–1503) was a Spaniard who bribed his way to the papacy in 1492. In 1493 he used his spiritual authority to divide the world from North to South Poles, between Portugal and Spain, in an attempt to distribute the new colonies and to avoid conflict. Spain received the western hemisphere and Portugal the eastern hemisphere.

Alexander the Great. ▼

Alfred the Great, dividing England into provinces. ◀

ALFRED THE GREAT

Alfred the Great (*c.* AD 849–901) succeeded his brother Ethelred as king of Wessex in AD 871. He defended England against Danish invasion, founded the first English navy, and put into operation a legal code. He encouraged the translation of works from Latin and promoted the development of the *Anglo-Saxon Chronicle*, a history of England from the Roman invasion.

ALI IBN ABI TALIB

Ali (*c.* AD 600–661) was a cousin of the Prophet **Muhammad** and was adopted by him as a child. He married Fatima, the daughter of Muhammad. On the death of the prophet, he was seen by the Shi'ite sect as the rightful successor and he did eventually become the 4th caliph. Shi'ites treat him as the 1st imam. He was murdered in a mosque by opposing Muslims in AD 661.

AMIN, IDI

Ugandan soldier and politician Idi Amin (b. 1925) joined the British (later to become Ugandan) army and rose through the ranks, becoming a colonel in 1964. He was made commander-in-chief of the army and air force, but when relations between them worsened, Amin staged a coup in 1971, dissolving the parliament and establishing a military dictatorship. Amin then proceeded to expel all Ugandan Asians and many Israelis in 1972, seized foreign-owned businesses and estates and ordered the execution of thousands of his opponents, making his bloodthirsty regime notorious worldwide.

AMUNDSEN, ROALD

The 'race' to the South Pole began in 1910, between a Norwegian team led by Roald Amundsen (1872–1928) and a British one led by **Robert Scott**. Using Inuit survival skills, dog sledges and fur clothing, the Norwegians advanced faster than the mixture of horses, dogs and motor-sledges used by Scott. Amundsen took seven weeks to reach the pole in December 1911.

ANNE, QUEEN

It was during the reign of Queen Anne (1702–14) that the Parliaments of England and Scotland merged, in 1707.

Queen Anne. ▲

ANSELM

Anselm (1033–1109) was a true revolutionary and the first great theologian of medieval Europe. His most famous *Cur Deus Homo* was written in exile in 1098, and in this he asks 'why did God become man?' and answers 'because it was necessary'. If God's honour were not satisfied then man's soul would be left to the devils. Only by God becoming human and sacrificing himself could mankind be saved. On a more practical level, Anselm believed the pope, as head of the church on earth, had to take precedence over every earthly ruler.

AQUINAS, THOMAS

Thomas Aquinas (1225–74) was the greatest of the Scholastics and his writings remain as the ultimate statement of Catholic theology. His principal contribution was his *Summa Theologiae* in which he argues that the teachings of **Aristotle** were fully in accord with the traditional teachings of the church. Here he argues that knowledge can be obtained both through reason, as Aristotle had done, and through faith in revelation. Revelation comes in two forms, the Scriptures and the natural world. His *Summa contra Gentiles* was an attempt to use reason alone to convince the Arabs of Spain and North Africa of the truth of Christianity.

ARCHIMEDES

The world had one of its great mechanical geniuses in Archimedes (287–212 BC), who devised remarkable weapons to protect his native Syracuse from Roman invasion, and applied his powerful mind to such basic mechanical contrivances as the screw, the pulley and the lever. The Archimedes screw was a machine for raising water and consisted of a circular pipe enclosing a helix and inclined at an angle of about 45 degrees to the horizontal, with its lower end dipped in the water. Rotating the device caused the water to rise in the pipe. He also discovered the principle of water displacement whilst having a bath.

ARISTOPHANES

Comedy has its roots in Greek drama, especially in the farcical satires of Aristophanes (*c.* 448–388 BC), of whose 54 plays only 11 are extant (including *Lysistrata* and *Frogs*).

ARISTOTLE

Aristotle (384–322 BC), one of the greatest Greek thinkers, advocated moderation in behaviour and the use of logic for investigation. Aristotle studied at **Plato**'s Academy from 367 BC, and became a teacher to **Alexander the Great**. Whilst developing many of Plato's ideas he rejected the theory of Forms, arguing that material things were the primary reality and that any properties they had, such as colour or taste, were just aspects or properties of that matter. His thought covered almost every subject, from politics to literature, logic to psychology and ethics to science.

Greek philosopher Aristotle. ▼

Richard Arkwright's spinning-frame. ▶

ARKWRIGHT, RICHARD ✉

Richard Arkwright (1732–92), a British inventor and businessman, created the spinning-frame, which could produce strong cotton thread. These machines could spin not just one thread, as on a hand-powered spinning wheel, but hundreds of threads. The popularity of such machines grew rapidly during the Industrial Revolution.

ARMANI, GIORGIO ✷

When Armani (b. 1934) launched his own label in 1974, he became the biggest-selling European designer ever in the US. Even now, his silhouette seldom changes; this is the secret of his longevity. Seasonally, collections are refined – shoulders may be widened or slimmed, jackets are shown with two buttons or three, trousers are sent out flat-fronted or pleated – but the softness, consummate minimalism and use of high-quality fabrics remain. Other labels include 'Emporio Armani', 'Mani', 'AX', 'Armani Exchange' and 'Giorgio Armani Calze'.

ARMSTRONG, NEIL

One of the greatest missions of the twentieth century was the 'race' to the Moon. On 20 July 1969 the United States beat their rivals, the USSR, when Neil Armstrong (b. 1930) and Edwin Aldrin landed their module on lunar soil. Armstrong was the first man to walk on the Moon, and Aldrin the second. The third member of the party, Michael Collins remained in the shuttle, the *Apollo XI*. After a short time, Armstrong and Aldrin returned to the shuttle and made a successful flight back to Earth, bringing with them soil specimens from the lunar surface.

ARNOLD, MATTHEW

Matthew Arnold (1822–88) believed the 'peace of God' was the Christian phrase for civilisation. In *Culture and Anarchy* (1869), he described London's East End as containing 'these vast, miserable, unmanageable masses of sunken people'. In reality he battled with belief and un-belief and gave up orthodox Christianity as a 'fond but beautiful dream'.

ÁRPÁD

Magyar chieftain Árpád (AD 869–907) led his people to sack and pillage in Moravia, Italy and Germany. They raided as far as Burgundy, which they devastated in AD 955.

Neil Armstrong, the first man to walk on the moon. ◀

ARTHUR, CHESTER A.

Republican Chester A. Arthur (1829–86) was the 21st president of the USA, holding office 1881–84.

ARTHUR, KING

Arthur was a military leader who defeated the Anglo-Saxons in 12 battles during the sixth century. He was fatally wounded in AD 537. His importance, or myth, has endured thanks to historians through the ages. Tenth-century Welsh literature eulogised Arthur. The legend of his court and Round Table emerged in the twelfth century. In 1998 a slate bearing Arthur's name was discovered in Cornwall and hailed as proof of his existence.

King Arthur and the Knights of the Round Table. ▼

ASOKA

Asoka (291–232 BC), the third Mauryan king, was known for his benevolent rule and for making Buddhism the official religion of the kingdom. He established laws based on Buddhist principles and these were carved on pillars throughout India. With his encouragement, Buddhism spread to Sri Lanka, where the simple and formal Theravada tradition took root, and also to Central Asia, where the emphasis was on the more intellectual Mahayana tradition.

ASQUITH, HERBERT

Over £40 billion was spent by the powers to sustain the war effort between 1914–18. Britain spent the second highest amount, £7.8 billion. Despite the propaganda that Britain was at one during the war, this was evidently not the case. No more was this better demonstrated than in government. When the war began Britain was ruled by the Liberal party headed, by Herbert Asquith (1852–1928). But internal factions led to this becoming a coalition government by 1915. By December 1916 Asquith had been replaced by **David Lloyd George**. Asquith differed from other politicians, including Lloyd George

Attila the Hun. ▶

and **Winston Churchill**, about the need for conscription.

ASSAGIOLI, ROBERTO

Dr Roberto Assagioli, founder of Psychosynthesis, was a student of **Freud**. Whilst valuing Freud's insights, he felt that they did not reveal anything about the higher aspirations of the human mind. Through his research at his Centro di Studi di Psicosintesi, in Florence, he developed the idea that people have multiple personalities, some conscious, some unconscious, and that a central goal of therapy is to integrate these and so make a whole and united mind.

ATAHUALPA

Atahualpa (*c.* 1502–33) was the last emperor of the Incas of Peru. He was taken prisoner in 1532 when the Spanish arrived, and agreed to pay a substantial ransom, but he was accused of plotting against the conquistador **Francisco Pizzaro** and was sentenced to be burned. On his consenting to Christian baptism, the sentence was commuted to strangulation.

ATTILA THE HUN

Attila (*c.* AD 406–453), king of the Huns came to power in AD 433 and, after invading the Balkans in 440–447, he crossed the Rhine and faced the Visigoths and Romans at Champagne, where he was defeated. In 451, he invaded northern Italy but was induced to withdraw by Pope Leo I. He died on the night of his marriage to the German Ildico, either by poison or, as **Chaucer** represents it in his *Pardoner's Tale*, from a nasal haemorrhage induced by drunkenness.

AUGUSTINE

Latin Christianity was to come to Britain in the person of Augustine (AD 354–430). On Augustine's arrival he was met by King Ethelbert, who had a Christian wife and some sympathy for the Christian faith. The king was baptised and other conversions followed rapidly. Augustine was made a bishop. Such enthusiasm for the faith may have been encouraged by weariness with the Teutonic gods, but more certainly by a keen interest to link with mainland Europe.

AURANGZEB

Aurangzeb (1618–1707) was the last of the Mogul emperors. He seized power in 1658, when he rebelled against the Emperor Shah Jahan, the builder of the Taj Mahal. Under Aurangzeb the Mogul Empire began to break up. Aurangzeb faced opposition from the Hindu Maratha princes from southern India and from the British, who had arrived in India in the early seventeenth century. When he died in 1707, the Mogul Empire disintegrated.

The castle at Winchester, where Jane Austen is buried. ▼

AUSTEN, JANE

Few novelists can have had quite such an uneventful life as Jane Austen (1775–1817), living with her mother and sisters throughout her relatively short life. Her tomb in Winchester Cathedral includes no mention of her novels, although her genius was recognised before her death. Along with *Pride and Prejudice*, *Emma* is probably her most enduring novel, but it is one in which she deliberately moved away from the comedy of manners to create a dangerously high-spirited heroine, whom she feared nobody would like but herself.

BABAR

Babar (1526–30) established the Mogul Empire in North India in 1526. The Moguls, descendants of Tamberlaine, the fourteenth-century Mongol leader, ruled until dethroned by the British in 1857.

BABBAGE, CHARLES

The idea of mechanically calculating mathematical tables first came to inventor Charles Babbage (1792–1871) in 1812 or 1813. Later he made a small calculator that could perform certain mathematical computations to eight decimals. Then, in 1823, he obtained government support for the design of a machine with a 20-decimal capacity. In the 1830s Babbage developed plans for the so-called analytical engine, the forerunner of the modern digital computer.

The Mogul emperor Babar. ▼

The English monk Roger Bacon. ▲

BACON, FRANCIS

Bacon (1561–1626) is generally seen as one of the founders of modern science. He stated that science should be about the collection and organisation of observed facts, so that general principles could be derived from them. Before him, the tendency was either to indulge in theoretical speculation or simply to describe the world without explaining it.

BACON, ROGER

Roger Bacon (*c.* 1214–94), an English monk, was the first to record the process and composition of gunpowder in 1260, but it would be 50 years before anyone took the concept seriously. Many other discoveries have also been credited to him, including the magnifying lens.

BADEN-POWELL, ROBERT STEPHENSON SMYTH

Sir Robert Stephenson Smyth Baden-Powell, 1st Baron Baden-Powell of Gilwell (1857–1941), was a British general who founded the Boy Scout and Girl Guide (Girl Scout) movements in the UK. The American organisation, Boy Scouts of America, was founded on Baden-Powell's model in 1910. Boys attain rising rank within the organisation through various accomplishments, each of which earns a rank or merit badge.

BAH'U'LL'H

Bah'u'll'h, 'the splendour of God', (1817–92), who was born in Tehran, was the founder of the Baha'i faith. In 1844 he joined the Babi movement – an Islamic

Shi'ite sect led by Hadrat-I A'la, 'the Bab'. In 1863, following revelations in a dungeon in Tehran, he declared that he was the Divine Messenger prophesied by 'the Bab'. His book, the *Kitab-I-Aqdas* ('the most holy book'), is the principal scripture of the faith, but the Scriptures of all the major faiths are used in Baha'i worship. His teachings bring together mysticism and contemporary concerns such as inter-religious harmony, disarmament and world government – concerns that are strongly promoted by the seven million Baha'is throughout the world today.

BAIRD, JOHN LOGIE

In 1926 Scottish electrical engineer, John Logie Baird (1888–1946), demonstrated a mechanical scanner able to convert an image into a series of electronic impulses that could then be reassembled on a viewing screen as a pattern of light and shade. In 1929 the British Broadcasting Company began broadcasting experimental TV programmes using Baird's system.

BALFOUR, LADY EVE

The organic-farming movement, known also as biological, regenerative or sustainable farming, was started by Lady Eve Balfour. Not only a talented jazz trombonist and pilot, Lady Balfour was an assiduous agricultural researcher and in 1944 published *The Living Soil*. Two years later the Soil Association was formed. Organic farming as much as possible excludes the use of synthetically produced fertilisers, pesticides, feed additives and growth regulators.

Lady Eve Balfour was a pioneer of organic farming. ▶

Roger Bannister. ▲

BAN CHAO

In AD 97 a Chinese general named Ban Chao (AD 32–102) reached the shores of the Caspian Sea. He sent a subordinate of his, named Gan Ying, further west, and he reached the Black Sea, where he came into contact with the Roman Empire, which he called Da Qin. This was described as a land of great wealth, but the length of the journey further westwards was too daunting for Gan Ying, and both he and Ban Chao returned to China.

BANNISTER, JOHN

Until 1672, people heard music by going to church or organising their own private performances. That year, however, a violinist named John Bannister, sacked from the King's Musik for misappropriating money, began a series of paid concerts, 'over against the George Tavern in White Friars, near the back of the Temple'. Other concert societies followed, taking the names from the taverns where they played.

BANNISTER, ROGER

Running a mile in under four minutes was a symbolic, but apparently unreachable, goal for athletes, and the world record – set by Gunther Hargg – had been unchallenged for eight years before 1953, when Christopher Chataway ran two miles in a world-record time of 8 minutes 49.6 seconds. Middle-distance runner Roger Bannister (b. 1929) finally passed the magic four-minute mark in 1954 on the Iffley Road running track in Oxford, with a time of 3 minutes 59.4 seconds. His achievement was crucial to the development of British athletics, inspiring the next generation of Olympic athletes.

BARBAROSSA, KHAIRREDEN

By the mid-sixteenth century, Spain had become the dominant European sea power in the Mediterranean, but the western expansion plans were a key part of **Suleiman the Magnificent**'s overall policies. His chief allies in this aim were the Barbary Corsairs, led by Khairreden Barbarossa (d. 1546). They quickly built up a fleet and decisively defeated a Christian force off the Albanian coast in 1538. This meant that the Ottomans had sea supremacy east of Italy. Dragut captured Tripoli in 1559 for the Corsairs, but the massive Turkish attempt to capture Malta in 1565 failed. **Philip II** of Spain had, by this time, massively increased his fleets and after Suleiman died in 1566, the tide began to change in favour of the Christians.

Khairreden Barbarossa. ▼

BARNARD, CHRISTIAAN

South African surgeon Christiaan Barnard (d. 1922) performed the first human heart transplant, on 3 December 1967 in Cape Town. The patient, 54-year-old Louis Washkansky, lived for 18 days. Barnard's success was followed by numerous attempts at other medical centres, with 101 heart transplants undertaken around the world within 12 months. Despite problems with immune rejection and poor survival rates, Barnard continued developing his methods until 50 per cent of patients lived for at least five years after surgery.

BARNARDO, THOMAS ☒

Dr Thomas Barnardo (1845–1905) was a British philanthropist who had, by the time of his death, assumed responsibility for almost 60,000 lives by providing homes for destitute children.

BARNUM, PHINEAS TAYLOR ☻

Phineas Taylor Barnum (1810–91) was a US showman. In 1871 he established the 'Greatest Show on Earth', which included the midget 'Tom Thumb', a circus, a menagerie and an exhibition of 'freaks' conveyed in 100 railway carriages.

BARRIE, J. M.

J. M. Barrie (1860–1937) was the ninth of 10 children of a Scottish hand-loom weaver, and was already a successful playwright when he met the Llewelyn-Davies family in Kensington Gardens. His friendship with their children led to the enormous success of *Peter Pan*, first performed in London in 1904.

BATES, HENRY

Henry Bates (1825–92) was an English naturalist and explorer. He spent 11 years collecting animals

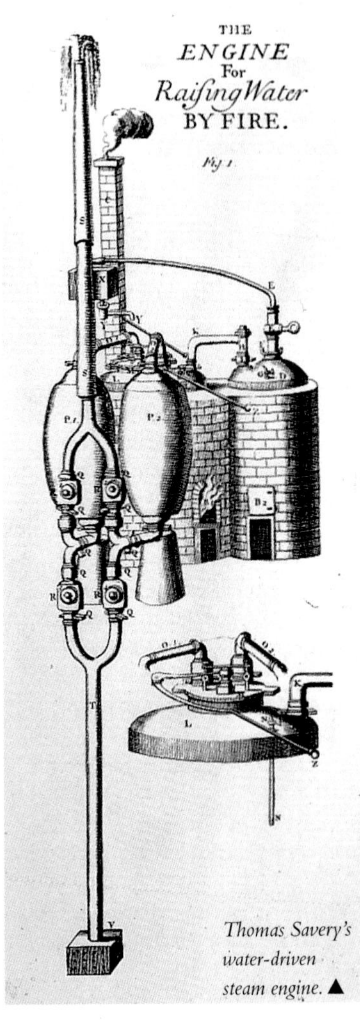

Thomas Savery's water-driven steam engine. ▲

and plants in South America and identified 8,000 new species of insects. He also made a special study of camouflage in animals.

BAUER, GEORG

The German Georg Bauer, or 'Agricola' (1494–1555), investigated mining technology and described diseases that affected miners. Such work had added importance because of the increasing use of coal to replace the wood formerly used for fires. In 1712, **Thomas Newcomen** invented the 'atmospheric engine', designed to pump water from mines and so reduce the danger of flooding, which would otherwise overtake workers underground. He was preceded by Thomas Savery, inventor of the water-driven steam engine in 1696.

BEATON, CECIL

Sir Cecil Beaton (1904–80) was an English photographer, well known for his elegant and sophisticated fashion pictures and society portraits, as well as his wartime photographs of bomb-damaged London. He also worked as a stage and film designer, notably for the musicals *Gigi* (1959) and *My Fair Lady* (1965).

Cecil Beaton's costume designs for My Fair Lady. ▲

BEATRIX

The eldest of four daughters of Queen Juliana and Prince Bernhard Leopold, Beatrix (b. 1938) went into exile with her family when the Germans overran the Netherlands in the Second World War, and she spent the war years in Britain and

Canada. In 1965 her betrothal to German Diplomat Claus von Amsberg caused a furore because of his past membership of the Hitler Youth and German army. They married in 1966 and the hostility dimmed at the birth of Willem-Alexander (1967), the first male heir to the Dutch throne in over a century. Beatrix succeeded to the throne following her mother's abdication in 1980.

BECKER, BORIS

When a 16-year-old German by the name of Boris Becker (b. 1967) entered the 1984 Wimbledon championships, he ended up leaving the tournament in a wheelchair nursing torn ankle ligaments, but he was not to be kept down for long. A year later, Becker rewrote the record books, by becoming the tournament's youngest winner, the first unseeded player to take the title and the first West German champion.

BECKET, THOMAS

Thomas Becket (1118–70) had been Archdeacon of Canterbury when Henry II made him Chancellor of England in 1155. When the post of Archbishop of Canterbury fell vacant, Henry insisted Becket be consecrated. From that day Becket became an opponent of the king, and the manner of his life changed. Becket yielded nothing to the king, and even the Pope encouraged him to take a more conciliatory tone. Becket spent five years in exile in fear for his life. In 1170 he returned, but he had enemies at court and among his brother bishops. On 29

Boris Becker. ◀

The murder of Thomas Becket in Canterbury Cathedral. ▲

December 1170 Becket was murdered in his own cathedral in one of the most notorious incidents in British history.

BECQUEREL, ANTOINE-CÉSAR

The solar cell was developed in 1839 by French physicist Antoine-César Becquerel. Becquerel discovered the photovoltaic effect while experimenting with solid electrodes in electrolyte solution, finding that voltage developed when light fell upon the electrode.

BEETHOVEN, LUDWIG VAN

Ludwig van Beethoven (1770–1827) was a musician and composer of great genius before he reached his teens. He went to study in Vienna under Haydn, but the relationship was strained, and Beethoven continued to study under the patronage of the noble families of Vienna. He began to turn deaf in 1799, causing him to become withdrawn and isolated. This was, however, the most productive period of his life, in which he produced most of his sonatas and piano variations, and despite his hearing difficulties, his symphonies from the last decade of his life are among his best known. His prolific output and undisputed genius have made him arguably the most famous composer of all time, certainly of his era.

BELISARIUS

Belisarius (*c.* AD 505–565), the great Byzantine commander, reorganised the Eastern Empire's troops in the AD 520s. In 532, he was given the task of defeating the Vandals in North Africa with 15,000 men and over 500 ships. He met them outside Carthage and by repeated charges, annihilated them. By 535, the Vandals were conquered. Landing in Italy, Belisarius defeated the Ostrogoths with a force of only 7,500. His emperor, Justinian, had drained the east of troops, despite the building of 700 fortifications. With Belisarius committed in Italy defending Rome and attempting to prevent the fall of the country to the Lombards, Antioch fell to the Persians in 540.

BELL, ALEXANDER GRAHAM

Alexander Graham Bell (1847–1922) began his career teaching the deaf, during which time he began to formulate the idea of electronic speech. He pioneered long-distance voice communication in 1876, when he invented the telephone as a result of **Michael Faraday**'s discovery of electromagnetism. Bell granted a patent for his idea the same year. His invention was to change the idea of communication for ever.

BELL, DANIEL

Sociologist Daniel Bell (b. 1919) argues that the original Protestant Work Ethic underlying capitalism will collapse as a result of the massive productive capacity of modern technology. This is argued in his books, *The End of Ideology* (1960), *Towards a Post Industrial*

Alexander Graham Bell. ◀

Society (1973), *The Cultural Contradictions of Capitalism* (1976), and *The Coming of Post Industrial Society* (1973).

BELL, GERTRUDE

Gertrude Bell (1868–1926), English traveller, author and archeologist, was one of the foremost explorers of the twentieth century. Her voyage across the Arabian Desert in 1913–14 was an unprecedented document of Middle Eastern culture and archeology, and brought about a new understanding of nomadic tribes. Among her books are *Amurath to Amurath* (1911) and *The Palace and Mosque of Ukhaidir* (1914).

BENESE, RICHARD

In 1539 Richard Benese, the man who defined the area of an acre, issued a comprehensive volume of instructions on surveying and the use of associated tools and instruments. He had set a precedent that marked the way for modern cartography. In 1592 the first fully surveyed map of England was published, showing villages, market towns and rivers.

BEN-GURION, DAVID

David Ben-Gurion (1886–1973) was born in Poland. Attracted to the Zionist Socialist movement he emigrated to Palestine (1906), where he worked as a farm labourer and in 1915 formed the first Jewish trade union. From 1921 to 1933 he was general secretary of the General Foundation of Jewish Labour, and in 1930 he became leader of the Mapai party. As defence minister he presided over the Israeli army's development into one of the Middle East's strongest forces. A founder of the state of Israel in 1948, he became the country's first prime minister, holding office 1948–53 and again 1955–63. On retiring from politics he remained a symbol of the Israeli state until his death.

Map of early Jerusalem, the capital of Israel. ▶

BENNETT, FLOYD

With the explorer **Richard Byrd** as navigator, Floyd Bennett (1890–1928) piloted a plane non-stop from Spitsbergen to the North Pole and back. Both men were awarded the Congressional Medal of Honor for their achievement. In 1928, on a flight to rescue stranded flyers in the Gulf of St Lawrence, Bennett was stricken with pneumonia, from which he later died in Quebec.

BENTHAM, JEREMY

Born in the City of London, Bentham (1748–1832) began training for the law but was influenced by **David Hume** and produced *Fragment on Government* (1776). Bentham took the optimistic spirit of the time and gave it philosophical expression. His basic premise was: 'Nature has placed mankind under the governance of two sovereign masters, pain and pleasure.... They govern us in all we do, in all we say, in all we think'. A consequence of Bentham's hypothesis is that punishment, for example, is not a retribution for past action but the prevention of future harms. He wished to reform the law so it was not determined by custom and practice but by reason independent of history. Bentham's utilitarian theory of ethics is that an act is good to the degree that it contributes to the greatest happiness of the greatest number. If an act gives one unit of pleasure to three people and causes two units of pain to another person then it is better to do this act than not to do it.

David Hume, the inspiration for philospher Jeremy Bentham. ▲

BERG, DAVID

David Berg, self-styled 'Moses David', founded The Children of God in the 1960s. The group was known for its hold over the minds of its adherents.

BERING, VITUS

Vitus Bering (1681–1741) was a Danish navigator. In 1724 Tsar **Peter the Great** hired Bering to lead an expedition from the Pacific coast, to sail west in search of a possible route along the north coast of Russia and Siberia to the Far East. In 1728, Bering put to sea, and sailed north into the strait that today bears his name. They found that just north of here the coast of Asia turned westwards, and concluded that a sea separated Asia and North America. The Great Northern Expedition, which took place between 1736 and 1743, made extensive explorations along the northern coast, both from the White Sea and the Pacific. Bering's role took him across the Bering Strait to the Alaskan coast, but he died of scurvy while returning to Siberia.

BERKELEY, GEORGE

Born and educated in Ireland, Berkeley (1685–1753) first visited England in 1723 and became Bishop of Cloyne in 1734. The works on which his reputation is built were published when he was a young man, and the chief target of

Peter the Great examining the ships before Bering's expedition. ▼

his criticism was **John Locke**. Berkeley held that the consequence of Locke's theories would lead to atheism and therefore the submersion of all morality. It was Berkeley's misfortune, and perhaps a comment on the Christian response to the world of his time, that he opposed the 'scientific world-view' when it was in the first flush of ascendancy.

BIGGS, RONNIE ⊠

The ripples of the Great Train Robbery still touch politics and crime today, with the request for Ronnie Biggs's extradition from Brazil. Yet he was a small player in an audacious crime that allegedly netted around £1 million. Faking a stop light on a line in Buckinghamshire, the gang intercepted a Royal Mail train at about 3 a.m. on 8 August 1963. With military precision, they took 120 mailbags stuffed with notes. The driver later died, arguably from injuries sustained that night, but this has never been proven. Several of the gang were caught, convicted and sentenced. They have retained their notoriety, especially Buster Edwards, the flower-seller, whose life was turned into a hit film.

BIKO, STEPHEN

Stephen Biko (1946–77) was an influential leader of the Black Consciousness Movement in South Africa, who became a martyr to the anti-apartheid cause. In 1968, as a medical student, Biko founded the South African Students Organization (SASO), which actively campaigned against racial discrimination. In 1975 and again in 1976 he was arrested and held for more than 100 days without being charged or put on trial. In August 1977, Biko was arrested for a third time at Port Elizabeth, where he died in custody after being taken by truck while unconscious to Pretoria, 1,190 km (740 miles) away. Although the police claimed that he died as the result of a hunger strike, the post-mortem examination disclosed that his death was caused by blows to the head. The police were absolved of blame, leading to public outcry around the world.

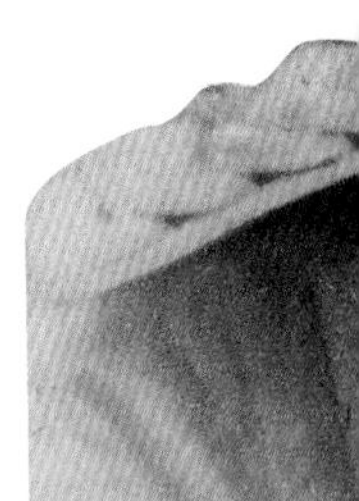

BINGHAM, HIRAM

Machu Picchu, in Peru, is an ancient Inca town. The abandoned site remained essentially unknown until its discovery by the American archeologist Hiram Bingham (1875–1956) in 1911. The famous feature of the site is a carved natural stone, known as Intihuatana.

BISMARCK, OTTO VON

Otto von Bismarck (1815–98) was the driving force behind the unification of Germany in the mid-nineteenth century. He worked to secure Germany's position as a world power. He became chancellor of Germany in 1862. He was a conservative Prussian politician, who wanted to extend Prussia's dominance in Germany by uniting the country under the king of Prussia. He followed the policy of *realpolitik*, which meant that he was ready to use any means to achieve his ends. In 1864 Bismarck, in alliance with Austria, declared war on Denmark and took Schleswig. In 1866 he signed a treaty with France and then picked a quarrel with Austria. The French remained neutral, but the Austrian army was crushed in seven weeks. When the peace terms were discussed, Bismarck insisted on being lenient to Austria, knowing he would want its support in the future.

Otto von Bismarck. ◀

Tony Blair. ▲

BLAIR, TONY

Tony Blair entered Parliament in 1983 and was given the shadow cabinet's energy portfolio in 1988, employment in 1991 and home affairs in 1992. Leadership victory after John Smith's death made him the party's youngest leader. By mid-1995 he had revamped the Labour party platform with commitments to free enterprise, anti-inflation policies and a hard line on crime. Despite criticism from the left of the party he successfully won the voters' favour, heavily defeating the Conservatives in the 1995 council elections.

Having led a highly successful 'New Labour' campaign in the run-up to the 1997 general election, he achieved a landslide victory on 1 May, ending 18 years of Conservative government in Britain.

BLAKE, WILLIAM

The engraver, poet and artist William Blake (1757–1827) was an enigmatic and unrecognised genius, ending his life in an unmarked grave in a public cemetery. He claimed to see angels, developed his own complex mythology and at the low-point of his life found himself arrested on trumped-up charges of sedition. His pictures were of a kind never seen before and his verses were stark and complex. They grow more influential with each century that passes. It is his poem *Jerusalem* that is best known; part of a cycle of poems about **John Milton**, written and engraved between 1803–08. The famous tune was finally added to turn it into a patriotic song during the First World War.

BLAVATSKY, HELENA

Theosophy is a populist occult school that mixes a range of Eastern, Ancient Egyptian and Neoplatonic ideas. It was promoted by Madame Helena Blavatsky

(1831–91), who claimed to receive the teachings telepathically from Tibetan mahatmas. The school, founded in New York in 1875, introduced Eastern ideas, in a rather confused form, to large numbers of Westerners.

BLÈRIOT, LOUIS

By 1908, Louis Blèriot (1872–1936) had perfected his powered monoplane and established the standard layout for future aeroplanes. Blèriot made the first channel Crossing in 1909, in a monoplane of his own design and construction. The 37-km (23-mile) crossing took 35.5 minutes.

BODHIDHARMA

The Chan school was traditionally brought to China by the sixth-century Indian monk, Bodhidharma, and was systematised by Hui-neng (the '6th Patriarch') during the T'ang Dynasty. The name derives from *Dhyana*, Sanskrit for 'meditation', and the central practice is the direct realisation of reality through meditation. Chan was influenced by the *Diamond Sutra* and also by the teachings of Taoism and the Hua-Yen school. Hui-Neng's Southern School taught that enlightenment was instantaneous whereas Shen Xui's Northern School taught that it was gradual.

Louis Blèriot. ▼

Humphrey Bogart. ▲

BOGART, HUMPHREY ☻

Humphrey Bogart (1899–1957) was a US film actor. Playing gangsters in 1930s movies and classic *film noirs* such as *The Maltese Falcon* (1941) and *Casablanca* (1942), he became a tender-hearted tough-guy in *The African Queen* (1952) – and a Hollywood institution.

BOKASSA, JEAN-BEDEL

Jean-Bedel Bokassa (b. 1921) was commander-in-chief of the Central African Republic from 1963 until, in December 1965, he led the military coup that gave him the presidency. On 4 December 1976 he proclaimed the Central African Empire and one year later crowned himself emperor for life. In all, £30 million was spent on his coronation, with £2 million spent on the crown alone, paid for by his patron, the president of the French Republic. His regime was characterised by state violence and cruelty. Overthrown in 1979, he remained in exile until 1986. Upon his return, he was sentenced to death, but this was commuted to life imprisonment in 1988.

BOLIVAR, SIMON

Simon Bolivar (1783–1830), 'The Liberator', was Venezuelan by birth. He led a series of campaigns against the Spanish colonialists and liberated Venezuela, Colombia, Ecuador, Peru and Bolivia.

BONAPARTE, NAPOLEON

Napoleon Bonaparte (1769–1821), emperor of France (1804–15) and commander in Italy (1796–97), seized power in 1799. When he conquered his empire from 1804 to 1811, Napoleon destroyed the political system of Europe. Every country in Europe was defeated or became allied to France, with the exception of Britain. In place of the old order, Napoleon created new countries, which were given to members of his family or to his marshals. These changes were redressed in the Treaty of Vienna in 1815 after the final defeat of Napoleon at the Battle of Waterloo. Napoleon's creations were swept away and the principle of legitimacy was enforced. The rulers of 1789 were restored. In Germany, Austria and Italy Napoleon's influence remained, however, and his nationalist ideas were to reappear later in the century.

Napoleon Bonaparte. ▲

BONNIE and CLYDE

The incredible four-year criminal career of Bonnie Parker (1911–34) and Clyde Barrow (1909–34) ended in the most dramatic of ways in Louisiana. Apparently working on a tip-off, Texas Rangers ambushed the pair, riddling their bodies with over 50 bullets. They died as they had lived, with shotguns and revolvers in their hands. The criminal duo left a trail of murders and robberies across the south-west of America. They are credited with the murder of at least 12 people and numerous woundings. Both were still in their mid-20s when they were killed. Their exploits have passed into folklore around the world.

Hubert Booth invented the first electrical carpet cleaner. ▲

BOOTH, CHARLES ☒

Charles Booth (1840–1916) was a wealthy Liverpool businessman who, in 1886, set out to discover the extent and nature of poverty in the East End of London and sent investigators to interview the poor and observe their conditions. The approach was strictly factual, and Booth's findings, published in 1903, contained no hint of emotion, even though among its conclusions was the damning fact that, for nearly 31 per cent, poverty derived from inadequate wages and precarious employment. Booth's work later influenced the provision in 1908 of state pensions for the aged.

BOOTH, HUBERT

The first electrical vacuum cleaner was invented in 1901 by the Scot Hubert Booth. He had the idea when he saw how much dust was blown out of a carpet by a jet of compressed air. His system used an electric pump to remove the dust from a carpet by sucking air along a tube and through a cloth filter.

BOOTH, WILLIAM ☒

William Booth (1829–1905) founded the Salvation Army, which was modelled on army lines, abandoned the sacraments of Baptism and Holy Communion and gave equal status to men and women.

BORDES, FRANÇOIS

The French archeologist, François Bordes (1919–81), was a renowned authority on the European Paleolithic period. Noted for his research on Neanderthal culture, Bordes was also known for his flint knapping (stone toolmaking) skills.

BORLAUG, NORMAN E.

Norman E. Borlaug (b. 1914) is a US microbiologist and agronomist and is often considered to be the founder of the Green Revolution – the term used since the 1960s to describe the effort to increase and diversify crop yields in developing countries.

BOTHAM, IAN

In the 1980s, one man bestrode English cricket like no other in the modern era: Ian Botham. From the very beginning of the decade, when he was England captain at just 24 years of age, to its end, Botham's influence on English cricket was unparalleled. His achievements with both bat and ball will never be forgotten. An immensely talented all-rounder, deeply committed to winning and a genuine crowd-pleaser, Botham was an incomparable hero.

Norman E. Borlaug began a revolution in agriculture. ▲

BOUDICCA

Resistance to the Roman invasion among Britons was patchy. Some tribes fiercely resisted, others helped the invaders. Many in the south welcomed the Romans as it ended the political dominance of the local Catuvellauni tribe. The most famous resistor – in England at least – was Boudicca. Queen of the Iceni tribe in East Anglia, she led a revolt against the Romans in AD 61. On his death, Boudicca's husband Prasutagas divided his kingdom between his daughters and the Romans. However, Roman agents seized all the land. When Boudicca protested, she was flogged and her daughters raped. Driven by fury, Boudicca's troops inflicted massive defeats on the Romans in Colchester, London and St Albans. After she was eventually defeated, Boudicca committed suicide in 61.

Boudicca, the queen of the Iceni tribe, who resisted the Roman invasion in Britain. ▲

BOULANGER, PIERRE

In 1936, Citroen conceived the idea of a low-priced car with a small engine to compete with the German 'people's car', the Volkswagen Beetle. The result was architect-engineer Boulanger's 2CV, launched in 1939. This economic and straightforward car was produced until 1990, when it was superseded by the lighter-weight AX. The Citroen 2CV completely rejected streamlined styling; its uncompromisingly functional bodywork was described by some critics as a product of the 'garden-shed school of auto design'. Nevertheless, its simplicity made it popular, and the 2CV introduced a new dimension in European small-car design. Supply never kept up with demand for this car, and it became a design classic, which visually or by association summed up the best of its time.

BOWES-LYON, ELIZABETH

Lady Elizabeth Bowes-Lyon (b. 1900) was the youngest daughter of the 14th Earl of Strathmore and Kinghorne. The family can trace its descent right back to Robert the Bruce. Elizabeth married Albert, the Duke of York, on 26 April 1923. On 11 December 1936 **Edward VIII** abdicated and her husband became King **George VI**, while Elizabeth became the Queen Consort. She had two daughters: **Elizabeth** – the future Queen – and Margaret. When her husband died in 1952, their daughter ascended to the throne, and the Queen Consort became known as the Queen Mother.

The Queen Consort became the Queen Mother on the ascension of her daughter Elizabeth II. ▼

BRADMAN, DONALD GEORGE

Many cricketers might be thought of as the greatest. However, few have stood the test of time quite like Donald George Bradman (b. 1908), the jewel in Australia's cricketing crown for over 20 years.

Donald George Bradman. ▼

Bradman's career batting figures speak for themselves: an all-time average of 95.14 and a Test average of 99.94, all-time records in both categories. Bradman missed out on a Test career average of 100 by just four runs. His top scores are equally impressive, with a first-class record of 452 and a Test record of 334.

BRAMAH, JOSEPH

The first hydraulically operated machine was a press, made by Joseph Bramah (1748–1814) in 1795. The use of a small piston feeding a larger one, results in a gain in power measured against a loss in movement. As well as machinery, other modern applications for hydraulics are seen in vehicles' braking systems, jacks and suspension units, which actually use fluid to dampen sudden movements.

BRANSON, RICHARD

Richard Branson (b. 1950) is a British entrepreneur, whose Virgin company developed quickly, diversifying from retailing records to the airline business and more. Today Branson is one of the most successful – and wealthiest – businessmen of the twentieth century.

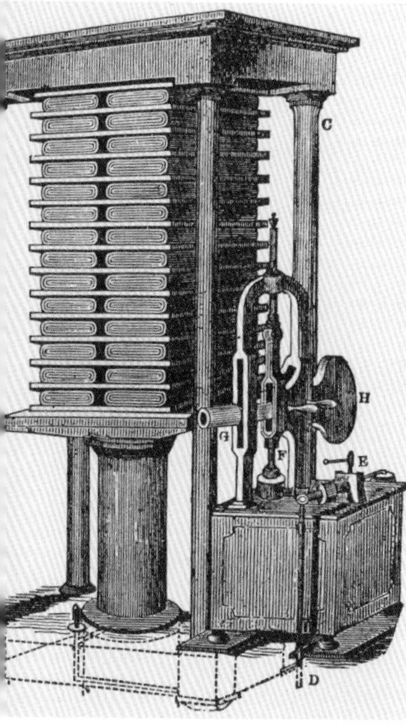

Joseph Bramah's hydraulic press. ▲

BRITTEN, BENJAMIN

'If wind and water could write music, it would sound like Ben's,' wrote the violinist **Yehudi Menuhin**, about the composer Benjamin Britten (1913–76). Britten revolutionised British opera in 1945 with *Peter Grimes*, based in an East Anglian fishing village, and followed it up with a string of songs designed for the voice of his lover and collaborator Peter Pears. Both Britten and Pears founded the Aldeburgh festival in 1948, in another East Anglian fishing village, and it grew into one of the top concert halls in Europe. Britten dominated British music in the middle years of the century, and became the first composer to be given a peerage, just six months before his death.

BRODY, NEVILLE

Brody (b. 1957) is the best-known British graphic designer of his generation. He began his career designing record covers, and from 1981 to 1986 was art director of the ground-breaking British style and music magazine *The Face*. Brody, heavily influenced by the chaotic ethos of punk, used computers to manipulate new and existing letter forms to create a look independent of the limitations imposed by old-fashioned printing techniques. He used typography as a visual language, shaping and emphasising the editorial message of the text. As a highly influential carrier of consumer information to free-spending young people, *The Face* transformed the way in which readers and designers approached the medium.

Charlotte Brontë. ▲

BRONTË, CHARLOTTE, EMILY AND ANNE

When the Brontë sisters, Charlotte (1816–55), Emily (1818–48) and Anne (1820–49), published their first poems in 1846, they used the androgynous pseudonyms Currer, Ellis and Acton Bell. They used the same names the following year when all three published novels. Charlotte's *Jane Eyre* and Emily's *Wuthering Heights* were both immediate successes, and Anne's *Agnes Grey* remains in print a century and a half later. Within two years, all had revealed their real names – causing astonishment that a woman could have written a novel as brutal as *Wuthering Heights* – but Emily, Anne and their alcoholic brother Branwell were already dead. Charlotte lived until 1855, but succumbed to complications in pregnancy.

BROOKE, RUPERT

Following his untimely death, Rupert Brooke (1887–1915) became the poet hero of the First World War. He was a fellow at Cambridge University, and travelled in the United States and the South Pacific. When war broke out he immediately enlisted as an officer. He died on a hospital ship, before he could witness the bloodiness of the fighting. Brooke became a symbol of all the gifted youth killed in the conflict. He is best remembered for his patriotic poems, such as 'The Soldier' and 'Granchester', where his romantic view of the war was reassuring to those not fighting at the Front.

BROWN, LANCELOT 'CAPABILITY'

A grateful nation had bestowed Blenheim Palace on the **Duke of Marlborough**. The palace was designed by the playwright and architect Sir John Vanbrugh, but the grounds were laid out in the new style – with 2,700 acres of natural parks and lakes instead of formal gardens – associated with Lancelot 'Capability' Brown (1716–83). The trees are said to have been planted, not in formal lines, but in accordance with the troop dispositions at one of Marlborough's victories. Brown won his nickname by telling clients their gardens had 'capabilities for improvement', and by the end of a successful career, starting with experience under the great landscape architect William Kent, he had designed more than 140 estates.

Blenheim Palace Gardens, laid out in the style of Capability Brown. ▼

The Clifton Suspension Bridge, designed and built by Isambard Brunel. ▲

BRUNEL, ISAMBARD KINGDOM

The Industrial Revolution is often remembered for the great achievements of the ambitious engineers of the period. Isambard Kingdom Brunel (1806–59) is probably the most famous of these pioneers. He designed and built some impressive structures in iron and steel, which made a significant contribution to transport. A series of iron-hulled steam ships – *The Great Britain*, *The Great Western* and *The Great Eastern* – were built by him between 1837 and 1858, and his bridges include the Clifton Suspension Bridge. He also assisted his father in the Thames Tunnel project.

BRUNO, FILIPPO

Filippo Bruno (1548–1600) was born in northern Italy and took the name Giordano when he became a Dominican monk. As a monk he studied **Aristotle** and **Thomas Aquinas**, but in 1576, fearing prosecution for heresy, he fled and then wandered in northern Italy and Switzerland, where he encountered Protestantism. His writings, such as *On the Infinite Universes and World* (1584), attracted the attention of the Inquisition. After imprisonment for eight years he refused to recant and was burned at the stake by the Church. Although many of his ideas seem strange today, his freedom of thought and his views on the unity of the world had much influence on seventeenth-century philosophy.

BUCHANAN, JAMES

Democrat James Buchanan (1791–1868) was the 15th president of the USA, holding office 1856–60.

BUDDHA, SIDDHARTA GAUTAMA

Siddharta Gautama Buddha was born *c.* 586 BC in Nepal, the latest in a continuing line of buddhas; his life lies at the heart of Buddhism.

Although Buddha did not deny the existence of gods, his teachings centred upon the insight that liberation comes through meditation and the renunciation of desire. Buddhists believe that humans have free will, but that all actions have consequences (*karma*). If desires and suffering (*dhukka*) are allowed to die down, *karma* too dies down.

BUNYAN, JOHN 📖

Typical of Puritan thought is *Pilgrim's Progress* (1678–84) by John Bunyan, for it is primarily concerned with individuals' search for peace and salvation. Bunyan (1628–88) does not appear to have been a strict Calvinist. He spent 12 years in Bedford Gaol (1660–72), so had much time to reflect on his allegory of religious life.

BURBAGE, JAMES ☻

The first purpose-built theatre in England opened in Shoreditch, London in 1576, built by the actor and carpenter James Burbage, the father of Richard Burbage. It became the home of the Lord Chamberlain's Men, one of whom was the young playwright **William Shakespeare**. When the lease ran out in 1597, they dismantled it, carried it to the south bank of the Thames and used it as building material for the famous Globe Theatre. Richard Burbage was also a shareholder of the Blackfriars Theatre, in the abandoned Blackfriars monastery on the other side of the river, and went on to

The Buddhist faith centres on the life of Siddharta Gautama Buddha. ▶

play the leading roles in *Hamlet*, *Othello*, *King Lear* and *Richard III*.

BUREN, MARTIN VAN

Martin van Buren (1782–1862) was the 8th president of the USA, in office 1836–40. He was a Democrat.

BURGESS, ANTHONY

In Anthony Burgess's (b. 1917) best-known work, *A Clockwork Orange*, gangs of disaffected youths roam the streets of a shabby town, causing mayhem. Old people are beaten and young girls raped. It is a chilling and bleak novel, told through the voice of Alex, one of the young criminals. He is morally vicious but mentally alert and he chooses evil as a reaction against the dulled society in which he lives. The soundtrack for Alex's life is **Beethoven**'s music and his violence is expressed in the 'droog' argot, a kind of gang slang. A complex, imaginative language dominates the texture of the book. Later **Stanley Kubrick**'s film version proved so controversial that Kubrick himself prohibited its public release.

The storming of the Bastille during the French Revolution, the object of Edmund Burke's Reflections. ▼

BURKE, EDMUND

In his *Reflections on the French Revolution* (1790) Burke (1789–97) affirmed that the glory of Europe would be gone for ever if the alliance between Church orthodoxy and the monarchical state were to be destroyed by mob forces. His thinking has appealed to successive generations of politicians. He was renowned as a boring speaker but his causes gathered support: freedom for the American states; freedom for Ireland; freedom for India from the East India Company; freedom of Parliament from the influence of the king; and opposition to the atheism indicative of the French Revolution. He thought of political power as a trust and politicians had to maintain the tradition of hierarchical, social and political order. His appeal lay in instinctive feelings of loyalty and he rejected the call made by the reformers and revolutionaries to individuality and individual rights.

Burke and Wills making their crossing of Australia. ▲

BURKE, ROBERT

Robert Burke (1821–61) was an Irish-born Australian explorer who made the first crossing of Australia (1860–61) together with ex-miner William Wills riding on camels; the first use of the animals in the country. Both perished on the return journey.

BURNS, ROBERT

Robert Burns (1759–96) was born William Burnes, the son of a Calvinist small farmer, and his verse – often in Scottish dialect – was published only for the last 10 years of his life, before he died of rheumatic heart disease at the age of 37. He was lionised as an untutored rustic genius with striking good looks, although his life was constantly beset by poverty. Scots people around the world still celebrate his birthday on 25 January. His songs include *O my Love's like a Red, Red Rose*, *Ye Banks and Braes* and *Auld Lang Syne* – the reworking of an older song by Sir Robert Ayton (1570–1638) of the same name, which was published in 1794 in a collection called *The Scots Musical Museum*.

BUSBY, MATT

Arguably one of the best English football teams of the decade was decimated in a tragic air crash on 6 February 1958. The Manchester United squad, on their way home from a successful quarter-final game with Belgrade, were on a BEA flight to Munich when the pilot lost control while landing. The aircraft ploughed into an airport building, killing seven players outright along with eight journalists and three Manchester United employees. Matt Busby (1909–94) survived the crash, but five of the dead were international players: Roger Byrne, Tommy Taylor, David Pegg, Bill Whelan and Duncan Edwards. Three months after the crash Manchester United met Bolton at Wembley in the FA Cup Final. The depleted squad lost 2–0.

Kuwaiti soldiers during the Gulf War. ▲

BUSH, GEORGE

Republican George Bush (b. 1924) was director of the Central Intelligence Agency (CIA) from 1976 to 1981, and the US vice-president from 1981 to 1989 under **Ronald Reagan**. He succeeded Reagan and became the 41st US president in 1989. His initial response to Soviet leader **Mikhail Gorbachev**'s initiatives in the arms race was considered inadequate, but he raised his popularity with success in the 1991 Gulf War with Iraq. He signed the Strategic Arms Reduction Treaty in July 1991 and began unilateral reduction in US nuclear weapons two months later. However, Bush's reneging on his election pledge of 'no new taxes' cost him the 1992 presidential election, when he lost to Democrat **Bill Clinton**.

BYRD, RICHARD E.

On 9 May 1926, Admiral Richard E. Byrd (1888–1957) and **Floyd Bennett** became the first men to fly to the North Pole by aeroplane. In 1928, Byrd organised an expedition to Antarctica, establishing a base called Little America on the Ross Ice Shelf near Roosevelt Island. A year later he flew with three companions to the South Pole and back. In 1946, Byrd returned to Antarctica to lead the largest expedition ever mounted to that inhospitable continent. Operation Highjump involved a fleet of 13 ships and 4,700 men. Highjump charted a large extent of the coastline of the ice-pack covering the pole.

CABOT, JOHN

John Cabot (*c.* 1450–98) was a Genoese merchant who settled in England in 1495. He had travelled extensively in the eastern Mediterranean and, when he heard about Christopher Columbus's discoveries, decided to sail west to try to find a short cut to Asia. He set sail on 2 May 1497 and reached land on 24 June; almost certainly this was the coast of Newfoundland. He returned to England and then led a second expedition the following year with five ships. One turned back, but the other four were lost. Cabot's expedition had

John Cabot. ▶

come to nothing, but he had begun a tradition in English seafaring and had started the English occupation and conquest of North America.

CAEDMON

Caedmon was the first important English writer, and one of the central figures in the flowering of Christian culture and learning known as the Northumbrian Renaissance in the period of peace before the arrival of the Vikings, some time between AD 658 and 679. Caedmon, a north Yorkshire cowherd, became the first Christian poet in Britain after he dreamt he was commanded by God to set down the story of the Creation. The illiterate Caedmon was apparently given some of the verses and the poetic talent to write more. At first, Caedmon's claims were sceptically received at nearby Whitby Abbey. However, the cowherd proved to the monks' satisfaction that he had, indeed, received a heavenly gift when he wrote down several verses within a few hours. Later, Caedmon became a monk at Whitby Abbey. The source for Caedmon's story, told some 50 years later, is The Venerable Bede, the Anglo-Saxon historian.

Emperor Julius Caesar in battle. ▼

Bust of Julius Caesar. ◀

CAESAR, AUGUSTUS

Octavian (b. Gaius Octavius, 63 BC–AD 14), the great-nephew of **Julius Caesar**, became emperor of Rome in 27 BC. As he was unwilling to upset the Roman people by taking the title of King, he took the title of Princeps and referred to himself as the 'First Citizen'. However, when the Senate decided to offer Octavian the title of 'Augustus', meaning 'respected one', he was quite prepared to accept. Augustus then set about reforming the empire, which had grown up haphazardly over the last two centuries. He took charge of the appointment of governors of the 30 or so provinces of the empire. He reorganised the army, reducing the number of legions from 62 to 28 and appointing all senior commanders.

CAESAR, JULIUS

In 59 BC, at the age of 41, Julius Caesar (100–44 BC) was thrust into prominence when he became governor of Illyricum, Cisalpine and Transalpine Gaul. He made an immediate impact, however, checking the threat of the Helvetti in 58 BC and advancing north of the old Roman frontier to clear Alsace of the German tribes. In the spring of 57 BC, he defeated a 300,000-strong Belgae army on the Aisne and by 56 BC had added nearly all of Gaul to the empire. He landed in Britain in 55 BC, but was forced to turn his attention elsewhere. The Gauls, under Vercingetorix, rebelled in 52 BC and at the siege of Alesia they were crushed for many years. By 50 BC, Julius Caesar had defeated all Gaul (France) and the Low Countries, and had brought under Roman rule much of modern Tunisia and Libya. In 49 BC Julius Caesar marched on Rome, and declared himself dictator. He faced Pompey in a civil war that lasted until 45 BC. He was murdered in 44 BC by his former friends Brutus and Cassius, but he had in effect created the Roman Empire.

CALIGULA

The four-year reign of Caligula (AD 12–41), began in AD 37 and ended with his assassination in 41. His reign has become a byword for tyrannical excess. He is said to have made his horse a consul.

CALVIN, JOHN

John Calvin (1509–64) was a French theologian, and one of the leaders of the Reformation in Geneva. He emphasised justification by faith and the sole authority of the Bible. He was inspired by the Protestant teachings of **Martin Luther**. Expelled from France in 1533 he moved to Geneva, where he turned the city into a repressive theocratic dictatorship. Worship, beliefs and morals were imposed by force and opponents were excommunicated or executed. His follower, John Knox, introduced a similar regime into Scotland. Calvin's teachings, whilst they shared the simplicity of Lutheranism, differed in that he believed in predestination and opposed the ordination of bishops. These differences later became the basis for several wars between the Protestant states of Germany.

John Calvin. ▼

Tommaso Campanella. ▲

CAMPANELLA, TOMMASO

Tommaso Campanella (1568–1639) was born in southern Italy and became a Dominican monk when he was 14. He rejected the Scholastic and Aristotlean philosophies he had been taught, and claimed that all knowledge of the world was obtained directly through the senses. This strictly empirical position contrasts with his later interest in astrology and white magic. Although denounced as a heretic and imprisoned for almost 30 years for holding these views, he spent several of his final years acting as astrological adviser to the pope. His *The City of the Sun* (1602) depicts an imaginary society governed by philosophers, in which the state provides education for all, there is no private property and all things, including wives, are held in common.

CAMPBELL, DONALD

When Donald Campbell (1921–67) learned, shortly after his father's death, that American industrialist Henry Kaiser intended to beat **Sir Malcolm Campbell**'s water speed record, he was stung into defensive action. He purchased the old *Bluebird K4* hydroplane from his father's estate, and refitted the Rolls-Royce R piston engine that had been replaced by the de Havilland Goblin jet. In July 1964 he finally succeeded in breaking the official land speed record, with a speed of 648.708 kph (403.1 mph) on Lake Eyre in the Australian outback. On the last day of December, he became the only man ever to break land and water speed records in the same year, when he achieved 444.69 kph (276.33 mph) on Australia's Lake Dumbleyung. Campbell was killed on 4 January 1967, when *Bluebird* took off at an estimated 528 kph (328 mph) on Coniston Water and somersaulted to destruction.

CAMPBELL, MALCOLM

British Captain Malcolm Campbell (1885–1948) repeatedly broke the world land speed record throughout his illustrious and unprecedented career, using ever bigger and more powerful vehicles – most of which he called *Bluebird*. Campbell devoted his life to achieving and then holding the land speed record for Britain, and he set new records in 1927 at 280 kph (74 mph); 1928 at 332 kph (206 mph); 1931 at 394 kph (245 mph); 1932 at 407 kph (253 mph); 1933 at 440 kph (274 mph); and in 1935 at 444 kph (276 mph). Later that same year he broke the 300 mph barrier, clocking up 484.6 kph (301.1 mph). He died on the last day of 1948, still planning to go faster. His son, **Donald**, took over as world speed champion, carrying on the *Bluebird* name.

CAMUS, ALBERT

Albert Camus (1913–1960) was born in North Africa in 1913. Before becoming a writer he had many jobs, including goalkeeper for the Algiers football team. He abandoned the pitch for the typewriter and became a journalist in France. He was involved in the resistance movement, editing a clandestine newspaper called *Combat*. His novels, full of images of the desert, sky, light and the sea, were an attempt to understand happiness and responsibility in an 'absurd world'. *The Stranger*, a book

George Canning ▲

about truth and murder, focused attention on his work. Camus was awarded the Nobel Prize for Literature in 1957, and died in a road accident in 1960.

CANNING, GEORGE

The modern British Conservative Party dates from Robert Peel's *Tamworth Manifesto* of 1834, but the term 'Conservative' was probably first used by George Canning (1770 –1827) in 1824. After **Viscount Castlereagh**'s suicide in 1822, George Canning became foreign secretary. Although he had fought a duel with Castlereagh in 1809, and the two men had been enemies ever since, their approaches to foreign policy were very similar. Canning believed even more strongly that the great powers should not interfere in events outside their own countries. He supported the Greek rebellion in the 1820s, which led to the creation of the Greek state and he threatened to use the British navy to prevent intervention in the revolts, that broke out against Spanish rule in South America. He said, 'I have brought in the New World to redress the balance of the Old'.

King Canute. ◀

CANUTE

Canute (1016–35), son of the Danish king Svein Fork-Beard, became King of England after defeating Edmund Ironside. He brought firm government and security from external threat. He forged strong links with the Viking successors, the Normans and other Scandinavian civilisations.

CAPONE, AL

Gangster Al Capone (1899–1947), in an attempt to protect his stake in illegal alcohol, extortion and prostitution rackets, had seven men gunned down, all members of a gang led by George 'Bugsy' Moran. This incident was the latest in what Police Commissioner William F. Russell described as 'a war to the finish'. Men dressed as police officers successfully passed themselves off as a raiding party and killed the seven victims. The men, armed with tommy-guns, lined their victims up against a wall at the back of a beer house in Chicago before murdering them with a hail of bullets. The Police Commissioner was furious that the gangsters chose to dress up as policemen, particularly since half of his force was under investigation for corruption.

CAREY, WILLIAM

In 1785 William Carey (1762–1834) was given permission to preach as a Baptist although he had no formal training. Soon he was challenging his fellow ministers with the Great Commission: 'Go forth and teach all nations.' He formed the Baptist Missionary Society in 1792 and a year later he decided to go to India. He had been in India for seven years before he baptised an Indian, but he did translate the Bible into six Indian languages and he is a model of the fortitude of the early British missionaries. He founded schools and colleges at a time when Britain was doing precious little at home. He was buried in Serampore. His epitaph reads: 'A wretched, poor and helpless worm, on Thy kind arms I fall.'

CARLING, WILL

Will Carling made his England debut in January 1988 and within 10 months had been named as captain in a bold move by the English RFU (Rugby Football Union). Carling went on to captain England more times than any other player, taking them to the forefront of the game as the top northern-hemisphere side. In 1991 and 1992, his side won back-to-back Grand Slams for the first time since 1924, and sandwiched between the victories they reached the World Cup final. Revelations about his private life, in particular his association with **Diana, Princess of Wales**, saw him fall from public grace during the later 1990s.

Missionaries in India; William Carey translated the Bible into six Indian languages. ▼

CARLOS I

King Carlos I was king of Portugal from 1889. In 1906 João Franco, a monarchist sympathiser, was appointed premier and was later accused of illegal money transfers to Carlos. Carlos was assassinated in Lisbon with his elder son, Luis. It is not known who killed them but the deed was applauded by Republicans. He was succeeded by his younger son, Manuel, who was only 18 and unable to cope with the Republican attacks on the monarchy. After the murder of a leading Republican a revolution began, taking control in October 1910. Manuel fled the country, settling in England where he remained an exile until his death in 1932.

Thomas Carlyle was one of many writers to reflect on the French Revolution. ▼

CARLOS III

Spanish king Carlos III (1716–88) reformed his nation's economy and expelled the Jesuits. He lost Florida to Britain, but regained it in the American War of Independence in 1783.

CARLSON, CHESTER

Before 1938, techniques for duplicating documents were messy and too slow to be economically viable. Chester Carlson (1906–68) managed to solve this problem by inventing the xerographic copier. It

Charles Dickens, who was greatly influenced by Carlyle. ▶

used an electromagnetic plate to attract powder ink to the paper, which was then fixed. The photocopier was born, which worked on a quick-dry process; this was exactly what the office environment needed.

CARLYLE, THOMAS

The social theorist, historian and writer Thomas Carlyle (1795–1881) forced himself on to the attention of the country with his 1836 study *The French Revolution* – 'itself a kind of revolution', he wrote later. In this and later works, he attacked unfettered industrial capitalism, affirming moral certainties at a time of revolutionary change, and insisting on the importance of the individual. He was fascinated by heroism, and his lectures *On Heroes, Hero-Worship and the Heroic in History* (1841) marked the beginning of his search for strong leaders, which was so influential on the Victorians who came after him. Those deeply influenced included the novelist **Charles Dickens** and the critic John Ruskin.

CARROLL, LEWIS

Lewis Carroll was the pen-name of the reclusive Oxford mathematics don and photography enthusiast, Charles Lutwidge Dodgson (1832–98). Both he and his friends were astonished when the story he told on a children's picnic in 1862, and published as *Alice's Adventures Under Ground*, became an immediate best-seller. The illustrations, by the political cartoonist Sir John Tenniel, became almost as famous as the story. In fact the book and its sequel, *Through the Looking Glass and What Alice Found There* (1871), revolutionised children's literature.

The guard statue to the tomb of Tutankhamen, discovered by Howard Carter. ◀

CARTER, HOWARD

In 1922, Howard Carter (1873–1939) discovered the tomb of King Tutankhamen (a pharaoh of the 18th dynasty; r. 1361–52 BC) in Egypt's Valley of the Kings. The tomb was filled with extraordinary treasure, including a solid gold coffin, and the famous death mask of the young pharaoh. The tomb was believed to have been cursed.

CARTER, JIMMY

Democrat Jimmy Carter (b. 1924) became the 39th US president (1976), narrowly winning victory over **Gerald Ford**. Carter was concerned with the establishment of peace in the Middle East, and he organised the Camp David peace agreements. Other features of his presidency were the return of the Panama Canal Zone to Panama and the Iranian seizure of US Embassy hostages. In 1980, prompted by the Soviet invasion of Afghanistan and instability in Iran, he issued a doctrine stating that any outside attempt at control in the Persian Gulf would be met by military force if necessary. Defeated by **Ronald Reagan** in 1980, he re-emerged during the 1990s as a mediator and peace negotiator.

CARTIER, PIERRE

The Parisian jeweller, Pierre Cartier (1878–1964), was responsible for designing the first wristwatch (for French aviator Santos Duman). His work was recognised and sought after early in his career; he created 27 diamond tiaras for the coronation of King Edward VII, and

Ronald Reagan defeated Jimmy Carter to become president in 1980. ▲

his watches and clocks became collectors' items. They represented the height of Art Deco style and drew on many influences, including Cubism, Bauhaus and Orientalism. In the 1940s, Cartier's clocks were made in gold, silver, rock crystal and diamonds, and became essential household accessories for the upper echelons of society. The Cartier clock has now achieved icon status.

CARTIER-BRESSON, HENRI

First and foremost a painter and draughtsman, the French photojournalist Cartier-Bresson (b. 1908) is known as the master of the expressive documentary photograph. His technique is based on pre-visualising the finished print, waiting until the 'decisive moment', and then, with a single exposure, creating a photo that is both spontaneous and carefully composed.

CASAS, BARTOLOME DE LAS

Bartolome de las Casas (1474–1566) was a priest who became known as the 'Apostle of the Indies' for his work in urging on King **Philip II** of Spain the rights of natives as equal subjects of the Spanish Crown. Las Casas' mission was not only philanthropic. He believed that contented, unexploited natives were easier to convert to Christianity. His importunings, however, had their effect in Spain, where like-minded people were concerned to justify the American conquests. Gradually, over the years, las Casas' ideas were adopted and the brutal treatment of the early days was at least partly contained.

CASTLEREAGH, VISCOUNT

Viscount Castlereagh (1769–1822) was the British representative at the Congress ofVienna and remained foreign secretary until he committed suicide in 1822. In Britain he was regarded as a conservative re-actionary, but abroad he was seen as a dangerous liberal. He refused to agree to the demands of Russia, Austria and Prussia to be allowed to interfere in the internal affairs of countries in Europe. He could do little about the Austrian domination of Italy, but he used his influence to protect France, Spain and Portugal. His position led to a split between the allies at the congresses after 1815. Castlereagh's policies were published in his state paper of May 1820, in which he set out his belief that the internal affairs of countries were their own concern.

Cuban leader Fidel Castro. ▼

CASTRO, FIDEL

Fidel Castro (b. 1927), lawyer and revolutionary, ousted the Cuban dictator Batista in December 1958, replacing his corrupt regime with a Marxist-Leninist programme of reforms. In 1961, the US government invaded the Bay of Pigs in Cuba, in an attempt to overthrow the Cuban government, fearful of the strength of the Communist regime there, but Castro's forces defeated the US. The following year, the US discovered Soviet missile bases in Cuba, and blockaded the island. Soviet leader Krushchev and President Kennedy met and an agreement was reached to dismantle the missile sites.

CATHERINE II (THE GREAT)

Catherine the Great (1729–96) became empress of Russia from 1762 after her husband Tsar Peter III was murdered in a coup. During her reign, Russia extended its boundaries to include territory from wars with the Turks. Russia also participated with the Habsburgs and Prussia in three partitions of Poland, which extinguished that once-powerful eastern European empire. She achieved notoriety for her love affairs with her courtiers.

CATON-THOMPSON, GERTRUDE

Gertrude Caton-Thompson (1889–1985) was an English archeologist noted for her work at the Zimbabwe Ruins in Africa. She inaugurated the first archeological and geological survey of the northern Fayum, Egypt (1924–28).

CAVENDISH, HENRY

Henry Cavendish (1731–1810) discovered hydrogen by experimenting with acids on metals. In 1781, he ignited a mixture of hydrogen and air and was amazed to find that he had created water, which was previously thought to be an element: he had accidentally shown that water must be made from a combination of elements.

Henry Cavendish. ▼

CAVOUR, CAMILLO DI

Count Camillo di Cavour (1810–61) was prime minister of Piedmont from 1852–59 and again from 1860 to his death. His aim was to unify Italy under the king of Piedmont, but he realised that would need powerful allies if he was to do this. In 1855 he sent the Piedmont army to fight in the Crimea alongside the Franco-British force. He hoped that this would win support from the powers for Italian unification. **Napoleon III**, the French emperor, sent forces against the Austrians in 1859 and won the battles of Magenta and Solferino. However, he was so shocked by the losses his army suffered, that he withdrew from the campaign. The Austrians handed over Lombardy, but retained Venetia. In 1860 Cavour cleverly took advantage of the campaign of **Garibaldi** to take over most of southern and central Italy. Cavour was prepared to use any means at his disposal to gain his objective. This policy became known as *realpolitik*, 'realistic politics'.

CEAUSESCU, NICOLAE

Nicolae Ceausescu (1918–89) was imprisoned in 1936 for Communist activities; it was in prison that he met the Communist leader, Gheorghe Gheorghiu-Dej, who became leader of Romania in 1952. When the Communists came to power (1947) he worked his way up until, under Gheorghiu-Dej, he was second-in-command. When Gheorghiu-Dej died (1965) he became leader and president of the State Council. In power he openly challenged the Soviet dominance of Romania, but his secret police kept rigid controls over his own people. His regime collapsed when he ordered security forces to fire on anti-government protesters in 1989, whereupon the Romanian army defected to the demonstrators and captured, tried and shot both Ceausescu and his wife.

CÉZANNE, PAUL

Cézanne (1839–1906) is considered by many to be the father of twentieth-century painting. His early work in Paris in the 1860s was crude, but in 1872, while working with fellow painter Camille Pissarro, he turned to an Impressionist style, with a lighter palette and small brush strokes. This style developed during the 1880s into a constructive one based on hatched brush strokes and blocks of colour. During this period,

The teaching of Chaitanya centred on worship of Krishna (left). ◀

Towards the end of his life, his style became more abstract, and he concentrated on fewer subjects, one of which was the landscape around Mont Sainte-Victoire.

CHAITANYA

Chaitanya was born in Bengal in 1485 and became the founder of the major Vaishnava sect, which is named after him. His teaching was that of passionate devotion, *bhakti*, directed towards Krishna, the latest avatar of Vishnu. His teachings follow on from the tradition of Ramanuja. The practice he taught of devotion and remembrance through continual chanting of the mantra *Hare Krishna* ('praise Krishna') is today principally associated with the International Society for Krishna Consciousness.

Cézanne lived at his family home in Provence and worked on landscapes, still lifes and portraits, such as *The Card Players* (1885–90), in which he achieved a sense of monumentality for the first time.

Neville Chamberlain encouraged a policy of appeasement towards Hitler. ◀

CHAMBERLAIN, ARTHUR NEVILLE

Neville Chamberlain (1869–1940) was a British Conservative politician and prime minister from 1937 to 1940. Chamberlain will always be associated with the discredited policy of appeasement towards **Hitler**. Strongly opposed by politicians such as **Churchill**, appeasement was actually quite popular among the people at the time. The guarantee of peace Chamberlain secured from Hitler in 1938 at the time of the Munich crisis, though, proved to be a mirage. Chamberlain joined the Churchill government but resigned just before his death in October 1940.

CHAMPOLLION, JEAN FRANÇOIS

Jean François Champollion (1790–1832), virtual founder of Egyptology as a serious discipline, scholar of Cryptic and other Oriental languages, was the first to decipher hieroglyphics (1822).

CHANDRAGUPTA

Chandragupta (d. 286 BC) was the first king (*c.* 321–298 BC) of the Maurya dynasty of the ancient kingdom of Magadha in north India. During Chandragupta's reign a strong centralised government grew up, supported by a sophisticated network of roads that allowed Mauryan control over most of India.

CHANEL, GABRIELLE 'COCO'

Chanel's (1883–1971) tailoring was always masterful and masculine. Like Jean Patou, her arch rival, many of Chanel's best ideas came from the male wardrobe, but also from the coastlines of Brittany and the boardwalks of Biarritz and Deauville, where she began life as a milliner working from her lover's apartment. Her heyday was the 1920s, her associations with names like **Picasso** and Le Corbusier putting her in touch with a 'less is more' aesthetic she made her own. Chanel adopted beige as her favourite colour, borrowed from the functionality of sportswear to put her women in trousers and designed skirts with 'walking pleats' to facilitate greater movement. In 1939, accused of aiding the Nazis, Chanel retreated to Switzerland, but in 1954 she returned to the Rue Cambon in Paris to run her couture house, where she continued to design and refine her look until her death.

CHANG TAO LING

Chang Tao Ling (b. AD 34) is traditionally described as a Taoist immortal who could 'ride the wind' and who received his powers and title of 'Heavenly Master' directly from Lieh Tzu. He was a magician who established a semi-independent Taoist state in south-west China.

CHAPLIN, CHARLIE

Charlie Chaplin was more than the first British film star, he was the first cinema star of the modern age and he went on to play a leading role in Hollywood. He was discovered in New York by film-maker Mack Sennett and after his first film in 1913, the cinema gathered a mass appeal, making it what some would say was the pre-eminent art form of the twentieth century. Chaplin had a prolific film output, but his later life was dogged by the Red Channels scandal, in which many US entertainment stars were accused of having Communist sympathies. Chaplin was amongst those who were defamed at this time.

Charlie Chaplin. ▶

CHARLEMAGNE

Charlemagne (AD 742–814) was Charles the Hammer's grandson and became king of the Franks in AD 768. Between 768 and 814, Charlemagne fought against the Saxons, Lombards, Spanish Muslims, Avars, Frisians, Bretons and Byzantium. His empire covered the majority of western Europe and the Pope crowned him emperor in Rome in 800. From his capital of Aachen he vigorously promoted Christianity and scholarship. It is for his wars against the Muslims in Spain that he is best remembered, but his introduction of the feudal system allowed him to maintain a strong cavalry force, so vital to defend the enormous borders and to strike out at his enemies. After his death, the empire fragmented under the pressure of the combined raids from the Arabs, Magyars and Vikings in the ninth and tenth centuries.

Charlemagne. ▶

CHARLES I, HOLY ROMAN EMPEROR

Charles I (1500–58) played a key role in developing a new order in Europe. He set up a centralised administration for the whole empire and founded the Habsburg family, which was to rule the Holy Roman Empire, and later Austria, until the end of the First World War. Charles spent most of his life defending his scattered domains against French, Turkish and Protestant enemies. The conquest of Mexico (1519–21) by **Hernan Cortes** and the conquest of Peru (1531–33) by **Francisco Pizarro** resulted in the influx of gold and silver from America, making Spain the greatest European power of the age. Charles abdicated in 1555, leaving Spain to his son, **Philip II**, and his German dominions to his brother, later Holy Roman Emperor Ferdinand I.

CHARLES I

In Whitehall on 30 January 1649, Charles I (1600–49) became the first monarch to be tried for treason and beheaded. The road to his execution was long and complex. He came to the throne on 1625, but his reign was dominated by disputes with Parliament over his attempts to raise revenues through taxation as well as being punctuated by protracted disputes over the long-standing issue of religion. Charles dissolved three Parliaments between 1625 and 1628. From 1629 he tried to rule without the aid of Parliament. Following a further failed attempt to work with Parliament civil war broke out. Captured by the Scots and handed over to the English, he escaped but was later caught and executed after his supporters were defeated.

CHARLES II

Charles II (1630–85) was restored to the throne in 1660 after the 11 years of the Republic. He was a very popular king, but as he grew older it became clear that he would have no legitimate children. Charles's successor would be his brother James, Duke of York.

The execution of Charles I. ▼

CHARLES V

Charles V, 'the Wise' (1337–80), acted as regent for his imprisoned father, John II. Crowned king in 1364, he reconquered the English territorial possessions in France.

CHARLES VII

Charles VII (1403–61) presided over the end of the Hundred Years' War with England, during which **Joan of Arc** raised the siege of Orleans in May 1429. His reforms set the basic organisational forms of modern armies, and his 25,000-man army stunned Europe with its effectiveness in Italy in 1496–97.

The Hundred Years' War, where Charles VII's military reforms were put in to practice. ▼

CHARLES VIII

After the Peace of Lodi (1454), a precarious balance of power had been maintained among the chief Italian states: Florence, Milan, Naples, the papacy and Venice. This equilibrium was upset when Ludovico Sforza of Milan appealed to France for aid against a secret league of Florence and Naples. The French king, Charles VIII (1470–98), descended into Italy with his army (1494), expelled the Florentine ruler Piero de'Medici and entered Naples in February 1495. Threatened by a coalition of Italian states allied with Emperor **Maximilian I** and King **Ferdinand II** of Aragon, Charles soon withdrew. A period of intermittent warfare followed, during which the Spanish general **Gonzalo Fernandez de Cordoba** conquered Naples (1503–04), bringing southern Italy under Spanish control, whereas France dominated the northern half of the peninsula.

CHAUCER, GEOFFREY

Geoffrey Chaucer's (*c*. 1340–1400) comic descriptions of the stories told by pilgrims were so successful that they were among the first books to be printed a century

The Miller, from the Canterbury Tales, *written by Geoffrey Chaucer.* ▲

later. Chaucer inspired his contemporaries to write in English as well, and did more than anyone else to make English the dominant language it is today, instead of French and Latin. His *Canterbury Tales* demonstrates the first full flowering of the English language. Chaucer had an eventful life himself, living above Aldgate as the Peasants' Revolt dashed underneath in 1381 and later becoming an MP. He is buried in Westminster Abbey, not as a poet – although his tomb later became the nucleus for Poets' Corner – but as a royal servant who leased a house in the abbey precincts.

CHEKHOV, ANTON

Anton Chekhov (1860–1904), a Russian dramatist and storyteller, developed a new kind of theatre. All the major events take place off-stage and the audience's attention is focused on the inner life of the characters. Dramatic events are replaced by close emotional observation, and each gesture of a character is full of intimacy, pessimism and tension. In *Uncle Vanya*, he uses these techniques brilliantly. Set on an estate in nineteenth-century Russia, the four-act play explores the interaction of characters with conflicting interests and desires. Although it focuses on the emotional upheaval of Vanya, Sonya and Serebryakov, the play finishes in a kind of deadly stasis.

CHENG-HO

The second Ming emperor, Yung Lo (1403–24), for a time considered the possibility of expanding his empire south-eastwards. He had assembled a huge fleet of 62 ships, which he sent into the Indian Ocean under Admiral Cheng-Ho (1371–1435). Cheng-Ho eventually made seven voyages around the Indian Ocean, visiting India, Sri Lanka and even the coast of East

Africa at Mogadishu. He also sailed into the Red Sea and anchored in the Arabian port of Jidda.

CHIH-I

The Chinese scholar, Chih-I (AD 538–597) made major strides in the integration and synthesis of the many different Buddhist ideas entering China. He classified these into eight teachings and developed T'ien Tai (Tendai in Japan) as an attempt to unite these into a single philosophical system. The school is named after the mountain where he founded his main monastery. He felt that each of these eight teachings came from the Buddha, and that each was suitable for a different audience. Each person should choose the teaching most suitable for their current situation. He felt, however, that all these teachings were compatible and that they were summed up most concisely in the text of the *Lotus Sutra*.

CHRISTIE, LINFORD

British athlete Linford Christie is the best-ever European sprinter. His form in the early 1990s broke American dominance in the sprints. Prior to his win in the Barcelona Olympics in 1992, only four non-Americans had won the gold medal in 11 Olympics since the Second World War.

CHUANG TZU

The earliest Taoist sage who is likely to have existed is Chuang Tzu (*c.* 369–286 BC), whose teachings

John Churchill. ▼

are to be found in a book of the same name. *Chuang Tzu* articulates the Taoist teaching that one should live in accordance with the Way (Tao), the order of nature, and abandon Confucian artificiality, the pursuit of wealth and power, and attempts to coerce either people or nature. The world is continually changing and so spontaneity and intuition are our only guides to a sane life. The person who lives this way will attain virtue (Te). The *Chuang Tzu*, the most philosophical and coherent of the Taoist scriptures, contains many amusing criticisms of orthodox Confucianism.

CHURCHILL, JOHN

John Churchill, 1st Duke of Marlborough (1650–1722), entered the army in 1667; he first distinguished himself by helping defeat the rebellion of the Duke of Monmouth (1685). King James raised him to the peerage and promoted him to lieutenant-general. Churchill soon shifted his allegiance to **William of Orange**, who deposed James and ruled as William III. Churchill campaigned for William during the war against France in Flanders and Ireland. When **Anne** became queen in 1702, she appointed Marlborough commander-in-chief and first minister. During the long war against France, he won victories at Blenheim (1704), Ramillies (1706), Oudenarde (1708) and Malplaquet (1709). Marlborough is acknowledged as a master military strategist.

William and Mary, the monarchs to whom Churchill shifted allegiance. ▼

CHURCHILL, WINSTON

Winston Churchill (1874–1965) was a British Conservative politician and prime minister 1940–45 and 1951–55. His political career began in 1900. A Liberal until 1923, he held the posts of Home Secretary in 1910, Lord of the Admiralty between 1911 and 1915 and Secretary of War between 1918 and 1921. He then became Colonial Secretary, playing a leading role in establishing the Irish Free State. He joined the Conservatives in 1923 and was made Chancellor of the Exchequer a year later. The start of the Second World War again saw him as Lord of the Admiralty, and in 1940 he was called to lead his country, which he did with passion and dedication for the remainder of the war. He was a popular and charismatic leader.

Winston Churchill. ▲

CLARKE, ARTHUR C.

In 1945 the British author-scientist Arthur C. Clarke (b. 1917) proposed the use of an Earth satellite for radio communication between, and radio broadcast to, points widely removed on the surface of the Earth. The station would be positioned at an altitude of about 35,900 km (22,300 miles) so that its period of revolution about the Earth would be the same as the period of the Earth's rotation. The first satellite communication experiment was the US government's Project SCORE, which launched a satellite on 18 December 1958.

CLARKSON, THOMAS

Thomas Clarkson (1760–1846) was a notable campaigner against slavery who gathered evidence on the slave trade, which he published in books and pamphlets. The Anti-Slavery Society (est. 1823), which led the campaign to stop the slave trade, continues to work towards abolishing types of slavery that still exist.

The emperor Claudius. ▲

CLAUDIUS

Claudius (AD 103–54), believed throughout his childhood to be mentally retarded, was proclaimed emperor by the Praetorian Guard. Following internal political disputes in Rome, the newly crowned Claudius turned his attention to Britain almost 100 years after **Caesar** first had. In AD 43 he assembled about 40,000 troops for a full-scale invasion of the islands. Despite fierce resistance, British troops could not match the weaponry of the Romans, nor did they have sophisticated body armoury like the invaders. Roman rule was confirmed when 11 British tribal kings submitted to the emperor. Claudius was present at the capture of Colchester and arrived in town complete with elephants. By 47, Roman forces had occupied as far north as the Trent.

CLAY, CASSIUS

Muhammad Ali is the adopted name of Cassius Clay (b. 1942) who was a US boxer. He was the Olympic light-heavyweight champion in 1960 and went on to become world professional heavyweight champion in 1964, and was the only man to regain the title twice. He was known for his fast footwork and extrovert nature.

CLEOPATRA

In the first century BC, corruption and intrigue became widespread in Ptolemaic Egypt and a number of kings were murdered. Cleopatra (68–30 BC) murdered her own brother in 44 BC. When Cleopatra committed suicide in 30 BC, Egypt became a province of the Roman Empire and one of its main sources of wheat. It remained under Roman, and later Byzantine, control for almost seven centuries.

CLEVELAND, GROVER

Democrat Grover Cleveland (1837–1908) was the 22nd and 24th president of the USA from 1884–88 and 1892–96.

CLINTON, WILLIAM

Bill Clinton (b. 1946) served as governor of Arkansas in 1979–81 and 1983–93 and established a liberal and progressive reputation. He won the 1992 presidential campaign by focusing on domestic issues and the ailing economy. In 1993 he became the 42nd US president and the first Democrat in the White House for 13 years. As president he brought in a variety of anti-crime measures and helped pull the US out of recession. In foreign affairs he backed the Israeli-PLO peace accord in Washington in 1993 and withdrew US peace-keeping forces from Somalia in 1994. Although his party suffered a

The White House housed its first Democrat in 13 years with the election of Bill Clinton in 1993. ▼

Bill Clinton. ◀

huge defeat in the November 1994 mid-term elections, he was himself re-elected as president in 1996. Revelations about his private life brought his professional integrity into question throughout 1998, but he continued in office.

COBB, JOHN

On 23 August 1939, British driver John Cobb (1900–52) set a new land speed record at the Salt Flats, Bonneville, Utah, driving his Railton Red Lion at 593.6 kph (368.85 mph). The aerodynamically designed car was created by Reid Railton and had a unique system of cooling the transmission brakes with ice. Cobb had previously set a world speed record of 563.6 kph (350.2 mph) on 15 September 1938, and he went on to set another official record, on 26 September 1947, clocking 634.38 kph (394.19 mph) in his Railton Mobil Special. That record wasn't broken until 1964, when **Donald Campbell**, in a Campbell *Bluebird*, smashed the record at an amazing 648.7 kph (403.1 mph).

COCTEAU, JEAN

The French artist and writer Jean Cocteau (1889–1963) was both an inventor and a producer of art in many forms. Enormously prolific and extremely influential among the Parisian *avant-garde* for over four decades, Cocteau had a lasting effect on a distinguished coterie of painters, composers, dancers, theatrical designers, actors and writers in every genre. His first volume of poetry was published in 1909, and his involvement with the Ballets Russes and Serge Diaghilev began the same year. After serving as an ambulance driver on the Belgian front during the First World War, Cocteau returned to Paris, and in 1917 produced his ballet *Parade*, with music by the modernist Erik Satie and scenery by **Picasso**.

COLERIDGE, SAMUEL TAYLOR

When two political radicals, **William Wordsworth** and Samuel Taylor Coleridge (1772–1834) met in the Quantock Hills in 1797, their conversation changed the direction of literature. They agreed with each other's sense that eighteenth-century poetry was emotionally artificial, and their *Lyrical Ballads* the following year pointed in another direction. Only four of the anonymous poems in the original edition were by Coleridge – although one was *The Rime of the Ancient Mariner*, described by one contemporary critic as 'the strangest story of cock and bull that we ever saw on paper'. *Lyrical Ballads* founded the Romantic movement in poetry, which became so important in the early years of the next century.

COLET, JOHN

Colet's (1466–1519) lectures on the 'Epistle to the Romans' marked a step forward in biblical research. He tended to be critical of the state of morality in the country, but still managed to be popular and well liked. He founded St Paul's School for 153 poor boys in 1509. His emphasis on the unity of divine truth, concern for historical context and his literal approach to texts excited **Desiderus Erasmus** and, no doubt, influenced **Thomas More**.

COLLINS, WILKIE

The detective story, where one intelligent outsider is able to see through the mists of confusion, was the invention of the American writer, Edgar Allan Poe, in the 1840s, but it was Wilkie Collins (1824–89) – the son of a landscape painter – who made the idea

Christopher Columbus. ▶

Christopher Columbus at San Domingo. ▲

British. His novel *The Moonstone* in 1868 introduced the character of Sergeant Cuff, and was serialised in **Charles Dickens**'s magazine *All the Year Round*. Along with his other great success, *The Woman in White* (1860), Collins used his own advice to himself: 'Make 'em laugh, make 'em cry, make 'em wait.' His career petered out in ill health and private confusion, at one point sharing his home with two of his mistresses simultaneously.

COLUMBUS, CHRISTOPHER

Christopher Columbus (1451–1506) was an Italian navigator and explorer who believed that Asia could be reached by sailing westwards. Sponsored by **King Ferdinand** and **Queen Isabella** of Spain he made four voyages to the New World. His first expedition embarked in September 1492, with three ships carrying 100 men. In October they first landed on Watling Island and then proceeded to sail round the Bahamas, Cuba and Hispaniola to find Asia, unaware of the significance of the discovery. Columbus was convinced these were Asiatic islands leading to China. His second voyage carried 1,200 people, tools, seeds and animals to begin colonising the largest and most accessible Caribbean islands. Columbus's 1498 voyage found mainland Venezuela and the 1502 voyage found Central America. Columbus lost support as the elusive route to the East, and the anticipated riches, failed to materialise. Columbus died in 1506 convinced the discovery of mainland Asia was imminent.

CONFUCIUS

China's great sage, K'ung Fu-Tze ('Master K'ung', 551–479 BC) is generally known in the West by his latinised name 'Confucius', and his teachings emphasised the importance of ethics and moral example. He came from an aristocratic but poor family in the state of Chou, and was orphaned at an early age. At this time China was in a state of chaos and had divided into many warring states. Many of Confucius's teachings, which could more accurately be described as moral and political than religious, were directed towards restoring the kind of social order that was believed to have existed in ancient times. To Confucius this was a matter of restoring to Earth the perfect Order of Heaven, *T'ien ming*. This could be done through virtuous living and the correct practice of the ancient rituals. Confucianism has no church organisation or dogma, and little emphasis is placed on a god or an afterlife, although Confucius himself is considered a superior being.

CONSTABLE, JOHN

John Constable (1776–1837) was one of the most popular English artists of his time. The son of a Suffolk miller, he specialised in rural landscapes, documenting the simplicity of nature just as **Wordsworth** was doing in poetry. His impressionistic method of portraying light caused a sensation when his most famous picture, *The Hay Wain* – originally called *Landscape, Noon* – was exhibited at the Salon in 1824, which probably had more of an influence in France than it did in Britain. His pictures, like *Flatford Mill* (1817), the first large painting he sent to the Royal Academy, and *Dedham Vale* (1828), remain etched on the national consciousness. His favourite area, around the Stour, is still known as 'Constable Country'.

Confucius. ◀

CONSTANTINE

Constantine (AD 280–337) divided his empire in half and built a new capital for the eastern half at Constantinople in AD 330. Constantine adopted Christianity as the state religion and in doing so, became in effect head of a religion that had previously been a threat to the state. With the power of the state behind it, the Church was able to resolve theological disputes by legal rather than philosophical means. At the Council of Nicea, called by Constantine in 325, the teachings of the theologian Arius, who taught that **Jesus** was not God, were declared heretical and religious orthodoxy was defined. At this time, the Church began to implement punishments for heresy; for example, Constantine ordered that Christians who refused to eat pork (which **St Paul** taught was suitable to eat) should be killed by drinking molten lead. Constantine was later canonised as a saint.

Emperor Constantine. ▲

COOK, JAMES

James Cook (1728–79) was a British naval explorer who helped answer many of the unresolved questions about the Pacific through his forages into the unknown seas in these parts. He plotted many unexplored areas in this part of the world from 1769. Cook produced a chart of New Zealand and, after

Captain James Cook arriving at Botany Bay. ▲

landing in Botany Bay, he claimed the Australian south-east coast for Britain, calling it New South Wales (1769). Cook also made an exploration of the Great Barrier Reef, and proved that New Guinea was not connected to Australia. He made another voyage to New Zealand between 1772 and 1775, before being killed in Hawaii in 1779.

COOLIDGE, CALVIN

Calvin Coolidge (1872–1933) was the 30th president of the USA, in office 1923–28. He was a Republican.

COPERNICUS, NICOLAS

Nicolas Copernicus (1473–1543), a Polish astronomer, was the first to suggest that the Earth was not the centre of the universe in post-medieval times; this came as a shock to European culture. His observations showed the Earth to be rotating around the Sun, which he in turn mistakenly took to be

Nicolas Copernicus. ▼

the centre of the universe, but nonetheless, the solar system hypothesis had been born. Christian beliefs were dominant at this time, so any idea which refuted the notion that the universe was centred around humanity, was not well received. Copernicus's major treatise – *On the Revolutions of the Celestial Spheres* – was not published until the year of his death.

CORDOBA, GONZALO FERNANDEZ DE

Gonzalo Fernandez de Cordoba (b. 1453) was a Spanish general known as *el Gran Capitan*. He fought in the wars to drive the Muslims from Spain and helped negotiate the surrender of the Moorish kingdom of Granada (1492). He was sent to Italy with an army in 1495 and he soon forced the French to withdraw. His victories at Cerignola and at Garigliano (1503) brought all of Naples under Spanish rule. He is credited with the introduction of the arquebusier, men armed with the latest handguns.

CORTÉS, HERNAN

Hernan Cortés (1485–1547) was a Spanish conquistador who, in 1519, set out from Cuba with a small force of only 508 men, landed at Tabasco and followed a mountainous route to Tenochtitlán – the vast capital of the sophisticated and wealthy Aztec civilisation. There he was greeted by a gorgeously garbed **Montezuma**, the Great Speaker, and treated like a God. Spanish troops with Indian allies later stormed the Aztec capital (now Mexico City) and seized control of the empire, after Montezuma was killed during an uprising in 1520.

Aztec warriors, defending Tenochtitlán against Hernan Cortés. ▼

COUSTEAU, JACQUES-YVES

Jacques-Yves Cousteau (1910–97), the French ocean explorer and pioneer in underwater research, became the foremost authority on oceanography and exploration, inventing (with Emile Gagnan), in 1943, the first scuba-diving device, which he called Aqualung. He commanded the prestigious research ship *Calypso* from 1950, and subsequently wrote a book about his findings, *The Calypso Log*. In 1957 he became head of the Conshelf Saturation Dive Program experiments, in which people live and work for extended periods in deep water along the continental shelves. He also conducted archeological research, exploring submerged shipwrecks. Cousteau did much to educate the public about the sea and sea creatures, and his books include *The Silent World* (1953) and *The Living Sea* (1963).

COWARD, NOEL

The actor and playwright Noel Coward (1899–1973) began by shocking his audiences with a play about drug addiction, *The Vortex* (1924), but made his reputation with patriotic set pieces, comic songs and stylish comedies. His song *Mad Dogs and Englishmen* caught the public mood, although his wartime *Don't Let's be Beastly to the Germans* caused a public furore and forced him to leave the country to perform to troops instead. But it was his comedy *Private Lives*, first performed in London in 1930, that was the pinnacle of his career. The play concerns a divorced couple who meet by accident on their respective honeymoons, and the cast of four included Coward, Gertrude Lawrence and **Laurence Olivier**.

CRANMER, THOMAS

Thomas Cranmer, Archbishop of Canterbury (1489–1556), was a key figure in the English Reformation, bold enough to marry the niece of a Lutheran theologian while clerical marriage was still illegal. He was also the main architect of the religious changes under Edward VI, constructing the Prayer Books of 1549 and 1552, the Ordinal of 1550 and the Thirty-nine Articles of the Anglican faith. But it was as author of the Prayer Book, the only legal liturgy in the Church of England between 1549–54 and 1559–1645, and the basis of the 1662 *Book of*

Mary I, who executed Thomas Cranmer under her Catholic regime. ▶

Marie Reine d'Angleterre
1515 - 1558

Common Prayer, that Cranmer is best remembered. His genius for prose and his soaring phrases have spread throughout English literature. He was eventually burned at the stake under **Mary I**.

CRIPPEN, HAWLEY HARVEY

In 1910, Hawley Harvey Crippen was trying to flee from the UK with his mistress Ethel le Neve. He had murdered his wife and buried her remains in the cellar of his London home. The suspicious captain of the Atlantic liner contacted Scotland Yard by radio telegraphy (its first use for police purposes) and a detective was dispatched in a faster boat and later arrested the couple. Crippen was executed at Pentonville, and is remembered as one of the most notorious criminals of all time.

Oliver Cromwell. ▼

CROMWELL, OLIVER

Oliver Cromwell (1599–1658) was an English general and Puritan leader of the Parliamentary side in the English Civil War (1642–49). **Charles I** was defeated at Newbury (20 September 1643) and the tide turned for the Parliamentarians for good in 1644, when the Royalists were beaten at Marston Moor in Yorkshire (2 July). In 1645 the Royalists were defeated by Thomas Fairfax's New Model Army at Naseby, and Charles, who had surrendered himself to the Scots, was turned over to Parliament and became a prisoner. After Charles I's execution (30 January 1649), his son **Charles II** renewed the war, sustained by Royalists in Ireland and Scotland. But Cromwell defeated the Irish and then invaded Scotland, where he crushed the Scots at Dunbar (1650).

CURIE, MARIE

Polish-born scientist Marie Curie (1867–1934) studied in Paris from 1891. Impressed by **Antoine-Cesar Becquerel**'s experiments, Curie decided to investigate the nature of uranium rays. In 1898 her husband Pierre abandoned his own researches to assist in her investigations of a new radioactive element in pitchblende ores, which proved to be polonium and radium. Both scientists refused to take out a patent and they were jointly awarded the Nobel Prize for Physics with Becquerel, for the discovery of radioactivity in 1903. After Pierre's death in 1906, Marie continued their work and in 1910 she succeeded in isolating pure radium, for which she won the Nobel Prize for Chemistry in 1911.

CUSTER, GEORGE ARMSTRONG

Lt-General George Armstrong Custer (1839–76) was a US Civil War general who campaigned against the Native American Sioux tribe from 1874 and was killed with a detachment of his troops by the forces of chief Sitting Bull in the Battle of Little Bighorn in Montana, also known as 'Custer's Last Stand'.

CYRUS THE GREAT

Cyrus the Great (*c.* 590–529 BC) founded the Persian Empire by conquering Asia Minor and Babylonia. Although a polytheist, he encouraged religious conciliation, allowing the Jews to return to Jerusalem. King of the Medes, he created a stable Middle Eastern empire. He was killed fighting the Scythians in 529 BC.

Oliver Cromwell at Dunbar. ▼

Louis Daguerre. ▲

DAGUERRE, LOUIS

Louis Daguerre (1787–1851) showed the world the possibilities of photography. Together with **Joseph Niepce**, who had taken the world's first-ever photograph, he experimented with ways of preserving an image on a metal plate. After Niepce died, Daguerre worked on, and in 1839 discovered that a plate coated with silver iodide would produce a satisfactory image, which he called a daguerreotype. Within a decade, thousands of photographic studios had sprung up around the world. The daguerreotype process permitted only one print to be made of each image.

DAIMLER, GOTTLIEB

Gottlieb Daimler (1834–1900) was a German engineer who, in 1889, pioneered the car and the internal-combustion engine. At first a plaything for the rich, the car enabled many townsfolk to venture out into the countryside for the first time. Country folk were not always pleased at the invasion, but when the car gave thousands a mobility the horse had never offered, it increased knowledge and understanding of rural life and brought people, however reluctantly, closer together.

DALÍ, SALVADOR

The Spanish artist Salvador Dalí (1904–89) combined great technical ability with a variety of artistic styles. He is probably best known for his Surrealist work, in which the commonplace is juxtaposed with the bizarre to create enigmatic, dream-like images. He frequently used double images, capable of interpretation on two levels at once, as well as other visual tricks. Dalí's genius blended with a rampant commercialism, and his prodigious energy sustained a vast Dalí industry in which his madness was artificially perpetuated as part of the myth. In 1957, he completed the illustration of Miguel de Cervantes' famous work *Don Quixote*, in which he used abstract calligraphy created in a number of more or less improbable ways, together with a brilliant colour palette.

DAMPIER, WILLIAM

William Dampier (1651–1715) was an English explorer and hydrographic surveyor who circumnavigated the world three times. He became the first Englishman to visit Australia on a buccaneering voyage (1679–91) and led an official expedition to observe the wildlife and indigenous Aborigines (1699–1701).

DARIUS I

When the Persians, under Darius I (550–486 BC), landed at Marathon, some 20 miles to the north-west of Athens, the Athenians were lured towards the landing site, while a second Persian amphibious force was poised to land at Phalerum and take the city. The Greeks under Miltiades, about 11,000

Gottlieb Daimler. ◀

strong, were hopelessly outnumbered. Frightened of being outflanked and overwhelmed by the Persians, the Greeks extended their lines across the whole valley. The Greek centre collapsed, but the wings drove the Persians back in confusion. The Persian force escaped by ship, leaving 6,400 dead. The Athenians then turned back and countered the second invasion force; they had lost just 192 men.

DARWIN, CHARLES

Charles Darwin (1809–82) was an English scientist whose studies of South American plant and animal life during the 1831–35 voyage of HMS *Beagle* to the Galapagos Islands contributed to his theory of evolution by natural and sexual selection. He reasoned that all living creatures must compete with each other in order to survive, and that nature must destroy those that could not compete. This led to his theory of the 'survival of the fittest' that was to revolutionise mankind's beliefs about their origins, and to shake the religious establishment to its core. He published his findings in 1859 in *On the Origin of Species by Natural Selection*.

Charles Darwin. ▶

DAVID I

David (1000–962 BC), Israel's greatest king, was originally a shepherd and musician from Bethlehem. He is best known for his allegorical defeat of the Philistine giant, Goliath – he probably became the leader of a small Hebrew army that defeated a larger Philistine one. He was elected king of the Hebrews, united the various Jewish tribes, and soon after captured the small town of Jerusalem, which he rebuilt as his capital. Since this time it has been known as the City of David.

King David I. ▲

DAVIS, BETTE ☻

Actress Bette Davis (1908–89) was given the role of Jezebel as a consolation prize for not getting the part of Scarlett O'Hara in *Gone with the Wind*. In the film she plays Julie, a perverse Southern belle, who ruins her own chances in love, as well as shaking up America's Old South. It is the Lupas Ball in New Orleans in 1852, and Julie turns up in a scarlet dress, while all the other unmarried women are dressed in pristine white. As she walks across the dance floor, couples shrink away from her. Her defiance threatens all the social conventions. Davis won an academy award for her performance.

DAWKINS, RICHARD

In *The Selfish Gene* (1976), Professor Richard Dawkins (b. 1941) argues that the process underlying life and evolution is the survival and replication of the fittest gene. Derived directly from **Darwin**'s theory of the survival of the fittest organism, Dawkins argues that plants and animals, as well as their nests, burrows, cars and even ideas, are merely the machines that genes use to survive. Although accused of reductionism by his opponents, his theories have taken a new twist. He argues that any basic unit that self-replicates, whether a gene, a process or an idea, is capable of evolution through natural selection. This means that not only would individual animals evolve, but so would artefacts, cultures, religions, communities and ecosystems.

DEAN, JAMES ☻

James Dean (1931–55) has come to represent the epitome of 1950s youth culture. He lived on the edge and died in a car accident at the age of just 24. Had he lived, his film career would have been prolific. His early death, however, elevated him to the position of an icon of tragic youth, and has gained his films a cult following. The most famous of these was *Rebel Without a Cause*, made in the year of his death, in which he co-starred with Natalie Wood and Sal Mineo.

DERRIDA, JACQUES

Jacques Derrida was born in Algeria in 1930. His thought developed as a response to that of Heidegger. He felt that metaphysical philosophy was without meaning, that it had reached the end of its history and that the only true philosophy concerned the nature of being. The question he asks is 'what can we say about Being without resorting to any metaphysical assumptions?' – and he tries to answer this by deconstructing philosophical statements on this matter and showing their limitations, contradictions and false assumptions. This exercise reveals that the structure of our language determines how we think.

DESCARTES, RENÉ

René Descartes (1596–1650) was a French mathematician who made significant discoveries in geometry and optics. By way of explaining the structure of the universe, he opted for a solution that employed mathematical physics, called analytical (or co-ordinate) geometry. He invented Cartesian co-ordinates as a means for using algebraic expressions to define and manipulate geometric shapes, which he saw as giving the universe its structure. Descartes argued that all matter ultimately consisted of measurable particles and that all man needed to do was to measure how these particles behaved. All other properties, such as colour and texture are unreal or could be reduced to the basic quantities of size and shape.

DEWAR, JAMES

The vacuum flask was invented in 1892 by the British chemist and physicist Sir James Dewar (1842–1923). He devised it to preserve liquefied gases, by preventing the transfer of heat from the surroundings to the liquid. The

René Descartes, who invented the science of analytical geometry. ▶

Diana, Princess of Wales. ▶

evacuated space between the walls (which are ordinarily glass or steel) is practically a non-conductor of heat; radiation is reduced to a minimum by silvering the glass or steel.

DIANA, PRINCESS OF WALES ☒

Diana, Princess of Wales (1961–97), was tragically killed in a Paris car crash in 1997. She died a commoner but her effect on the monarchy could hardly have been greater than if she had died the ruling monarch. Letters in the national press compared the public reaction to the revolutions in eastern Europe in 1989. Married in 1981 to the heir to the throne, Charles, Diana soon proved to be a popular choice. The couple provided an heir to the throne, William, in 1982, but the marriage was to end in divorce in 1996. She criticised the Conservative government, took up the cause of the banning of landmines – Britain was one of the biggest exporters of arms – and started a relationship with a wealthy Muslim, Dodi Al-Fayed, who was killed in the same accident.

DIAZ, BARTHOLOMEW

Bartholomew Diaz (*c.* 1450–1500) was a Portuguese explorer and the first European to reach the Cape of Good Hope in 1488, and to establish a route around Africa. He drowned during an expedition with Pedro Cabral.

DICKENS, CHARLES

Drawing inspiration from his own life of 'genteel poverty', Charles Dickens (1812–70) has become the best-known and best-loved English novelist of all time. His often dark portrayals of London life, and his obvious social criticisms are tempered by a range of intricately drawn characters and multitudinous plots, so cleverly exacted that the reader becomes totally involved in the lives and situations of the characters. His novels were first serialised in London papers, beginning with *Pickwick Papers* in 1836. He became the voice of nineteenth-century England, and inspired generations of future writers.

DIGGES, LEONARD

Precise mapping began in 1570 with the development of the theodolite by English mathematician Leonard Digges. The theodolite measures horizontal and vertical angles. It consists of a telescope mounted between two side supports in a trunnion. The angles through which the telescope moves are measured from circular, graduated scales.

Charles Dickens. ▶

DIOR, CHRISTIAN

In the war years women had dressed in utility clothing, short, drab and uncluttered in style. Material was rationed, and suits and frocks were asexual. And then Dior (1905–57) appeared. He said: 'I designed clothes for flower-like women, with rounded shoulders, full feminine busts and hand-span waists.' His dresses used metres of fabric and had hems rustling near the floor. The look was opulent and uncomfortable to wear, but a

sunburst after years of practicality. Women were enraptured and rushed to buy them. In England, senior politicians were outraged at the thwarting of fabric restrictions, but they could not stop the wave of the 'New Look', particularly after Princess Margaret adopted the style.

DISNEY, WALT

Walt Disney (1901–66) was travelling by train from New York to Hollywood, doodling on a drawing pad to pass the time. A shape began to appear on the page in front of him: 'out of trouble and confusion stood a mocking, merry, little figure; it grew and grew. And finally it arrived – a mouse. A romping, rollicking, little mouse.' He was named Mickey. Disney decided that his cartoon would have synchronised sound, Mickey would talk, and he would be the very first cartoon character to do so. The opening of the resulting animation, *Steamboat Willie*, featured Mickey whistling as he recklessly steered across the water. The tune 'Turkey In The Straw' became a concert, using the livestock cargo as musical instruments. It worked beautifully; critics said: 'Clever is a mild word to use. It is a wow.'

DISRAELI, BENJAMIN

Disraeli (1804–81), the son of a Spanish Jew, was a Conservative prime minister first in 1868 and later between 1874 and 1880. Notably, he was responsible for several pieces of social legislation passing through Parliament. These included the second Reform Law of 1867 and the Public Health Act in 1875. In the field of foreign politics he made **Queen Victoria** Empress of India in 1876, as well as beginning Britain's ownership of

Benjamin Disraeli made Queen Victoria Empress of India. ▼

the Suez Canal in 1875. A renowned novelist also, he once said, 'when I want to read a novel – I write one'.

DONNE, JOHN 📖

John Donne (1572–1631), Dean of St Pauls, had been brought up as a Roman Catholic, but had enjoyed a passionate lifestyle as a young man. In 1612 he resolved to become a priest and was ordained in 1615. His poetry lives on but it was as preacher, particularly his sermons on death, that he came alive to the people of his day.

DOYLE, ARTHUR CONAN 📖

The great detective Sherlock Holmes is probably the most imitated and parodied character in literature. He and Dr Watson appeared for the first time from the pen of the doctor-turned-writer Arthur Conan Doyle (1859–1930) in the novel *A Study in Scarlet*, published in *Beeton's Christmas Annual* for 1887. But it was not until the short stories began for *The Strand Magazine* in 1891 that Holmes acquired a mass audience. Conan Doyle borrowed some of the literary method from Edgar Allen Poe, and Holmes's scientific method from one of his teachers at

The great fictional detective Sherlock Holmes, created by Arthur Conan Doyle. ▲

Edinburgh University. He tried to kill his character off in *The Memoirs of Sherlock Holmes* (1894); popular demand brought him back from the dead, though, and by 1927 there had been four novels and 56 short stories.

DRAKE, FRANCIS

Francis Drake (*c.* 1540–1596) was an English buccaneer and explorer. Having enriched himself as a pirate against Spanish interests in the Caribbean, he was sponsored in 1577 by **Elizabeth I** for an expedition to the Pacific. He left Plymouth in the *Golden Hind*, sailed around South America, pillaging Spanish ports along the coast, and reached the Spice Islands in November 1579. He took on a cargo of cloves and continued eastwards, returning to Plymouth in September 1580. Drake also helped defeat the Spanish Armada in 1588 as a vice admiral in the *Revenge*. He planned to destroy the remnants of the Armada at anchor in Spanish ports and then land in Portugal and support Don Antonio of Portugal in an attempt to overthrow **Philip II**. He persuaded the queen to back him, to the extent of about £60,000, and the expedition set sail in April 1589. It was a disaster; the force marched on Lisbon, but failed to take it. When Drake returned home in disgrace he had lost 8,000 of his 15,000 men. He went into retirement, but planned one more expedition in 1595, along with his uncle John Hawkins. It was to be an attack on New Spain in the Caribbean. It, too, failed and Drake and Hawkins were both killed.

Francis Drake. ▶

DRYDEN, JOHN

The poet and playwright John Dryden (1631–1700) was born into a Puritan family, and spent his career adapting to the prevailing political climate, ending up as a Roman Catholic in 1686. But the adaptation was all the more important, because Dryden was appointed as Poet Laureate on the death of D'Avenant, the first poet to hold the title officially. He achieved the position with his poem *Annus Mirabilis* in 1667, describing the Great Fire of London and the naval war with the Dutch the year before. Towards the end of his life, dismissed as Laureate during the Protestant Revolution of 1688, he turned to the theatre and then to translating Latin classics, developing the heroic couplet which would be adopted by many poets in the next century.

DU BOIS, WILLIAM EDWARD BURGHARDT

William Edward Burghardt Du Bois (1868–1963) was a lifelong advocate of world peace and a leading champion of the liberation of Africans – in particular, African-Americans. Du Bois was the first black to be awarded a PhD from Harvard. In more than 20 books

Elizabeth I, who sponsored Francis Drake's voyages of discovery. ▲

and 100 scholarly articles, Du Bois championed the African-American culture through historical and sociological studies. *The Souls of Black Folk* was a pioneering effort, arguing that an educated black elite should lead Blacks to liberation. In 1905 Du Bois founded the Niagara Movement, a forerunner of the National Association for the Advancement of Colored People (NAACP), which he helped organise in 1909.

DUNSTAN ☯

Dunstan (AD 924–988) went on to become an able and powerful archbishop. Educated by Irish monks in Glastonbury, he became abbot in *c.* AD 943; this event has been called 'a turning point in the history of religion in England'. He set about establishing other monasteries based on the Rule of St Benedict. In about 970, a meeting was held to modify the Benedictine Rule to the English situation, for example prayers for the king were to be said at each service. Dunstan was Archbishop of Canterbury from 960–88 and he revitalised monasteries. Many monks became bishops, and he created a framework of monastic and church government that remained in place until the Reformation.

DYCK, ANTHONY VAN ✷

Anthony Van Dyck (1599–1641) was born in Antwerp, and studied under Peter Paul Rubens, before arriving in England as court painter to **Charles I**, where he painted almost everybody connected with the court – including the famous painting of the royal children. He lived in continual penury, finding it difficult to extract the money he was owed from the king, and he died broken-hearted at the outbreak of the Civil War. His new approach to portrait painting, with a poetic and graceful style, meant that his pictures are now in most of the best-known galleries in the UK.

Portrait of a Princess *by Anthony Van Dyck.* ◀

Thomas Edison. ◀

desire for that concept, so that the real and unnameable God may be free to be born in him. In recent years, the similarities of this approach to Buddhism have aroused great interest. His Latin theological works provide a philosophical defence of his teachings. Although denounced as a heretic in his lifetime, he has since been recognised as one of the most important Catholic theologians.

EDISON, THOMAS

The phonograph, invented by Thomas Edison (1847–1931), was an early forerunner of the record player. In 1878, both Thomas Edison and Joseph Swan were independently working on designs for commercially viable electric light bulbs. The first true filament bulb, containing an inert gas, was marketed by Edison in 1880. He also constructed the first central power station and distribution system in New York City in 1881.

ECKHART, JOHANNES

Johannes Eckhart, 'Meister Eckhart' (1260–1327), was a German theologian and mystic of the Dominican Order. His German sermons provided guidance in apophatic spiritual practice whereby the practitioners free themselves from any concept of God or

Edward I. ▲

EDWARD I

Edward I (1239–1307) was king of England from 1272. One of his great innovations was the longbow. It was during the Welsh Wars (1277–95), that it came to the fore and the English victory at Orewin Bridge (1282) owes much to this weapon. From 1252, all freeholders in England were required to possess a bow and regular archery practice was obligatory. It was also during Edward's reign that Parliament took its approximate modern form with the Model Parliament in 1295.

EDWARD III

Edward III (1312–77) was king of England from 1327 and it was his claim to the French throne that resulted in The Hundred Years' War. England won a comprehensive naval victory off Sluys in 1340, but it was not until 1346 that Edward felt strong enough to face the French in a decisive battle. Edward landed in France and headed for Calais with 15,000 men, he was immediately pursued by Philip VI who had at least 40,000 troops, including 29,000 mounted knights. Taking up a position overlooking a valley, Edward turned to face them. The French advanced to within 150 yards and the skies filled with English arrows. Wave after wave of Philip's soldiers were slaughtered. The French lost 10,000 to England's 200.

EDWARD THE CONFESSOR

The Anglo-Saxons, in the person of Edward the Confessor (1042–66), returned to the throne in 1042. Edward founded Westminster Abbey, where all subsequent coronations have been held. The controversy over his successor paved the way for the Norman

Conquest, as a result they included the last Anglo-Saxon king, **Harold II**, who was defeated by **William the Conqueror**.

EDWARD VII

Edward VII (1841–1910), the eldest son of **Queen Victoria**, came to the throne in his 60th year – 1901 – and he proved a huge success, despite his mother's misgivings and his well-earned reputation for gambling and debauchery as a young man. The beginning of the Edwardian era witnessed the build-up to the First World War. Edward, popular among his subjects, though tiresome to his mother for his playboy lifestyle, nevertheless proved an asset for his foreign-policy ventures.

EDWARD VIII

In January 1936, Edward VIII (1894–1972) came to the throne. His brief reign came to an end before the year was out. Although the story of his relationship with the American divorcee, Mrs Wallis Simpson, has often been told as one of history's greatest-ever love stories, it also sparked a constitutional crisis among the British establishment. The power of Parliament over the monarchy was proven when the prime minister Stanley Baldwin, backed by the Church, forbade the king from marrying Mrs Simpson if he wanted to retain the crown. Edward VIII chose to abdicate. Subsequently, it appeared that the politicians were fearful of Edward's pro-Nazi leanings, although whether they used the marriage crisis as a pretext to remove him from the throne is still unclear.

Edward VIII. ◀

EDWARD, THE BLACK PRINCE

After the Treaty of Bretigny in 1360, Edward, the Black Prince (1330–76), governed Aquitaine, the area in south-west France that included Gascony. He became involved in a series of campaigns against the French, led by Bertrand du Guesclin. The French avoided battle and concentrated on wearing out the English by a war of attrition. The people of Aquitaine became more and more opposed to the English as Edward raised extra taxes to pay for the cost of the war. Eventually, in 1371, he left France and returned to England. Edward died in 1376 from the plague, just a year before his father.

EGBERT, KING

Saxon Wessex, which was eventually to bring the Vikings under control, grew vastly in power in the early ninth century. King Egbert, who seized the throne of Wessex in AD 802, spread his territory into Cornwall (AD 815), overpowered his chief rival, King Beornwulf of Mercia (AD 825), and then moved to control Kent, East Anglia and Northumbria. This expansionist policy was not without its setbacks; in 836, Egbert suffered defeat at the hands of the Vikings. Within two years, however, he returned to destroy them in

The effigy of Edward, the Black Prince in Canterbury Cathedral. ▼

battle at Hingston Down, Cornwall. The king died in the following year, but he left behind a strong, well-organised realm.

EINSTEIN, ALBERT

Albert Einstein (1879–1955) formulated theories about the nature and structure of the universe that totally transformed human understanding of the way things behave. **Isaac Newton**'s theories had been accepted as fact for almost 200 years, because they worked as far as most observations were concerned, but scientists, especially astronomers, were noticing anomalies that couldn't be explained by Newtonian rules. In 1905 Einstein's *Special Theory of Relativity* was published. In it, he proposed various ideas on the subject of matter, light, space and time, not least that they are all inter-related. He provided complex mathematical formulae to reinforce his ideas and went on to release his *General Theory of Relativity* in 1915 and *Unified Field Theory* in 1953. Einstein's work led to the developments in nuclear fusion and fission, and to Arthur Stanley Eddington (1882–1944) proposing, in 1933, that the universe was expanding from a central point of origin.

Albert Einstein. ▲

EISENHOWER, DWIGHT

Dwight 'Ike' Eisenhower (1890–1969), a Republican, became the 34th US president in 1952. A general in the Second World War, he commanded the allied forces in Italy in 1943, then the allied invasion of Europe and from October 1944 all the allied armies in the West. He resigned from the army in 1952 to campaign for president, where the popularity he had gained in Europe swept him to nomination and ultimate victory. In power he promoted business interests at home during an era of post-war prosperity, and conducted the Cold War abroad. A popular politician, he was re-elected by a wide margin in 1956.

ELGAR, EDWARD

The composer Edward Elgar (1857–1934) began his musical career as bandmaster at the Worcester county lunatic asylum, but by the 1890s he had won himself an international reputation, leading to the 1899 performance of his best-loved orchestral portraits of his friends, *The Enigma Variations*. This was followed a year later by his celebrated oratorio, *The Dream of Gerontius*. In 1901, he was asked to write something for the coronation of **Edward VII**, and his *Pomp and Circumstance* marches – including the tune that became known as *Land of Hope and Glory* – was given its premiere in Liverpool. This was followed by a double encore at the Promenade concerts, and it has been played there ever since.

ELIOT, GEORGE

Mary Ann Evans (1819–80) was a powerful woman writer – probably the most powerful of the century – who chose not to publish under a woman's name. This was partly because she was living with the philosopher, George Henry Lewes, who was separated from his wife, a fact that would have confused the public reception if it had been known. It was as George Eliot that

T. S. Eliot. ▲

she created powerful women characters for novels like *Silas Marner* (1861) and *Daniel Deronda* (1876). *Middlemarch: A Study of Provincial Life* describes country life in the 1820s, but its concerns are about ardent and more modern characters, such as her heroine Dorothea Brooke.

ELIOT, T. S.

The poet and playwright T. S. Eliot (1888–1965) was born in America, but came to London in 1915 and worked as a clerk in Lloyds Bank. His poem cycle *The Waste Land*

(1922) was one of the most influential examples of modernist writing, edited into shape by the poet Ezra Pound – who was later discredited for broadcasting from Fascist Italy during the war. Eliot's work became increasingly religious during the 1920s, culminating in *The Four Quartets*, which were first published together in 1943. Eliot demonstrated a whole new way of writing poetry, obscure and spiritual, but it was his *Old Possum's Book of Practical Cats* (1939) that became his greatest success after his death. It was turned into the musical *Cats* by **Andrew Lloyd Webber** (b. 1948).

Elizabeth I. ▼

ELIZABETH I

Elizabeth I (1533–1603) became queen of England in 1558 when she was 25 years old. During her lifetime she had seen her father, **Henry VIII** grow old and increasingly unhappy, her brother **Edward VI** die at the age of 15 and her elder sister **Mary** become very unpopular after she married **Philip II** of Spain and tried to re-impose Catholicism on England. Elizabeth was determined to re-establish the authority of the crown. Traditionally the monarch in England was referred to as 'Your Grace', the same title used for a duke and an archbishop. Elizabeth forced her courtiers to address her as 'Your Majesty', implying that there was something different and remote about royalty. Known as the 'Virgin Queen', Elizabeth never married, and on her death the throne passed to the Scottish king, **James VI**.

Queen Elizabeth II and her husband Prince Phillip. ◀

ELIZABETH II

Elizabeth II (b. 1926) is the second monarch from the dynastic House of Windsor. Her family's name was originally Saxe-Coburg but this was changed in 1917 as its German associations were seen as inappropriate during the First World War. She came to the throne the year Britain tested its first atomic bomb (1952) and has survived 10 prime ministers, beginning with **Winston Churchill**. Her rule has overseen vast changes in Britain, politically, culturally and socially, as well as many changes to the royal family. Since the mid-1990s there have been increasing calls for a return to a republic. Elizabeth II has seen the British Empire transformed into a commonwealth of independent nations. She is respected for her grasp of foreign affairs and international politics.

EPICURUS

Epicurus (341–270 BC) was a materialist; he taught that the gods were immortal physical beings, but that they did not control the world or judge or punish humans. There was no life after death and the good life involved the enjoyment of reasonable pleasure, the cultivation of contentment, and freedom from responsibilities and from physical pain. Man should 'eat, drink and be merry – for tomorrow we die'. Epicurus established a school of philosophy in Athens, known as The Garden, to study and practice this way of life. He was opposed by the rival Stoic school.

ERASMUS, DESIDERIUS

Erasmus (1466–1536) was the central figure in the development of liberal-humanist Christianity during the Renaissance. Born in Rotterdam, he became a priest in 1492. He criticised the corrupt state of monastic life and scholarship, especially the stale dogmatism of the teachings of **Aquinas**, Ockham and Scotus – all derived from **Aristotle**. Instead, he advocated a return to the study of original texts such as the original Greek New Testament and the writings of **Plato**. His views were published in his satirical *In Praise of Folly* in 1511. Unfortunately, his moderate criticisms were attacked as heresy both by the Catholic authorities and by their new opponents, the evangelical Protestants, such as **Luther** and **Calvin**.

Desiderius Erasmus. ◀

ERATOSTHENES

A Greek geographer and mathematician called Eratosthenes (*c.* 276–194 BC) was the first map-maker to apply a mechanism to maps that made them practicable for navigation. He included lines of longitude and latitude so that a grid was created, which meant that different locations were referenced in relation to one another according to real space. It was also possible to determine a position at sea or on land on the map, according to the predictable movements of the stars throughout the year. Based on his astronomical observations, Eratosthenes was even able to make a surprisingly accurate calculation of the world's circumference at a time when most people still believed the world was flat.

ERSKINE, JOHN

John Erskine (1879–1951) was an American writer, educator and musician, who helped stimulate the Great Books movement in education while a professor at Columbia University in the US (1916–37).

ESQUIVEL, ADOLFO PEREZ

Adolfo Perez Esquivel (b. 1931), an Argentine human-rights activist, was awarded the Nobel Peace Prize in 1980. A sculptor and former professor of architecture, he became secretary-general of the Service for Peace and Justice in Latin America in 1974.

EUCLID

In the third century BC Euclid worked at the Museum of Alexandria, in addition to his studies in astronomy and music; he wrote a 13-book set *Elements* which detailed geometry, areas and the theory of numbers.

EVANS, ARTHUR JOHN

Arthur John Evans (1851–1941) was a British archeologist who, in 1895, began 40 years of excavation and discovery on the island of Crete. He uncovered what he termed the Minoan Civilisation, named after its king, Minos. King Minos was previously thought to be a mythical figure; Evans's work on the palace complex at Knossos proved otherwise. Here on a hilltop site specially chosen as a protection against earthquakes, he discovered buildings up to five storeys high, an elaborate throne room, beautiful friezes, gilded stone roofs, stone conduits and clay water pipes for drainage, staircases constructed on wooden columns and light wells designed to illuminate the interior.

EVERITT, PERCIVAL

Percival Everitt was the father of vending. He introduced a coin-operated, automatic, postcard-vending machine, to Mansion House Underground station, London, in 1883. By 1887, The Sweetmeat Automatic Delivery Co., launched by Everitt, was dispensing a wide range of goods from vending machines. They included: cigarettes, eggs, quinine, biscuits, scent, condensed milk, sugar and accident insurance! By the early twentieth century, there were coin-operated jukeboxes, telephone kiosks, gas meters and ticket machines.

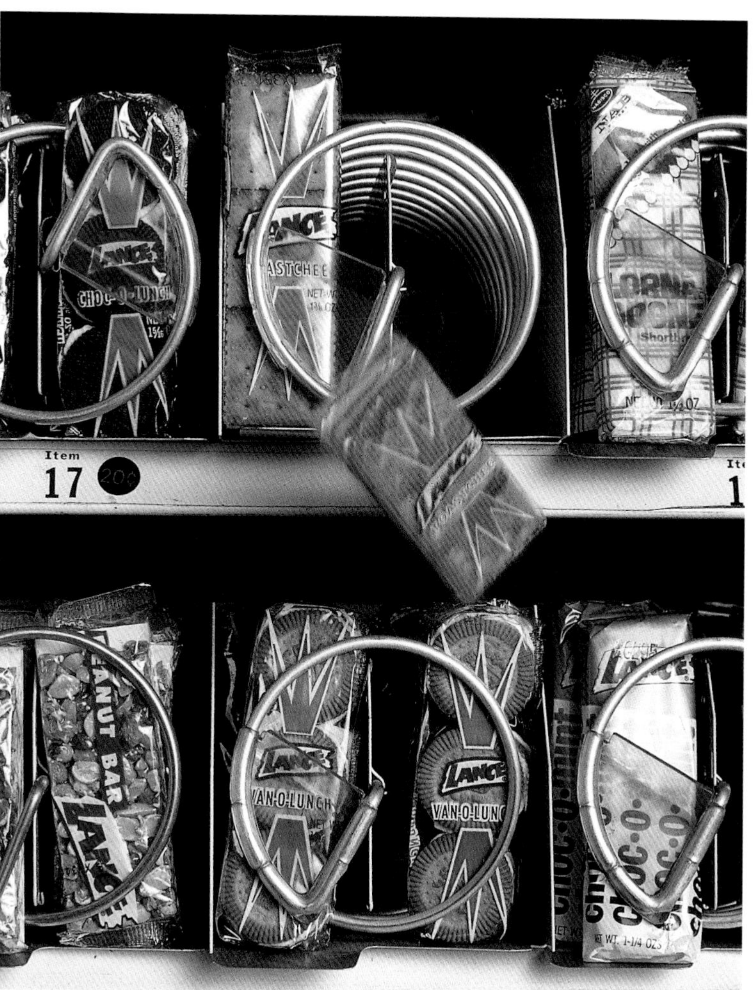

A modern vending machine, pioneered by Percival Everitt. ▲

FABERGE, KARL

This world-famous jewellery designer (1846–1920) made his name by creating a series of gem-studded eggs for the Russian monarchy. Extravagance and attention to detail are hallmarks of the Fabergé style, as is his love of coloured golds, translucent enamels, fine filigree work, and the unrestrained use of sapphires, rubies, emeralds and moonstones.

FARADAY, MICHAEL

In 1820 a man named Hans Christian Oersted inadvertently proved the connection between magnetism and electricity, by moving a compass needle to align itself with the flow of an electrical current. This led to Michael Faraday (1791–1867) making a prototype dynamo in 1821, by spinning a magnet inside a coil of copper wire that produced an electric current. He then tried a similar experiment to demonstrate that a reverse process would create a rotary motion; it was the first electric motor. Faraday's prototypes had shown the way to go, even though they were not designed to have a functional value.

FERDINAND II

Ferdinand II (1452–1516), king of Aragon from 1479, married his cousin **Isabella I**, who succeeded the throne of Castile in 1474. Ferdinand turned his attention to the conquest of Naples and to disputes with France over the control of Italy. In addition, he added Navarre and territories on the French border to the family's domains. In 1492, Granada was conquered, ending the Reconquest of Spain from the Arabs. Isabella died in 1504 and upon Ferdinand's death in 1516 both of their crowns went to their grandson **Charles I**.

Ferdinand II. ▶

FERRARI, ENZO

More than any other team, Ferrari has been shaped by one single person, 'Il Commendatore'; and more than any other team, Ferrari has left its mark on Grand Prix racing. Without Ferrari, Formula 1 seems impossible. Enzo Ferrari (1898–1988), who used to race for Alfa Romeo, launched his own company in 1947. The myth that emerged within a few decades shines far brighter than that of any other team.

FICINO, MARSILIO

Marsilio Ficino (1433–99) played an important role in reviving the thought of **Plato** during the

Marcilio Ficino revived the teachings of Plato (above) during the Renaissance. ▲

Renaissance. He established a Platonic Academy near Florence. His commentaries and translations of Plato (from Greek to Latin), which he produced at his Academy, include *Theologica Platonica* (1482). In these, he explores Plato's religious thought, his theory of the immortality of souls and his views on platonic love. His particular interest was in integrating the thought of **Plotinus** and the Neoplatonists with Christianity, although he felt that these teachings existed in all religions.

FIELDING, HENRY

Henry Fielding (1707–54) was a pioneering magistrate, starting the Bow Street Runners as a team of 'thief-takers' in Westminster with his blind half-brother, John, but he was also a prolific comedy writer and satirist, parodying the enormously successful *Pamela* by Samuel Richardson with his own *Shamela*, and then writing what has been claimed as the first great English novel, *Tom Jones*. The story describes the adventures of a 'foundling', and it established a narrative voice that involves the reader in a way that had never been done before. Fielding was also a successful dramatist, and opened himself to ridicule by marrying his dead wife's former maid.

FILLMORE, MILLARD

Millard Fillmore (1800–74) was the 13th president of the USA, in office 1850–52. He was a Whig.

FIORELLI, GIUSEPPE

Giuseppe Fiorelli (1823–95) was an Italian archeologist, best known for his excavations of Pompeii (1860). He helped pioneer the use of archeological stratigraphy, and he invented the technique of making plaster casts of human bodies and houses from the impressions they left in the ash.

FLEMING, ALEXANDER

Scottish bacteriologist Alexander Fleming (1882–1955) qualified as a surgeon at St Mary's Hospital in Paddington, where his career was spent. As a researcher, he became the first to use anti-typhoid vaccines on human beings and he pioneered the use of salvarsan against syphilis. As a medical officer in France during the First World War, he discovered the antiseptic powers of lysozyme, which is present in tears and mucus. In 1928 he made a chance exposure of a culture of staphylococci and noticed a curious mould, penicillin,

The Model T Ford, mass-produced by Henry Ford. ▼

which was found to inhibit the growth of bacteria and to have outstanding antibiotic properties.

FONTEYN, MARGOT ☻

Margot Fonteyn, stage name of Peggy Hookham (1919–91), was an English ballet dancer renowned for her perfect physique, clear line, musicality and interpretive powers. She formed a legendary partnership with **Rudolf Nureyev**.

FORD, GERALD R.

The Republican Gerald R. Ford (b. 1913) was the 38th president of the USA from 1974–76.

FORD, HENRY ⊠

Henry Ford (1863–1947) was a US automobile manufacturer, who built his first car in 1896 and founded the Ford Motor Company in 1903. His Model T was the first car to be constructed solely by assembly-line methods and to be mass-marketed. It was designed to be affordable by the layperson and by 1927, 15 million had rolled out of his factories. In 1913, Ford had introduced the first conveyor-belt assembly line and truly interchangeable parts, which revolutionised the car industry, as well as many others.

Henry Ford. ▲

FOREMAN, GEORGE

George Foreman, born into poverty in Texas in 1949, was, at just under 2 m (6 ft 4 in), a giant of a boxer. Although he dropped out of school at 14, it was not until he was 18 that he first put on a pair of boxing gloves; from then on he hardly looked back. Winning the Olympic heavyweight title in 1968, he turned professional in 1969 and won all of the 38 fights he had before his 1973 meeting with Joe Frazier.

FORSTER, E. M.

E. M. Forster (1879–70) came from a wealthy and privileged background; he studied classics and history at Cambridge. He visited India, which became the setting for his most famous novel, *A Passage to India*. Published in 1924, the book is a complex study of human misunderstandings in colonial India.

FOUCAULT, MICHEL

The French philosopher, Michel Foucault (b. 1926), sought to understand the origin and nature of institutional controls over how we see ourselves. In his *Discipline and Punish* (1975) and his *Madness and Civilisation* (1961) he explores the origins and development of concepts and normality by looking at the history of punishment and of asylums. State concepts of normality are internalised and determine how we see ourselves. The 'work of freedom' is to step outside these definitions and to create ourselves.

FOX, GEORGE

The Society of Friends, or 'Quakers', was founded in England by George Fox (1624–91). Following his own inner

George Fox. ◀

experiences in 1646 and 1647, he rejected the formal institutions of the church and emphasised direct awareness of the divine. Quaker meetings involve no liturgy or ritual and are characterised by long periods of silence and contemplation – during which the members were once said to 'quake' in awe of God, hence their name. Quakers are renowned for their active concern with peace issues and social justice and for the democratic way in which they run their affairs.

FRANCIS II

From 1273, the Holy Roman Empire was dominated by the Hapsburg family. Francis II (1768–1835), the last emperor, dissolved the empire in 1806 and thereafter ruled as Emperor of Austria.

Belvedere Palace, home to the emperors of Austria. ▼

FRANK, ANNE

Anne Frank (1929–45) was a Jewish girl who hid with her family in occupied Amsterdam between 1942 and 1944. She kept a diary while hiding from Nazi persecution, living in a secret apartment for two years before being discovered. Anne and her family were betrayed to the Gestapo on 4 August 1944, and deported with eight others in the last convoy of cattle trucks to the extermination camp at Auschwitz. Anne was shipped on to the Bergen-Belsen concentration camp, and died there in March 1945. Her three notebooks, left behind at 263 Prinsengracht in Amsterdam, contained her diary, chronicling the period in which she and her family hid from the Gestapo. This moving account was abridged in 1947 and became an international best-seller, acting as a poignant reminder of the plight of the Jews during the Holocaust.

FRANKLIN, JOHN

In 1819, Lieutenant John Franklin (1786–1847) was part of an expedition sent to map the north coast of Canada. In 1825, he returned to explore the Mackenzie River and in 1845 led a third expedition to try to find the north-west passage in his two ships, the *Erebus* and the *Terror*. Although Franklin was well prepared, his ships became trapped in ice during the winter of 1846–47. He himself died in June 1847 and the rest of the party died the following winter. The bodies of some of the men have been discovered recently and the cause of death was found to be lead poisoning. Franklin had carried supplies of food in lead cans, unaware of the risk that this entailed.

FRANZ FERDINAND, ARCHDUKE

The heir to the Austrian throne, Archduke Franz Ferdinand (1863–1914), and his wife were assassinated by Serbian nationalist Gavrilo Princip on 28 June 1914. This led to war between Austria and Serbia. When Russia mobilised in support of the Serbs, Germany automatically became involved and this brought in France. By

The assassination of Archduke Franz Ferdinand. ▲

12 August all the major European powers were involved and world war was imminent.

FREDERICK II (THE GREAT)

Frederick the Great (1712–86) became king of Prussia in 1740. In that year he started the War of the Austrian Succession by his attack on Austria. The struggle was renewed in the Seven Years' War (1756–63). Costly Prussian successes at Zorndorf in 1758 and again at Leignitz and Torgau in 1760 only drained Frederick's limited resources. He suffered another defeat against the Russians at Kunersdorf in 1759. By the end of 1761 the Austrians had moved into Saxony and Silesia, and

Russian troops held Prussian Pomerania. With enemy armies closing in around him, Frederick seemed incapable of further resistance. At this critical moment the Russian empress died (January 1762) and was succeeded by Peter III, one of Frederick's devoted admirers. Peter immediately withdrew from the war, and Austria, unable to defeat Prussia alone, was compelled to end the fighting in Germany.

FREDERICK II

Frederick II (1534–88), king of Denmark from 1559, led a war against Sweden between 1564–70. He built the magnificent castle at Elsinore, scene of **Shakespeare**'s *Hamlet*.

FREUD, LUCIAN

The early work of British painter Lucian Freud (b. 1922), grandson of **Sigmund Freud**, portrays people and plants in a bleached, realistic style with hard lines and an almost Surrealistic aspect. From the 1950s, his paintings became more truthful and meticulous, focusing on nudes in squalid settings. Typical of Freud's work are *Naked Man, Back View* (1991–92) and numerous self-portraits. *Girl with a White Dog* portrays the artist's first wife, Kathleen, with an English bull terrier, and is emblematic of Freud's mastery and near-obsessive portrayal of human flesh, with all its flaws exposed.

Frederick the Great of Prussia. ◀

FREUD, SIGMUND

Sigmund Freud (1856–1939) was an Austrian psychiatrist whose controversial studies into sexual repressions helped many people whose mental distress had long been without sympathy or explanation. Inventor of psychoanalysis, his first major work was *The Interpretation of Dreams*, which he was inspired to write in response to the many dreams that he had following the death of his father. His principal concept was of the unconscious mind, which he analysed in terms of competing forces – the *ego*, the *superego* and the *id*. Behaviour patterns in his patients, such as anxiety, phobias, hysteria and obsessions, were classified as neuroses – the consequences of repressing disturbing thoughts. He pioneered the study of the unconscious mind and developed the methods of free association and interpretation of dreams, which were the basic techniques of psychoanalysis.

FRITTS, CHARLES

Charles Fritts constructed the first true solar cells in the 1890s. He coated the semiconductor selenium with an ultra-thin layer of gold. Less than one per cent of the absorbed light energy was converted into electrical energy.

Sigmund Freud. ▲

FROEBEL, FRIEDRICH WILHELM AUGUST

Friedrich Wilhelm August Froebel (1782–1852) was a German educator who created and developed the kindergarten. Froebel's educational philosophy and practice was based on his belief in the unity of the universe.

FRY, ELIZABETH

Elizabeth Fry (1780–1845), was an English prison reformer and philanthropist. In 1813 she investigated prison conditions and publicised abuses – seeking separation of the sexes, classification of prisoners, and improvements in food, clothing and supervision. Her pioneering work was responsible for much improvement in the prison system.

FU HSI

The very first Chinese emperor was Fu Hsi, whose birth was said to have occurred in the twenty-ninth century BC.

GABOR, DENNIS

Dennis Gabor (1900–79), a Hungarian-born British scientist, invented holography in 1948, for which he received the Nobel Prize in physics more than 20 years later. Gabor considered the possibility of improving the resolving power of the electron microscope, first by utilising the electron beam to make a hologram of the object and then by examining this hologram with a beam of coherent light.

Yuri Gagarin. ▶

GAGARIN, YURI

On 12 April 1961, the Soviet cosmonaut Yuri Gagarin (1934–68) became the first man in space, as he was launched into orbit in the *Vostok 1* spaceship. Gagarin, an air force jet pilot, was chosen with the first group of Soviet cosmonauts in March 1960. His ship reached a maximum altitude of 327 km (203 miles) and circled the Earth once before landing near the Volga River. After the flight, Gagarin became training director of the womens' cosmonaut programme and returned to space for the Soyuz programme. He was killed in a MiG trainer jet crash in 1968. A crater on the far side of the Moon is named after him.

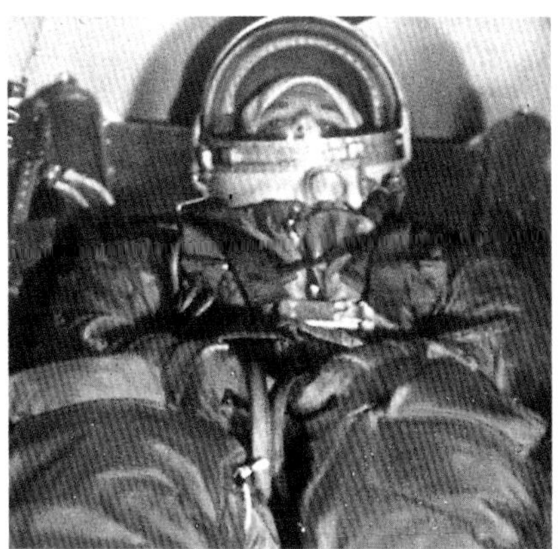

GAINSBOROUGH, THOMAS

The great landscape and portrait artist Thomas Gainsborough (1727–88) had moved his practice to fashionable Bath in 1759, developing a distinctive style of painting in the grand tradition of Van Dyck. But it was not until his arrival in London in 1774, setting up in Pall Mall, that he became the most successful portrait painter of the century, developing a fluid and impressionistic style, portraying country gentlemen posing in front of their land. He was the only rival to Sir Joshua Reynolds, the first president of the Royal Academy, and the embodiment of the artistic establishment. Gainsborough caught a chill listening to the trial of Warren Hastings in Westminster Hall in 1788, and died shortly afterwards.

GALEN, CLAUDIUS

Most notable among those who strove to advance anatomical understanding was Claudius Galen (AD 131–200). Galen's monumental work, *On the Use of the Parts of the Human Body*, served as the standard medical text for 1,400 years.

Claudius Galen. ◀

GALILEO, GALILEI

By the time **Isaac Newton** started his astronomical observations, it was very difficult to make telescopes any larger. The design developed by Galileo (1564–1642) was a refracting telescope, which required lenses to become bigger and bigger if a greater magnification of the stars was desired. Making larger lenses was becoming prohibitively expensive because of the level of expertise involved, so an alternative design needed to be invented. In 1581 Galileo noticed the phenomenon of the pendulum. A hundred years later the pendulum would set a new benchmark in time-keeping accuracy.

Isaac Newton. ▲

GAMA, VASCO DA

Vasco da Gama (*c.* 1469–1524), a Portuguese navigator, finally made the voyage by sea to India with four ships, which sailed round the Cape of Good Hope in 1497. Explorations of Mozambique, Malindi and Mombasa revealed abundant trade with Indians and Arabs. Frictions between the Christian explorers and African Muslims led to clashes, but da Gama secured a pilot who guided them to Calicut, an Indian commercial centre, in May 1498. Da Gama had found a passage to Asia by finding the best Atlantic winds to enable a journey around the Cape of Good Hope, and had crossed to India in three weeks. Trading fleets emerged to carry cargo between India and Lisbon, which became a major commercial centre. In 1502 the first permanent European naval force in Asian waters appeared when da Gama led an armed fleet to meet any threats.

GANDHI, INDIRA

Nehru's daughter, Indira Gandhi (1917–84), joined the central committee of Indian Congress in 1950, becoming president in 1959 and prime minister in 1966. After her conviction for election malpractices in 1975, she declared a 'state of emergency', with civil liberties curtailed and censorship imposed, until she lost the 1977 election. Acquitted from a corruption charge (1978), she resigned from the Congress party, becoming leader of the new Indian National Congress. She became prime minister again in 1980, but was assassinated in October 1984 by members of her Sikh bodyguard, resentful of her employment of troops to storm the Golden Temple at Amritsar and dislodge dissenters. Her murder provoked a Hindu backlash and 3,000 Sikhs were massacred.

The Golden Temple at Amritsar, to which Indira Gandhi sent troops. ▼

GANDHI, MAHATMA

Mahatma Gandhi (1869 –1948), honorific name of Mohandas Karamchand Gandhi, became the leader of the Congress party when he returned to India in 1915. He began a campaign of satyagraha, or peaceful, civil disobedience, to force the British to leave India. Gandhi began to spin cotton, in defiance of British laws which said that raw cotton had to be sent to Britain, and in 1930 organised a 'March to the Sea' to make salt. His self-restraint won him a place at the Round Table Conferences in London in 1930 –32. These were intended to find a compromise between the British and the Indians. The result was the Government of India Act in 1935. For the first time Indians played a significant part in the government of their country. He was assassinated by a Hindu fanatic on 30 January 1948. Gandhi is revered today as the father of the Indian nation.

Mahatma Gandhi, the father of the Indian nation. ◀

GARFIELD, JAMES A.

James Garfield (1831–81) was the 20th president of the USA from 1880–81. The Republican president was assassinated.

GARIBALDI, GIUSEPPE

Giuseppe Garibaldi (1807–82) was a Republican guerrilla leader. He first became famous when he defended Rome against the French army after it had been seized by Italians in 1848. He surrendered after a siege lasting a month. In 1860, after the Piedmontese army had occupied Lombardy, Garibaldi sailed from Genoa and landed with a thousand men on Sicily, which was part of the kingdom of Naples. In less than three months he had driven the Neapolitan army out of Sicily, and in August invaded the mainland. Garibaldi planned to invade the Papal States and then attack Venetia, but before he could implement this, the Piedmontese army invaded the Papal States from the north and Garibaldi handed over all his conquests to Victor Emmanuel, the king of Piedmont. Garibaldi played a crucial role as a catalyst in the unification of Italy and in the development of modern Europe.

GARRICK, DAVID ☻

For four years, David Garrick (1717–79) worked in the wine trade and took part in amateur theatricals, but he caused a sensation performing in **Shakespeare**'s *Richard III*, at an unlicensed performance in Goodman's Fields in 1741. For the rest of his career, including 30 years as manager at Drury Lane, he transformed the theatre and made acting into a respectable profession, writing a large number of plays and farces – and even a musical adaptation of *The Tempest*.

GATES, BILL ⊠

Bill Gates formed the company Microsoft with a school friend, Paul Allen. They adapted the language BASIC to form an operating system MS-DOS and sold it to IBM for the new PC they were working on. Their system was an overnight success, arriving as it did on the brink of the technological revolution, and spawned an empire that no other computer company has been able to match since. Bill Gates was believed to be one of the richest men in the world by the end of the 1990s.

Bill Gates' Microsoft is now a household name. ▼

GAULLE, CHARLES DE

Charles de Gaulle (1890–1970) was a French general. From 1940 –44 he based himself in England as leader of the Free French troops fighting the Germans, becoming head of the provisional French government in 1944–46. When national bankruptcy and civil war in Algeria loomed in 1958, de Gaulle was called on to form a government. As prime minister he changed the constitution to make a presidential system, and became the first president of the Fifth Republic in 1959. He was re-elected in 1965. A staunch nationalist, he opposed British entry to the EEC, withdrew French forces from NATO in 1966 and pursued development of a French nuclear deterrent. He resigned in 1969 after defeat in a referendum on constitutional reform.

Charles de Gaulle ▲

GAULTIER, JEAN PAUL

Trained at the couture houses of Cardin and Patou, Gaultier (b. 1952) is undoubtedly fashion's clown-prince of kitsch. In 1982, he produced the 'Corset' dress; in 1984, his spivvy pinstripes parodied 'City Man' tailoring and he introduced conical bras; in 1985, in his notorious 'And God Created Man' collection, he shocked audiences by introducing skirts for men. Despite his anarchic approach, Gaultier never diverts from strict cut and a good finish.

GELDOF, BOB

An Irish rock singer, Bob Geldof (b. 1954) was the leader of the group Boomtown Rats between 1975 and 1986. In 1984 Bob Geldof had been appalled by pictures of the famine in Africa and decided to help. He persuaded 40 pop stars to come to a recording studio and the single 'Do They Know It's Christmas' was released. The proceeds raised £8 million for famine relief. Live Aid was the follow-up: a 16-hour concert that would take place in England and America simultaneously. It would be broadcast to every country in the world. By the end of the evening, an estimated 1.5 billion people had watched the event and £60 million had been raised to help the people in Ethiopia.

GEORGE V

George V (1865–1936) was a popular monarch due to his sense of royal duty during the First World War. George V was responsible for changing the Germanic name of the royal house in 1917 from Saxe-Coburg into Windsor, a name which remains today. His devotion to duty was evidenced after the war when he later formed the National government in 1931 in response to the economic crisis of the time.

GEORGE VI

George VI (1936–52) became king when his brother **Edward VIII** abdicated. By remaining in London and 'taking it' during the Second World War he restored prestige to the monarchy.

GEORGE, DAVID LLOYD

David Lloyd George (1863–1945) began his career as a Welsh Liberal politician. He was a pioneer of social reform and, as Chancellor of the Exchequer he introduced old-age pensions in 1908 and health and unemployment insurance in 1911. He was made prime minister of Britain in 1916 at the height of the First World War. His leadership proved inspirational during the war years.

GERSHWIN, GEORGE

In the 1920s the 'Jazz Age' was swinging and George Gershwin (1898–1937) was right at its centre. He composed vibrant, witty songs that had syncopated rhythms and expressive harmonies. The tunes seemed to sparkle and they had 'that high attribute of making people fall in love with them'. In 1924, Gershwin bridged the gap

David Lloyd George. ▲

between classical and popular music with 'Rhapsody in Blue', which captured the 'tempo of modern living with its speed and chaos and vitality' but was performed as a serious piece of music. In the same year he wrote 'Lady Be Good', to which witty lyrics were set by his brother Ira. It marked the advent of the Gershwin musical.

GILL, ERIC ✷

Gill (1882–1940) fully explored the relationship between art and craft, being himself a sculptor, sign maker, woodcut artist and carver of stone letters, as well as a religious thinker, essayist and lifelong campaigner against 'aesthetic snobbery'. With the encouragement of the typographer Stanley Morison, Gill began to design type for the printing trade. His first face, the classical roman Perpetua, was finally released in 1929, some years after its inception, but his most famous face is the sans serif Gill Sans.

GILLETTE, KING CAMP ✉

At the turn of the century a travelling salesman and inventor, King Camp Gillette from Wisconsin, developed a safety razor with disposable blades. He began to market this money-saving invention in 1901, and the Gillette name is still a household one. A utopian socialist, King Gillette set up a 'World Corporation' in Arizona in 1910 to advocate a world-planned economy.

Gillette's safety razor. ▶

GLADSTONE, WILLIAM

Although he was not a favourite of **Queen Victoria**, Gladstone (1809–98) proved himself to be an enduring politician of the Victorian era. He entered Parliament as a Tory but eventually became a Liberal prime minister in 1868. After spending six years in opposition he was prime minister again between 1880 and 1885. One of the most notable pieces of legislation to pass through Parliament during his leadership was the Reform Act of 1884, which gave the vote to farm labourers. He was prime minister again between 1892 and 1894 and

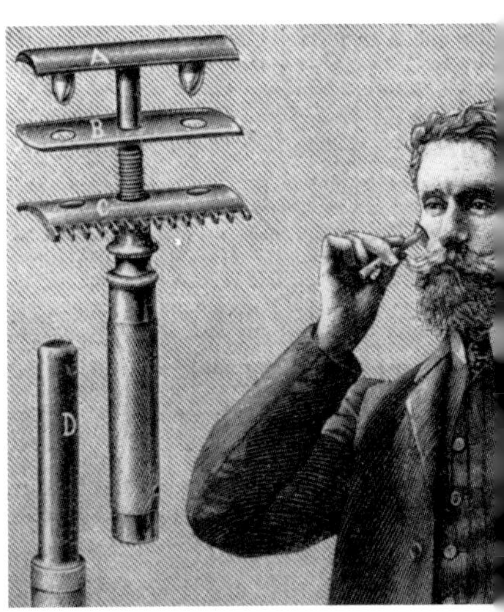

William Gladstone. ◀

unsuccessfully tried to push through a bill for Home Rule for Ireland in 1885 and 1893.

GOERING, HERMANN WILHELM

Hermann Wilhelm Goering (1893–1946) was second only to **Adolf Hitler** in the German National Socialist regime. During the 1930s, he had gained enormous power as Prussian minister-president and minister of the interior; chief of the Gestapo (secret police); minister of aviation and, with the rank of field marshal, commander-in-chief of the air force; and economic dictator of the Third Reich, directing the four-year plan. During the Second World War, Goering was the instigator of many of the atrocities undertaken by the Nazis, but as the war drew to a close, his influence on Hitler was undermined by the failure of the air force against the British and the Soviets. Captured by the allies in 1945, he was tried as a major war criminal by the International Military Tribunal at Nuremberg. He was condemned to execution, but took poison before he could be killed.

GOETHE, JOHANN WOLFGANG VON

Johann Wolfgang von Goethe (1749–1832), Germany's greatest literary figure, was one of the foremost critics of reductionist science in the eighteenth century. He argued that as the natural world can only be known through subjective and qualitative experience, the process of reducing these experiences to mathematical quantities was not empirical. He felt that scientists were deliberately blinding themselves to the reality of the natural world and replacing it with an abstraction. This allowed them to treat nature as an inanimate object and to exploit it for their own ends. To counter this problem he attempted to develop a theory of colour that incorporated the direct sensory experience of different colours.

GORBACHEV, MIKHAIL

Mikhail Gorbachev (b. 1931) became president of the Soviet Union in 1985 and announced his policies of *perestroika* and *glasnost*. *Perestroika* involved the restructuring of the Soviet economy and *glasnost* meant openness. He was able to develop a close friendship with the Western leaders, which enabled a number of treaties to be signed in the years from 1986 to 1991. In 1989 Gorbachev and President **George Bush** of the USA were able to announce that the Cold War was over. He was awarded the Nobel Peace Prize in 1990 for his attempts to halt the arms race, but early in 1991 he tried to placate the right wing of his party and produced a

Johann Wolfgang von Goethe. ◀

Mikhail Gorbachev. ◀

plan for a reformed union treaty. Alarmed hard-liners staged a coup in late summer but he was he rescued by Boris Yeltsin. His power was weakened by then, though, and he resigned in December 1991.

GOUDY, F. W. ✷

Goudy (1865–1947), a printer and designer of typefaces, established his business in New York, where he also lectured on typography. Goudy designed more than a hundred new typefaces, among them Garamond, Goudy Old Style, Forum and Trajan, produced for American Type Founders and the Lanston Monotype Machine Co. Goudy was also a fine calligrapher, but tragically many of his drawings were destroyed when his workshop burned down in 1939.

GRABLE, BETTY ☻

One of the most enduring images of Betty Grable is as the 'forces' favourite', looking back over her shoulder in a white swimming costume, and displaying her 'million dollar legs', the amount for which Lloyds of London insured them. She was trained at Hollywood Professional School from the age of 12, and was in chorus lines before she was 14. She got her break at Fox, where she starred in 18 musicals, high on gloss and Technicolor. *Coney Island* is typical of them; 95 minutes of Betty singing and dancing, with Coney Island as a background, with the story of two guys after the same girl to link the routines.

GRACE, WILLIAM GILBERT

When Dr William Gilbert Grace (1848–1915) began his career in first-class cricket at the age of 16, the game was still rough and ready. By the time he retired at the age of 50, the rules were set and – partly through his influence – cricket was established as England's national summer game. His heavy frame and large black beard made him the most famous cricketer in history, winning a total of 54,904 runs in his first-class career – including 126 centuries and 877 catches. He captained England 13 times, but the pinnacle of his career came when he scored the first-ever test century, against Australia in 1880. In 1903, he also became the first president of the English Bowling Association.

English cricketer William Gilbert Grace. ▲

GRANT, ULYSSES S.

Republican Ulysses S. Grant (1822–85) was the 18th president of the USA from 1868–76.

GROSHOLTZ, MARIE

There had been waxworks in London – notably at Westminster Abbey, where the unkempt representations of royalty were known as the 'ragged regiment' – before Madame Tussaud (Marie Grosholtz, 1760–1850) set herself up in England in 1802. She had been imprisoned for three months in Paris during the French Revolution, and had even modelled some of the revolutionary leaders from their heads after being taken from the scaffold. Her collection of 300 figures was first seen at the Lyceum in the Strand, but moved to a permanent home in London's Baker Street in 1835. The Chamber of Horrors was opened there, and included the knife from the Paris guillotine that had executed 22,000 people in the French Revolution.

GUEVARA, CHE

The Argentinian Communist revolutionary leader Che Guevara (1928–67) graduated in medicine at the university of Buenos Aires in 1953 but left Argentina soon after because of his opposition to **Perón**'s government. He then joined **Fidel Castro**'s revolutionary movement in Mexico in 1955 and played a significant role in the Cuban Revolution in 1956–59. Following this he held government posts under Castro. An activist of revolution elsewhere, he became a hero of left-wing youth in the 1960s. After leaving Cuba in 1965 to become a guerrilla leader in South America, he was captured by government troops while trying to stage a revolt and was executed in 1967.

Che Guevara. ▶

GUSTAVUS ADOLPHUS

Gustavus Adolphus (1594–1632) was king of Sweden from 1611, when he succeeded his father Charles IX; he was known as 'The Lion of the North'. He allocated half of Sweden's budget to military expenditure and waged successful wars with Denmark, Russia and Poland. The Thirty Years' War (1618–48) marked the beginning of modern warfare. During that conflict Gustavus greatly improved army organisation and discipline, introducing more powerful artillery and a lighter infantry musket that permitted soldiers to load and fire faster. This success is tempered by the fact that he was accidentally killed by his own side during a fog.

GUTENBERG, JOHANN

It was the inventive genius of a German goldsmith called Johann Gutenberg (*c.* 1400–68) that brought printing of age. During the late 1450s, he devised a system for using individual type characters, cast in moulds from an alloy of lead, tin and antimony, which were interchangeable within a frame. It was quick and easy to assemble whole pages of type that could all be used time and time again for other jobs. Within 30 years most of the western European countries had several printing works, and by the early sixteenth century most classical manuscripts were made available in print. In 1609, the first newspaper went on sale in Germany, where it had all started.

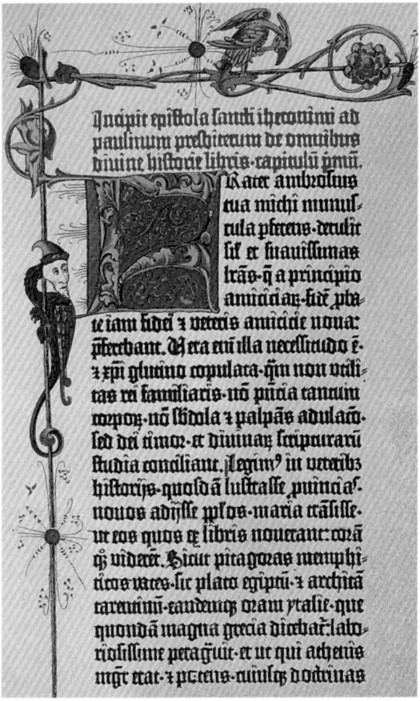
Incipit epistola sancti iheronimi ad
paulinum presbiterum de omnibus
divine historie libris. capitulū p̄mū.
Rater ambrosius
tua michi munus-
cula pferens. detulit
sil et suavissimas
lrās. q̄ a principio
amiciciaꝝ. fidē pba-
te iam fidei ⁊ veteris amicicie nova:
pferebant. Vera enī illa necessitudo ē.
⁊ xp̄i glutino copulata. q̄m non utili-
tas rei familiaris. nō p̄ncia tantum
corpoꝝ. nō subdola ⁊ palpās adulacō.
sed dei timor. et divinaꝝ scripturarū
studia conciliant. Legimꝰ in veteribꝫ
historiis. quosdā lustrasse pvincias.
novos adiisse p̄plos. maria trāsisse.
ut eos quos ex libris noverant: corā
q̄ viderēt. Sicut pitagoras memphi-
ticos vates. sic plato egiptū. ⁊ architā
tarentinū. eandemq̄ oram ytalie. que
quondā magna grecia dicebat: labo-
riosissime peragravit. et ut qui atheris
mḡr erat. ⁊ potens. cuiusq̄ doctrinas

HADRIAN

Roman Emperor Hadrian (AD 76–138) is best known for the immense wall he had constructed in the north of England. Roman Britannia was a dangerous place, requiring strong fortifications – for instance the stone walls built round the rich trading port of London in AD 195 – to keep out marauding bands of rebels. Built by 142, Hadrian's Wall ran between Arbeia (South Shields) and the Solway Firth and was intended to keep the Selgovae, Novantae and other Scots tribes at bay. It was manned by

A page from Gutenberg's Bible. ◀

The Roman Emperor Hadrian. ▶

nearly 12,000 soldiers. Only three years later, another defence line, the Antonine Wall, was constructed even further north. Under Hadrian, Rome's empire contracted under pressure from insurrections in the east.

HAIG, DOUGLAS

On 1 July 1916, the British and French launched the Somme offensive. This brought them up against some of the heaviest German fortifications on the entire Western Front. The British general Sir Douglas Haig (1861–1928) resisted the idea, but French Commander Joffre won the argument and the campaign began. The general slaughter of allied troops that occurred is infamous, with the British suffering 65,000 casualties on the first day alone. Haig's method of sending soldiers 'over the top' has since been condemned as one of the biggest strategical mistakes in the history of warfare.

HAILE SELASSIE

The name of Rastafari was taken from the name of Haile Selassie (1892–1975), Lord Ras Tafari (Head Creator), King of Kings, Lion of the Tribe of Judah, Emperor of Ethiopia. Rastafari festival days are 23 July, Emperor Haile Selassie's birthday, and 2 November, the day of his coronation. Rastafarianism was founded in Jamaica during the 1930s by a group who believed Haile Selassie to be the true Messiah.

HALLEY, EDMUND

Edmund Halley (1656–1742) was an English astronomer who became a friend and collaborator of Isaac Newton. He was primarily concerned with the movements of astronomical bodies over long periods of time. He compiled a catalogue of all the stars he could see with his telescope and referred to historical records to trace the proper motion of stars. He also began work on calculating the astronomical unit or AU, which is the average distance from the Earth to the Sun during its orbit, and the unit by which astronomers measure the distances of other planets. Halley was fortunate enough to witness the comet named after him in 1682, which he correctly identified to be the comet previously sighted in 1456, 1531 and 1607. He predicted its return in 1785, reasoning that it must follow a parabola.

HAMMARSKJÖLD, DAG HJALMAR AGNE CARL

Hammarskjöld (1905–61) was an economist, statesman and later the second secretary-general of the UN. He was active throughout the 1950s in a variety of peace talks and mediations. He helped resolve the Suez Canal crisis, mediated in the 1958 Lebanon and Jordan problems and sent a UN force into the Congo in 1960 to suppress the civil disorders. He supported an independent UN, free to deal with international challenges. He died in a plane crash while on a peace mission to President Tshombe of the Congo on 18 September 1961.

Hammarskjöld helped resolve the Suez Canal crises. ▼

George Frideric Handel. ◀

HANDEL, GEORGE FRIDERIC

George Frideric Handel (1685–1759) was the son of a barber-surgeon from Lower Saxony who became the *kapellmeister* to the Elector of Hanover, later George I (1660–1727). He arrived in London in 1711 and went on to dominate the London opera circuit. An invitation to Dublin led to a feverish burst of 25 days' activity to write *The Messiah* in his home near Oxford Street in London, his meals left uneaten outside the door. It was admired in Dublin in its first performance, and George II (1683–1760) rose in his seat during the London performance – overwhelmed by the Alleluia Chorus. Handel later went blind, his eyes ruined by the same surgeon who had tried to save the eyesight of Johann Sebastian Bach (1685–1750).

HANNIBAL

Hannibal (247–182 BC) was a Carthaginian general and son of Hamilcar Barca. He transported 30,000 men, horses and elephants over the Alps and defeated the Romans at the Battle of Cannae by enveloping and destroying their army. Hannibal used cavalry against the Romans in the Second Punic War (218–01 BC), but the Romans finally deployed superior cavalry in the Battle of Zama (202 BC) and he was sent into exile.

HANNO

In the late third century BC, Carthaginian merchant Hanno sailed through the Strait of Gibraltar and south down the west coast of Africa, in search of precious metals, especially gold. He left an account of his voyage in a temple at Carthage, which was copied down by a Greek so that a complete text remains. However, the description does not exactly match the geography of the coast, and some scholars have speculated that there are intentional inaccuracies to prevent others from following in Hanno's wake. He certainly got as far as Senegal, and possibly all the way to Gabon.

HARDIE, KEIR

The Reform Act of 1884 in Britain extended the right to vote to much of the working class. Traditionally the working classes had sought representation through the Liberal Party but, with the extended franchise, a new Labour Party was formed in 1893 by Keir Hardie (1856–1915) of the Lanarkshire Miner's Union. With the support of the Trade Unions, and especially the miners,

Ramsay MacDonald, the first Labour prime minister, elected with the help of Keir Hardie. ▶

Keir Hardie became an MP in 1892, and the Labour Party won 40 seats in 1910. In 1924 Labour, in alliance with the Liberals, won their first election and Ramsay MacDonald was elected prime minister.

HARDING, WARREN G.

Warren G. Harding (1865–1923) was the 29th president of the USA, from 1920–23. He was a Republican.

HARDRADA, HARALD

Harald Hardrada was king of Norway and a descendant of Canute, one of the Danish kings of England, who reigned from 1016 to 1042. When he heard news of the king's death, he decided to try to seize the throne of England. Harald was a famous warrior and he was supported by Sweyn, the king of Denmark and by Tostig, the brother of Harold Godwinson, who had been exiled in 1064. He was obviously a very dangerous opponent and in September he landed in Yorkshire and defeated an English army at the Battle of Fulford Gate, near York.

Harald Hardrada was a descendant of the Danish king Canute. ▶

HARDY, THOMAS

When the former architect's apprentice Thomas Hardy (1840–1928) reached the pinnacle of his career as a novelist with *Tess of the D'Urbervilles* in 1891, he faced a campaign of outrage about the novel's 'indecency' led by his wife – and promised to give up novels altogether if he ever faced such a reception again. But the clamour was even stronger about *Jude the Obscure*, a novel that reflected some of the tensions in his own marriage, and it was the last one he ever wrote. In the years that followed, he devoted himself to poetry and became the Grand Old Man of English letters.

HARGREAVES, JAMES

In about 1764 James Hargreaves (d. 1778) conceived the idea for his hand-powered multiple spinning machine, when he observed a spinning wheel that had been accidentally overturned by his young daughter, Jenny. As the spindle continued to revolve in an upright rather than a horizontal position, Hargreaves reasoned that many spindles could be so turned. He constructed a machine with which one individual could spin several threads at one time. After he began to sell the machines to help support his large family, hand spinners, fearing unemployment, broke into his house and destroyed a number of the machines, which he called 'jennies', causing Hargreaves to move to Nottingham in 1768.

HARRISON, BENJAMIN

Benjamin Harrison (1833–1901) was the 23rd president of the USA from 1888–92. He was a Republican.

HARRISON, WILLIAM HENRY

Whig William Henry Harrison was the 9th president of the USA from 1840–41.

James Hargreaves's 'spinning jenny'. ▶

HARVEY, WILLIAM

William Harvey (1578–1657) was an English physician who, in 1628, discovered the circulation of blood, thanks to the invention of the microscope by Dutchman, Zacharias Janssen.

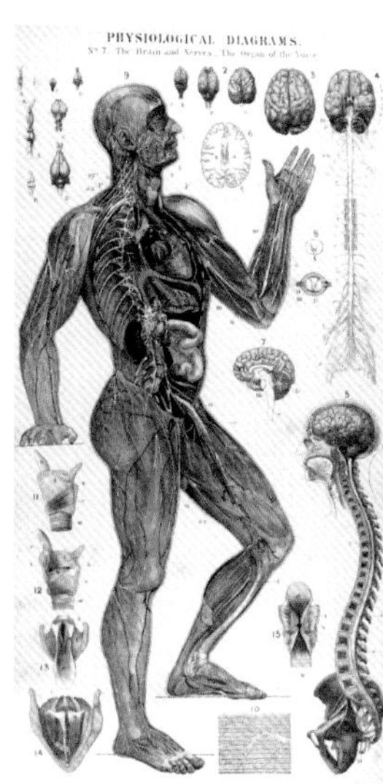

William Harvey's studies led to the discovery of blood circulation. ◀

HASTINGS, WARREN

Warren Hastings (1732–1818) was the governor of Bengal from 1772 to 1785, who began a programme of reforms, introducing a new coinage and tax system and beginning the study of Muslim and Hindu law. In 1773 a supreme court was set up and the actions of the Company's officers were controlled. They were prevented from trading privately and taking gifts. When war broke out with France in 1778, Hastings seized the remaining French trading stations and also attacked the Maratha confederacy. Hastings sometimes acted high-handedly, and, after his retirement in 1785, he was accused of corruption by one of his colleagues, Philip Francis. His trial dragged on from 1788 to 1795, when he was acquitted.

HENDRIX, JIMI

Jimi Hendrix (1942–70) was born in Seattle, but started roaming after playing in local bands and doing a stint in the army. In London in 1966 he formed the Jimi Hendrix Experience, and set about taking the music world by storm. His electric-guitar playing was legendary, a kind of innovative buzz of controlled feedback and melodic riffs. He was also a dazzling showman, slinking on stage in velvet and then smashing or burning his guitar. His first album *Are You Experienced?* was a psychedelic blaze of chords with Dylan-inspired lyrics. His later recordings anticipated dub and ambient music. He died of an overdose on 18 September 1970.

HENRY I

Henry I (1068–1135) was **William the Conqueror**'s son. He was a vigorous and efficient ruler, organised a secretarial department called the Chancery and a treasury department known as the Exchequer. The latter got its name from the custom of laying out tax payments on a long cloth marked out in squares, or chequers. Each square indicated a certain amount of money. Special markers were placed on them to show how much money had been received and how much was still owing. Thus even an illiterate tax collector could see how much money he had yet to collect.

HENRY III

When **King John** died in 1216 he was succeeded by his nine-year-old son, Henry III (1207–72). Henry made several attempts to invade France and these were partly responsible for his increasing unpopularity with the Barons. In 1264–65 there was a civil war between the Barons led by Simon de Montfort and Henry's forces led by his son Edward. When Henry died in 1272, his son succeeded as **Edward I**.

The massacre of the Huguenots; Henry IV instigated a gradual acceptance of this Protestant religion in France. ▼

HENRY IV

From 1562 to 1598 there was a series of eight wars between Catholics and Protestants (called Huguenots) in France. The Huguenots were concentrated in the south-west of France, but Paris and the north-east remained Catholic. The wars came to an end when Henry of Navarre became King Henry IV (1553–1610) in 1589. He was a Huguenot, but converted to Catholicism to ensure that the Catholics would accept him. In 1598 he issued the Edict of Nantes, which gave Huguenots equal political rights with Catholics and allowed the Protestant religion to be practised in some parts of France, but not in Paris and some other cities. It was the first example, however, of acceptance of Protestantism in a major Catholic country.

Henry the Navigator. ▲

HENRY THE NAVIGATOR

Henry the Navigator (1394–1460) was a Portuguese prince who, while in North Africa, had seen Asian cargoes arriving and this encouraged him to search for a passage for Portugal. His second motive was to bring Christianity to pagans. It was believed that sailing beyond Morocco led to waters boiled by liquid flames from the sun. Sailing west led to swamps. To prepare crews for these hazards and to overcome fears, Henry established a maritime centre in 1419. Storms drove Henry's first expedition in 1420 to the Madeira islands. The islands of the Azores, reached in 1431, became a base for subsequent expeditions. By the time of Henry's death his ships had sailed a third of the way down the African coast to present-day Sierra Leone.

HENRY V

Henry V (1387–1422) proved himself a brave soldier and an outstanding king. He signed a peace treaty with France in 1396, but it did not last very long. Henry V, keen to press his claim to the French throne, took advantage of French indecision and renewed the Hundred Years' War in 1415. He captured Harfleur and marched on Calais. A huge French army was lured out in pursuit against his army of less than 6,000. The armies met at Agincourt, where the French showed that they had ignored the lessons of previous encounters with the English. In a little more than half and hour, Henry's archers slaughtered 6,000 of the 25,000-strong French army.

Henry VII in the Tower of London. ▲

HENRY VI

When King **Henry V** of England died in 1422, his nine-month-old son, Henry VI (1421–71), was unable to rule. When he took power he was a poor ruler and failed to hold on to the English empire in France. His failures encouraged his enemies, the Yorkists, to try to seize power and eventually Henry was captured in 1461 and held prisoner in the Tower of London. He was almost certainly murdered in 1471.

HENRY VII

Henry VII (1485–1509) brought prosperity and stability to his realm after 100 years of unrest. He financed exploration of the Canadian sea-board and encouraged trade with Europe. His immediate aim was to pacify England after the Wars of the Roses, which had lasted on and off for 30 years. Any possible rivals to the throne were imprisoned and executed. Henry also built up a strong treasury, which gave him a high degree of independence. Henry VII set a pattern which later monarchs followed; but few had his ability to manage their resources as effectively.

Henry VIII. ▼

HENRY VIII

During his first years of rule Henry VIII (1491–1547) concerned himself largely with foreign policy defeating both the French and the Scottish in battle in 1512 and 1513. However, continued fighting, prompted by Henry's belief that war was the 'sport of kings', left England near bankruptcy in the 1520s. Henry fell in love with Anne Boleyn while married to his first wife, Catherine of Aragon. Exasperated by Catherine's failure to produce a male heir, Henry sought a divorce. The marriage was sanctioned by Rome, however, and despite his appeal to Pope Clement VII, his request was denied (the pope's political master was Catherine's nephew). To divorce Catherine, the king had to prove Rome had no dispensation over his case; this he was eventually able to do during the 1530s, installing himself as head of the new Church of England. Anne was already pregnant when she married Henry, but bore him a daughter, **Elizabeth I**, instead of the son he so wanted. She was later executed for adultery. Henry's third wife, Jane Seymour, gave him his heir, but died shortly afterwards, and the king married a further three times. His sixth wife, Catherine Parr, outlived him.

HERBERT, GEORGE, 5TH EARL OF CARNARVON

George Herbert, 5th Earl of Carnarvon (1866–1923), was an English Egyptologist and collector of antiquities who sponsored excavations around Thebes (1906–1922). These culminated in the discovery of the tomb of Pharaoh Tutankhamen.

HEREWARD, THEGN

The year after he took part in the looting of Peterborough Abbey, Thegn Hereward, known as Hereward the Wake, staged an uprising near Ely. The Normans came in force to deal with him, and although Hereward and his men held out for months against assaults from both land and sea, their cause was ultimately doomed. Cunningly, the Normans confiscated lands belonging to monks near Ely, precipitating their surrender, and with that Hereward's resistance was critically weakened. Inevitably, his own men were obliged to follow suit, but Hereward himself managed to escape. He was never heard of again, but legends about this great hero-patriot from Lincolnshire proliferated long after he was dead.

HERTZ, HEINRICH

The development of radar can be traced to the work of German physicist Heinrich Hertz (1857–94). Hertz proved the existence of radio waves and demonstrated that they can be reflected like light waves. The possibility of using the radio

Hilda of Whitby. ▼

Edmund Hillary reaching the top of Mount Everest. ▶

reflection phenomenon for detection purposes was further explored after the engineer **Guglielmo Marconi** elaborated its principles in 1922.

HILDA

Hilda (AD 614–680), who ruled over the double monastery (male and female) at Hartlepool and Whitby, until her death, showed how devotion to the new religion of Christianity could capture powerful, outstanding women. She promoted education, and social welfare for the young, old and destitute.

HILLARY, EDMUND

In 1953, Hillary (b. 1919) and the Nepalese explorer Tenzing Norgay achieved the 8,848-m (29,028-ft) summit of Mount Everest. An earlier attempt had been foiled by fierce winds, but on 29 May 1953 at 11.30 a.m. the two men stepped on to the 'symmetrical, beautiful snow cone summit'. They spent 15 minutes taking photographs and eating mint cake, before leaving the Union Jack, the Nepalese national flag and the United Nations flag, as well as sweets and biscuits as a Buddhist offering from Tenzing Norgay. Hillary was knighted for his achievement, and Tenzing was awarded the George Cross.

HIPPOCRATES

In 450 BC Hippocrates of Cos (*c.* 460–377 BC) undertook the first anatomical studies of man and by AD 175 the physician **Claudius Galen** had established the basic principles of anatomy and physiology. The Hippocratic oath is the most enduring tradition in Western medicine, and has been the guiding ethical code for physicians since ancient Greece.

HIROHITO

Hirohito (1901–89) succeeded his father, Yoshihito, as emperor of Japan in 1926. His reign was marked by rapid militarisation and the wars against China (1931–32 and 1937–45) and the US (1941–45), which ended with the two atomic bombs on Hiroshima and Nagasaki. Under American occupation in 1946, Hirohito renounced his legendary divinity and many of his powers to become a democratic constitutional monarch. A keen scholar of botany and zoology, he wrote books on marine biology. He died in 1989, having been the longest-reigning emperor of the longest-reigning dynasty in the world.

HITCHCOCK, ALFRED

Alfred Hitchcock (1899–1980) was an English film director and a US citizen from 1955. He was a master of the suspense thriller, and noted for his meticulously drawn storyboards that determined his camera angles and for his cameo walk-ons in his own films.

Greek physician Hippocrates. ◀

HITLER, ADOLF

Hitler (1889–1945) published the first part of *Mein Kampf* ('My Battle') in 1925 while in prison. He completed it in 1927 and the book was to become one of the most notorious Nazi documents of the era. He became chancellor of Germany in January 1933 and was given total power when the Enabling Act was passed in March. This allowed him to govern without the Reichstag, the German Parliament, for the next four years. By then, Germany had been changed completely by the Nazis. A total dictatorship had been set up in Germany. When the president, von Hindenberg, died in 1934, Hitler took control of the country under the title 'der Führer'. He led Germany throughout the Second World War and implemented some of the most terrible schemes against humanity in history, in particular his campaign against the Jews, which he called the 'Final Solution'. Hitler committed suicide in April 1945 in Berlin.

Adolf Hitler. ▲

HO CHI MINH

Communists were frequently involved in the highest councils of independence movements, which therefore became suspect in the eyes of the United States. The worst offenders, from this perspective, were the Indo-Chinese Communists led by Ho Chi Minh (1890–1969). When the French finally agreed to the independence of Indo-China, the United States supported an anti-Communist regime in its own state in the South. The war continued, because political leaders in the United States had adopted a strategy of containment. Friendly governments were established in states bordering the Communist bloc, and linked by means of military alliances, such as the Baghdad Pact of 1955 between Turkey, Iraq, Iran and Pakistan. The strategy was publicised under the less aggressive name of the 'Domino Theory'.

HOBBES, THOMAS

Appalled by the Civil War violence around him, Hobbes (1588–1679) was searching for a more logical basis for ordering human society, following on from the humanism of his friend Sir **Francis Bacon**. The publication of the immensely influential and materialistic *Leviathan* caused outrage among politicians and theologians, and although he was given a pension by **Charles II**, he was forbidden to write by Parliament and his books were publicly burned. He was suspected of atheism, and after the mid-1660s could find no one to publish his works. His life and work is a reflection of that moment in time when there was a shift from the age of Christian humanism to the age of humanism and secularism.

A Gin Lane *engraving by William Hogarth.* ▲

HOCKNEY, DAVID

Hockney (b. 1937) studied at the Royal College of Art in London, and his work first became widely known as a result of the 'Young Contemporaries' exhibition (1961–62). In Hockney's earliest, most irreverent phase, he treated popular imagery in a quirky, graffiti-like manner interlaced with visual puns. One of the finest draughtsmen of his era, Hockney has executed several series of prints, of which *The Rake's Progress*, inspired by **William Hogarth**, is the best known.

HOGARTH, WILLIAM ✷

Our view of the mid-eighteenth century is coloured by the moral engravings of William Hogarth (1697–1764), the first British artist of the century to win an international reputation for himself. His pictures, such as *Gin Lane* and *Chairing the Candidate*, provided a raucous and brutal view of ordinary life, but it was his moral series, like *Rake's Progress* (1733–35) and *Marriage à la Mode* (1743–45), that made him famous.

HOLBEIN, HANS ✷

Hans Holbein the Younger (*c.* 1497–1543) was a European humanist, one of **Erasmus**'s wide circle of friends, many of whom made their homes in England. He arrived in 1526, and after 1532 he rarely left, building up a unique memory of **Henry VIII**'s court with his superb portraits of the most eminent people in the land. His portraits included some of the candidates for Henry's various marriages, and it was on one of these rare visits abroad, that Henry asked him to paint Anne of Cleves. Enchanted, Holbein 'expressed her imaige verye lyvelye' and Henry married her – dismissing her shortly afterwards as a 'Flanders mare'. Holbein died of the plague in 1543.

Portrait of a woman by Hans Holbein. ▼

J. Edgar Hoover was the director of the FBI. ▶

HOMER

According to Herodatus, the *Iliad* and the *Odyssey* were written about 850 BC, but they may actually have been written up to a century earlier than this. Both are attributed to the blind poet, Homer, and are the earliest and greatest Greek epic poems, providing a detailed picture of early Greek religion. The *Iliad* tells the tale of the great siege of Troy (Ilium) by the Greeks from 1194–84 BC, while the *Odyssey* recounts the journeys of the legendary Greek figure Odysseus.

HOOVER, HERBERT

Herbert Hoover (1874–1964), born to Quaker parents in Iowa, became the 31st US president. During the First World War he was closely associated with relief of distress in Europe. He became secretary of commerce under **Harding**. A Republican candidate, he defeated 'Al' Smith in the presidential election of 1928, but his opposition to direct government assistance for the unemployed after the world slump of 1929 made him unpopular and he lost to **Roosevelt** in 1932.

HOOVER, J. EDGAR

John Edgar Hoover (1895–1972) was director of the Federal Bureau of Investigations from 1924 until 1972. A controversial figure, he was noted for his rigorous investigations into all radical movements: Ku Klux Klan; Malcolm X; Martin Luther King; communists and fascists – but criticised for his leniency towards the Mafia. Hoover reputedly kept the country's politicians on his side by keeping exhaustive (potentially damaging) files about them. Hoover also led the investigation into the death of long-term sparring partner John F. Kennedy – it was Hoover who made the much-disputed announcement that Lee Harvey Oswald had acted alone in Kennedy's murder.

HUBBARD, L. RON

In 1950 L. Ron Hubbard (1911–86), the American science-fiction writer, founded the pseudo-science of Dianetics, which he later developed into the Church of Scientology. Since Hubbard's death, both Dianetics and Scientology have continued to be controversial, but still attract increasing numbers of new converts.

HUBBLE, EDWIN

The astronomer Edwin Hubble (1889–1953) proved that the galaxies are systems independent of the Milky Way, and by 1930 had confirmed the concept of an expanding universe.

HUMBOLDT, ALEXANDER VON

Baron Alexander von Humboldt (1769–1859) was a German geophysicist, botanist, geologist and writer who, in 1799, was commissioned by the Spanish monarchy to conduct a thorough exploration of parts of South America, in search of valuable mineral deposits. Humboldt made two expeditions, one along the Orinoco River in Venezuela in 1799–1800, and one along the Andes in 1801–03. His studies increaseded botanical knowledge considerably and also mapped the blank spots in northern South America.

The Hubble Telescope. ◀

HUME, DAVID

David Hume's (1711–76) best-known work, *A Treatise of Human Nature* (1739), disappointed him on publication. It fell 'dead-born from the press,' he wrote. He was a sceptic and a free thinker. His emphasis lies on the value of custom and instinct as guides to life. If reason is taken as fundamental this will lead to confusion, so custom, which is a summary of knowledge, is a better guide. To early readers Hume appeared to argue against the existence of God and in his *Dialogues Concerning Natural Religion* he demolished the principal arguments for the existence of God. His purpose was to halt the pretensions of reason and put instinct in its place.

David Hume. ▲

HUSSEIN, IBN TALAL

Hussein ibn Talal (b. 1935) became king of Jordan in 1952. The king struggled to maintain rule despite political upheavals inside and outside his country. His federation of Jordan with Iraq in 1958 came to an end with the Iraqi military *coup d'état* in July. By 1967 he had lost all his kingdom west of the River Jordan in the Arab-Israeli wars. In 1970 he suppressed the Palestine Liberation Organization, which was acting as a guerrilla force against his rule on the East Bank territories. Subsequently, he became a moderator in Middle Eastern politics, signing a peace agreement with Israel in 1994.

HUSSEIN, SADDAM

In 1980 Iraqi president Saddam Hussein (b. 1937) invaded Iran hoping to reverse the 1975 border settlement and perhaps to gain control of the rich, oil-producing Iranian province of Khuzestan. Although Iraqi forces won early successes, Iran rallied, held the invaders, formed new armies, and took the offensive. An agreement for a cease-fire was eventually reached in August 1988 with the help of the United Nations. The crisis began again in August 1990, when Hussein invaded and annexed Kuwait. Between August and November the United Nations Security Council passed a series of resolutions that culminated in the demand that Iraq withdraw unconditionally from Kuwait by 15 January 1991. By that time, some 500,000 allied ground, air, and naval forces were arrayed against an Iraqi army estimated at that time to number 540,000. The land offensive, Desert Storm, was launched and within 100 hours, the city of Kuwait had been liberated, and thousands of Iraqi troops had deserted, surrendered, or been captured or killed. Throughout the 1990s, tension in the area remained, culminating in 1998 when Saddam Hussein's refusal to allow United Nations arms' investigations in Iraq led to British and US attacks.

Iraqi president Saddam Hussein. ◀

HUXLEY, ALDOUS

In *Brave New World*, Aldous Huxley (1894–1963) describes a world where the arts of the salesman are used by the government; where people are genetically engineered and psychologically normalised to fit into society; where brainwashing and subliminal advertising are used to keep people consuming and to prevent them thinking. It was intended to be the possible future of the consumer society.

IBN ARABI

Ibn Arabi (1165–1240), mystic, philosopher, poet and sage, was given the title Muhyiddin ('The Revivifier of Religion') by his followers. He was born in Andalusia, Spain, at the height of Islamic culture there, and came in touch with the teachings of all three Western religions. His highly influential *Fusûs al-Hikam*, the 'bezels of wisdom', is a brief summary of his teachings, whilst the *Futûhât al-Makkiyya* is a vast encyclopedia of his ideas. His key doctrine is the Unity of Being; that ultimately there is no self but God and that all things are ultimately one because they are ultimately God.

IBN RUSHD

Ibn Rushd, known in the medieval West as Averroës, was a twelfth-century Islamic philosopher best known for his interpretation of the works of **Aristotle** and his reconciliation of these ideas with monotheistic religion. It is through him that Western Europe discovered Aristotle and it is as a result of his interpretation that Aristotle became a major

Aldous Huxley. ◀

source of inspiration for **Thomas Aquinas** and for Christian Scholastic theology.

INNOCENT III

Innocent III (1198–1216) asserted papal control over reluctant rulers and states. In 1209 he excommunicated **King John** of England for refusing to accept Stephen Langton as Archbishop of Canterbury. He attempted to reorganise the crusading efforts under papal auspices, lack of funds to pay for the passage of the 10,000 crusaders in Venice forced a diversion of the army. At the request of the Venetians, the crusaders first attacked the Christian city of Zara, in Dalmatia. Then they sailed on to lay siege to Constantinople. The Byzantine capital fell in 1204; it was looted and became the residence of a Latin emperor, Baldwin, Count of Flanders.

Carvings of crusader knights. ▼

ISABELLA I

Isabella I's (1451–1504) accession to the throne of Castile in 1474 and of her husband **Ferdinand II** to that of Aragon in 1479 meant that the two most important kingdoms of Spain were joined. They were known as the 'Catholic Monarchs' because after 700 years of rule by the Moors they catholicised Spain. They were exceptionally gifted, Isabella in internal politics and Ferdinand in foreign policy. She also introduced the Inquisition into Castile, expelled the Jews and the Moors and financed Columbus's expedition to the Americas in 1492. Their youngest daughter was Catherine of Aragon, first wife to **Henry VIII**.

Isabella I. ▼

ISAIAH

The Prophet Isaiah lived at a time of great conflict and danger for Israel. Faced with the threat of invasion he prophesied that unless the people of Israel had faith and lived honestly the land would become desert and the nation would be destroyed. Isaiah forecast that the people would revive their faith and that in response the desert would blossom and the gardens of paradise would appear on earth. There is evidence that the biblical book of Isaiah was written partly by him and partly by one or two later prophets.

IVAN III (THE GREAT)

Ivan III (1440–1505) was the grand duke of Muscovy from 1462. In 1480, he defeated an attempt to reassert the right to tribute made by the heirs of Mongols, the Tatar khan of the Great Horde. Moscow had long been the most important principality in Russia in support of the rights of the Russian Orthodox Church and in dealings with the

Frontispiece from an early German Bible; it is believed that the Prophet Isaiah wrote part of the book that takes his name in the Bible. ▶

Tatars. Under Ivan III, the first of its rulers to call himself tsar, the territorial expansion of Muscovy moved rapidly. The great trading city of Novgorod, with its vast lands to the north, was annexed in 1478. Other states to the north-west of Muscovy were also added.

IVAN IV (THE TERRIBLE)

Ivan IV (1530–1584) was the grand duke of Muscovy from 1533. The first major step eastwards by Muscovy occurred in 1552, when Ivan conquered the khanate of Kazan. This brought the borders of the Muscovite principality to the Urals, the traditional boundary between Europe and Siberia. The tsar granted huge tracts of this new conquest to a leading Muscovite merchant family, the Stroganovs. They came into conflict with the neighbouring khanate of Sibir, and in return for help from the tsar handed over their estates to him. Fighting in the region continued for several years, but by constructing a chain of forts along the rivers, Russia asserted its control.

JACKSON, ANDREW

Andrew Jackson (1767–1845) was the 7th president of the USA from 1828–36. He founded the Democratic Party in 1828, and was the first Democrat President.

JACKSON, MICHAEL

Michael Jackson (b. 1958) is a US rock singer and songwriter, who turned professional in 1969 as the youngest member of the Jackson Five. His worldwide popularity peaked with the albums *Thriller* (1982), *Bad* (1987) and *Dangerous* (1991).

JACKSON, THOMAS J. 'STONEWALL'

Thomas J. 'Stonewall' Jackson (1824–63) was a Confederate general in the American Civil War. He organised the Shenandoah Valley campaign and helped to defeat the Union army at the Battle of Chancellorsville.

JAMES I

The reign of James I (1566–1625) – James VI of Scotland, 1603–25 – is noted for religious strife. Catholics hatched the Gunpowder Plot, while the Puritan *Mayflower* pilgrims left for America. James tried to avoid Parliament as much as possible; and by being frugal, he was able to avoid summoning Parliament for many years. For the first time, however, the crowns of England and Scotland were joined.

James I. ▲

JAMES, WILLIAM

William James (1842–1910) was an American with a huge range of interests. He was both philosopher and psychologist and his work *The Varieties of Religious Experience* (1902) (among others) has had a lasting effect. He was concerned with religious issues throughout his life and the above work studies the phenomena of mysticism and religious experience with an assessment of their validity. His work still retains its seminal significance. He developed a theory of a 'mother sea of consciousness', which plays some of the roles of an infinite God or Absolute, while leaving humans with an independence and integrity of personal choice.

JANSKY, KARL

In 1932 astronomer Karl Jansky (1905–50) detected the presence of 'radio noise' coming from outer space. This led to the development of radio telescopes, with the realisation that radio waves, instead of light waves, could tell scientists a lot more about the universe.

JEFFERSON, THOMAS

The third president of the USA, from 1800–08; Thomas Jefferson (1743–1826) was a Democrat-Republican. The Declaration of Independence was drawn up by Jefferson on 4 July. The actions of the Americans set a new precedent in power and politics. They asserted the right of a people to throw off their allegiance to their king and establish for themselves a new and different form of government. Jefferson expanded the English and American views of civil rights. He emphasised the primacy of human happiness and advanced the concept of religious freedom and church-state separation as a key element of civil rights.

JENNER, EDWARD

In 1796, a British scientist called Edward Jenner (1749–1823) managed to inoculate a boy against smallpox by using cowpox vesicles. Cowpox was a related disease, which caused the boy to develop the antibodies in his system necessary to fight off smallpox. This became known as a non variolous vaccination, and established the practice of using either dead or related pathogenic organisms for inoculating against serious diseases.

Edward Jenner administering the first vaccination against smallpox. ◀

JESUS CHRIST

Born in to a poor family in Galilee in around the year 7 BC, the son of a carpenter, Jesus showed interest in religious matters from an early age. His cousin, John the Baptist, was at that time a radical and ascetic preacher who was highly critical of the Jewish establishment. Jesus underwent the ritual of baptism in the Jordan River, which symbolised the cleansing of the spirit. Subsequently, after a retreat into the wilderness, he became a wandering preacher and attracted a large following. He rejected the pursuit of wealth and the use of violence, proclaiming that these would prevent man from entering the Kingdom of Heaven. This message is most explicit in his Sermon on the Mount. His message that all men could, like him, become sons of God, led to his persecution by the priesthood. The traditional teaching of the church is that, after his crucifixion, Jesus rose from the dead, but many early Christians and the Jews and Muslims (for whom he is a great prophet) did not share this belief.

The Crucifixion of Jesus Christ. ▼

JOAN OF ARC ☒

Joan of Arc (Jeanne d'Arc, 1412–31) was a French peasant girl, who led the French army against the English during the Hundred Years' War. Called the Maid of Orleans, she is a French national heroine and patron saint. When Joan was about 13 years old she began to hear voices that encouraged her to help liberate the French from the English. In 1429 she left her home in Champagne and led troops under her own command to relieve the city of Orleans, which she did in eight days. She was captured by the Burgundians in 1430, who sold her to the English. Joan of Arc was tried on a charge of heresy, treason and witchery and on 30 May 1431 she was burned at the stake in Rouen. There are monuments to her memory in many French cities and towns. She was beatified by the Pope on 18 April 1909 and canonised in 1920.

JOHN OF GAUNT

The Black Prince was replaced in France by his brother, John of Gaunt (1340–99). John proved to be an incompetent soldier and within three years most English possessions in France had been lost. By 1375 only five towns remained

Manuscript depicting the Hundred Years' War, in which Joan of Arc led the French against the English. ▲

in English hands: Calais, Cherbourg, Brest, Bayonne and Bordeaux. John of Gaunt returned to England in 1374 and tried to take power, but when **Edward III** died in 1377, he was succeeded by Richard II, the son of **Edward, the Black Prince**.

JOHN PAUL II

John Paul II, born in Poland, became the first non-Italian Pope in 450 years. He travels widely, often preaching to huge crowds at open-air venues.

JOHN, KING

King John (1167–1216), faced by enormous debts as a result of his brother **Richard I**'s continual campaigns on the Third Crusade, was forced to raise higher taxes. John's attempts to recapture the English possessions in France failed when he was defeated by **Philip II** of France at the Battle of Bouvines. Finally, John's barons forced him to accept the Magna Carta at Runnymede in 1215. In theory, this guaranteed the rights of free men, but in fact the most important clauses were attempts to limit the king's power and protect the rights of the Barons. John probably intended to disregard the Magna Carta as soon as he felt strong enough, but he died the following year and left the throne to his young son, who became **Henry III**.

King John signing the Magna Carta. ▼

JOHNSON, AMY

On 24 May, British aviator Amy Johnson (1904–41) became the first woman to fly solo from England to Australia; she was aged 27. She followed the 19-and-a-half-day flight with a record six-day solo flight from England to India, for which she received international acclaim. Johnson was one of the small, brave group of British women pilots who ferried aircraft from the factory to the airfield during the Second World War, a mission that held great danger. She was killed ferrying an aircraft in 1941.

JOHNSON, ANDREW

Democrat Andrew Johnson (1808–75) was the 17th president of the USA, holding office 1865–68.

JOHNSON, LYNDON B.

Democrat Lyndon B. Johnson (1908–73) was the 36th president of the USA from 1963–68.

JONSON, BEN

The annual Bartholomew Fair, held in Smithfield every 24 August, was used as the basis of the greatest play by Ben Jonson (1572–1637), the son of a master bricklayer and probably imprisoned after acting in the notorious play *The Isle of Dogs* in 1597. *Bartholomew Fair* was first performed in 1614 and depicted a range of outrageous characters, notably the hypocritical Puritan Zeal-of-the-Land Busy and the Justice Adam Overdo, who is eventually engulfed in the iniquities of the fair. The partnership between Jonson and the architect Inigo Jones (1573–1652) also created the spectacular masques of the Stuart court, combining drama, music, art and dance, brought to an end when the Civil War dispersed the court in 1642.

Bartholomew Fair at Smithfield, the subject of Ben Johnson's play of the same name. ▲

JOYCE, JAMES

One of the most important novels of the twentieth century was published in a small bookshop in Paris in 1922. James Joyce's (1882–1941) *Ulysses* told the events of a single day in the life of Dublin man Leopold Bloom. Using a technique that would later become known as 'stream of consciousness', Joyce positioned the reader inside the minds of the characters, carried along by the flow of their thoughts. The book is rich with puns and wordplay, symbolism and history. It is also sexually frank and was banned under obscenity laws in America until 1933.

JULIUS II

Julius II (1503–13) worked to restore papal sovereignty in its ancient territory. A patron of the arts, he commissioned **Michelangelo** to paint the ceiling of the Sistine Chapel.

JUNG, CARL GUSTAV

A student of **Freud**, Jung (1875–1961) rejected his emphasis upon sexuality as the principal driving force of unconscious thought. Jung focused instead upon the spiritual, and drew much inspiration from the study of the practices, beliefs and symbols of religions. He felt that man's unconscious thoughts were not unique to each individual, but rose instead from a collective unconscious, and therefore the symbols and thoughts that arose in our dreams were timeless and universal archetypes.

KABIR

Kabir (1440–1518) was born into a weaving family from the Hindu holy city of Benares. His father was a Muslim and his mother is believed to have been a Hindu. He sought to reconcile the mystical forms of Hinduism (in its Vaisnavi form) and Islam (in its Sufi form) through worship of Rama/Allah as the One Supreme God. He rejected the polytheism of popular Hinduism and taught that there was one God who had many names. He is known as the 'saint poet' and is remembered both for the many *bhajans* (devotional songs), that he wrote and as a teacher of Guru Nanak (1469–1539), the founder of the Sikh religion. His teachings helped to reduce conflict between Hindus and Muslims.

Carl Gustav Jung. ◀

KAFKA, FRANZ

Franz Kafka (1883–1924) was a Czech author who died of consumption in 1924. He published little in his lifetime, and had asked for his unpublished work to be burnt after his death. But his friend Max Brod rescued and printed his strange and mystifying texts. *The Trial*, Kafka's story of a man arrested for an unspecified crime, was published in 1925, earning the author a unique reputation in modern European literature. His style is crystalline and clear, but the subjects of his novels are claustrophobic. In all of them a character is involved in a nightmare situation over which he has no control, but which he must try to understand.

KANT, IMMANUEL

Kant's (1724–1804) philosophy is unique in its methods and aims. The critique of knowledge as a means of reaching philosophical conclusions is emphasised by Kant. This leads to the assertion that only mind exists so there is a rejection of utilitarian ethics in favour of systems which can be demonstrated by abstract philosophical arguments. In *The*

The Sikh Golden Temple at Amritsar; the Sikh religion was descended from the Hindu ideals of Kabir, through Guru Nanak. ▼

Critique of Pure Reason (1781) he showed that all arguments (for the existence of God, etc.) were grounded in contradiction and paradox. His own argument for the existence of God was that moral law demands justice and is not assured in this life, therefore there is a God and a future life.

KEATS, JOHN

The Romantic poet John Keats (1795–1821) died in Rome of tuberculosis at the age of only 25, yet his work marked the full flowering of the Romantic movement – in fact most of his great poems, such as 'The Eve of St Agnes' and 'Ode to a Nightingale' were written in two years of productivity in 1818 and 1819. It was a difficult time for Romantic poets; Keats struggled with money, as well as his love for Fanny Brawne; Percy Bysshe Shelley was drowned in the Bay of Spezia in 1822 and Lord Byron died of fever fighting for the Greek nationalists in 1824.

KELLER, HELEN ADAMS

Helen Adams Keller (1880–1968) was an author, speaker and philanthropist. She became blind and deaf at the age of 19 months as a result of brain fever, and was considered to be beyond help, communicating only with tantrums and wild laughter. She was patiently encouraged and taught by Anne Mansfield Sullivan, and she learned to read Braille and to write by using a special typewriter. In 1904, Keller graduated with honours from Radcliffe College and began a life of writing, lecturing and raising money for the handicapped.

KELLY, GRACE

Grace Kelly (1929–82) came from a wealthy family, went to good schools and was determined to prove that she could work. She modelled and did some work in commercials, and acted in a few Broadway plays before Hollywood beckoned. She was spotted by **Alfred Hitchcock** who cast her with exquisite taste in *Dial M for Murder*, and opposite James Stewart in *Rear Window*. While working on her third Hitchcock film, *To Catch a Thief*, she met Prince Rainier III, the ruler of the small principality of Monaco. In 1956, she married the prince in spectacular ceremony.

Returnees from the Bay of Pigs, Kennedy's unsuccessful invasion of Cuba. ▶

KENNEDY, JOHN FITZGERALD

John Fitzgerald Kennedy (1917–63) was born in Massachusetts, served in the navy in the Second World War, was elected to Congress in 1946 and to the Senate in 1952. He married Jacqueline Lee Bouvier in 1953. In 1960 he defeated **Richard Nixon** to become the 35th US president, the first Roman Catholic and the youngest person to be elected president. He mounted the unsuccessful Bay of Pigs invasion of Cuba, but in 1963 he secured the withdrawal of Soviet missiles from the island. At home he brought academics into Washington as advisers and set out a reform programme, 'New Frontiers', which was implemented by **Lyndon Johnson** after his death. He would die tragically in Dallas in 1963 at the hands of an assassin.

KEPLER, JOHANNES

Johannes Kepler (1571–1630) was a German mathematician and astronomer who used mathematics to formulate three laws of planetary motion, which are still the basis for man's understanding of the solar system. Kepler's work directly influenced the work of **Isaac Newton**. The laws state that: i) each planet has a elliptical path, with the Sun centred at one of the points of focus; ii) the plain swept out by the radius vector of a planet will always measure an equal area given the same length of time; and iii) the square of a planetary year is proportional to the cube of its average distance from the Sun.

Genghis Khan. ▲

KEYNES, JOHN MAYNARD

John Maynard Keynes (1883–1946) was a British economist who in 1936 put forward a blueprint for a more stable economy, which guaranteed secure employment. This, Keynes wrote, could be achieved by government spending and control of money to prevent the financial crises that, in the past, had so often destroyed jobs and with them, lives. Keynes' ideas were revolutionary in that they sought to remove the causes of the insecurity that had blighted human life for centuries and make sure that everyone could earn a decent living.

KHAN, GENGHIS

Son of a minor chieftain, Genghis Khan (*c.* 1167 –1227) moulded the warring Mongol clans into an unstoppable force. He organised his armies in multiples of 10, with the touman (10,000) being the largest tactical unit. By the time he unified all of the tribes, his empire stretched a thousand miles from east to west. The Horde, as his army was called, even breached the Great Wall of China in 1211, devastating China. Genghis was bought off by the Chinese and turned his attention to the West. By 1221, he had conquered the Khwarizarmians and had extended his empire from Tibet to the Caspian Sea and the Persian Gulf. Again, he turned on China, over-running the Hsia and southern China. He died in 1227.

Islam's holy book, the Qur'an. ▲

KHOMEINI, RUHOLLAH

Iranian Shi'ite Muslim leader Ruhollah Khomeini (1900–89) held the title ayatollah, which means 'sign of Allah', when he became the chief teacher of Islamic philosophy and law. He was exiled from Iran (1964) for opposition to the pro-western regime of the shah. Ayatollah Khomeini continued to campaign against the shah from his exile in France, demanding a return to the principles of Islam. The pressure on the shah became so great that he left the country in 1979 and the ayatollah made a triumphant return and became virtual head of state. Khomeini died in June 1989.

KHRUSHCHEV, NIKITA

In March 1953 **Stalin** died. After a period of rivalry he was replaced by Nikita Khrushchev (1894–1971), who immediately brought about a change in East-West relations, by introducing the policy of Coexistence. Khrushchev believed that there was nothing to be gained by trying to destroy the West, the Soviet Union had to accept that it existed and had to try to compete with it and prove that the Soviet system was better. Competition took the form of the 'Space Race', which the Soviet Union won with the first satellite in 1957 and the first man in space in 1961. Khrushchev was a lively character who enjoyed travel and meeting people. He set out to hit the headlines and produce a popular image for Communism.

KING, MARTIN LUTHER

Martin Luther King (1929–1968) was a US civil-rights campaigner, black leader and Baptist minister. An advocate of non-violence he was awarded the Nobel Peace Prize in 1964 and used peaceful, but determined, methods to promote black equality. He was assassinated in 1968, but remains one of the most influential figures in the campaign for the rights of Black Americans; his famous 'I have a dream' speech was the greatest and most passionate call for basic human rights of the twentieth century.

Martin Luther King.

KINGSLEY, MARY

One of the final expeditions in the 1800s was made by Mary Kingsley (1862–1900), a British amateur anthropologist and naturalist who travelled to West Africa to explore Angola and the

Lord Kitchener. ▶

Congo River (1893). While exploring in 1894, she encountered the Fang cannibal tribe and travelled in a native canoe up the Ogoové River. She ended her expedition by climbing Mount Cameroon (possibly the first woman to accomplish this). By the First World War the continent was under almost complete colonial control by France, Britain, Germany, Belgium, Spain, Portugal and Italy.

KITCHENER, GENERAL

In 1897 Sir Alfred Milner became British High Commissioner in South Africa. He demanded that the Uitlanders be given the vote and refused to compromise. The Boers declared war in 1899, realising the weakness of British forces. Until the end of the year, the British suffered defeat after defeat, but the arrival of General Roberts with reinforcements in January 1900 turned the tide. By September 1900 both Boer republics had been occupied and their capitals captured. General Kitchener (1850–1916), later field-marshall, had previously commanded troops at the Mahdist Battle of Omdurman and took over command in November 1900. He had to build block-houses to defend railway lines and herd Boer civilians into concentration camps before he could force their leaders to surrender. Kitchener, one of the great military leaders of his time, died during the Second World War, when his ship was destroyed by a mine in 1916.

KLAMMER, JEAN-CLAUDE

Klammer's (b. 1953) uninhibited, courageous and risk-taking skiing style endeared him to fans worldwide and made him a legend in his native Austria. Born in the town of Mooswald, Klammer entered the Winter Olympics with the full weight of the Austrian nation expecting nothing less than gold from their hero. In 1975, he had secured his first-ever World Cup downhill title by showing incredible form. That season, he won eight out of the nine downhills. In one race at Wengen, Switzerland, he destroyed his fellow racers, winning by a massive margin of 3.54 seconds. He missed out on the overall title, which takes into account the slalom event as well, only by losing in the final race.

KOCH, ROBERT

German bacteriologist Robert Koch (1843–1910) was awarded the Nobel Prize in 1905 for his work, which included the discovery of the bacillus responsible for tuberculosis (1882).

KORESH, DAVID

David Koresh formed the Branch Davidian sect in 1959. The sect was a splinter group, formed out of another group that itself had broken away from the Seventh Day Adventist Church. The charismatic leader took his followers to Waco, Texas, and formed a commune. Koresh became more dictatorial as time went on, instructing that he was a messiah and that all the women in the group were his God-given wives. Authorities were alerted over the stockpiling of weapons there and a siege was born. The fiery demise of the compound claimed the lives of Koresh and 74 of his followers, with four federal agents killed in the preceding shoot-out.

Peter Kropotkin furthered the ideas of Charles Darwin (below), but disagreed with the capitalist approach some groups derived from Darwinism. ▼

Kublai Khan. ◄

KROPOTKIN, PETER

Prince Peter Kropotkin (1842–1921) was born into a noble Russian family. Following exile from Russia for his anarchist views, he settled in London. His book, *Mutual Aid* (1902), was a refutation of the views of the Social Darwinists, who justified capitalism because it encouraged the survival of the fittest. As an outstanding biologist and anthropologist he was able to show that evolution in very many cases resulted in mutually beneficial co-operation between animals and between peoples in primitive societies. He rejected the communist alternative to capitalism because he felt his research proved that co-operation could arise naturally without being imposed by the state.

KUBLAI KHAN

In 1279 Kublai Khan (1215–94), grandson of **Genghis**, brought China under his control and his descendants ruled as emperors of China until overthrown by the Ming dynasty in 1368.

KUBRICK, STANLEY

Kubrick (b. 1928) is an American film writer, director and producer with a legendary status. Early films include *Fear and Desire* (1953) and *Killer's Kiss* (1955). *The Killing* (1956) caused critics to take notice of his taut, brilliant style and bleakly cynical outlook, while *Paths of Glory* (1957) solidified his reputation as a film-maker interested in depicting the individual at the mercy of a hostile world. *2001: A Space Odyssey* and *A Clockwork Orange* (1971), both made in England, where Kubrick has worked since 1961, engendered critical controversy, but the former has now become accepted as a landmark in modern cinema. It is a long film, obscurely symbolic, but intensely exciting from a visual point of view.

R. D. Laing. ◀

LAING, R. D.

R. D. Laing (1927–1989) was one of the most radical critics of psychiatric practice of the twentieth century. In his books *The Divided Self* (1960) and *Sanity, Madness and the Family* (1964) he rejected the orthodox view that schizophrenia is simply an illness, and saw it instead as a normal response to an impossible social situation. He therefore favoured group therapies and attacked chemical therapies and electric-shock treatments. He also viewed madness not as a sign of mental decline but as a phase through which the mind passed whilst healing itself. This led him to see the therapist as a companion on a journey through madness.

LANCASTER, JAMES

As a result of the war with Spain, a sustained assault by the English on the Portuguese spice trade was delayed until 1592, when James Lancaster (*c.* 1554–1616) reached Penang, in the Malay peninsula. From here he sailed into the Strait of Malacca and attacked every Portuguese ship he came across, before sailing for home. Unfortunately for Lancaster, part of his crew mutinied in Bermuda, and made off with his ship. Lancaster's voyage itself was a failure, but the knowledge he gained contributed to the foundation of the Honourable East India Company in 1600.

LANCASTER, JOSEPH

The British educator Joseph Lancaster (1778–1838), was one of the developers of the monitorial system of education. Lancastrian schools were an important factor in the growth of mass education.

LANDER, RICHARD AND JOHN

In 1830 British explorers Richard (1804–34) and John (1807–39) Lander discovered the mouth of the Niger River, which eventually became the passage into the African interior, making the once-great Saharan crossroads largely obsolete.

LAO TZU

Taoism centres on a number of philosophical works including the *Tao Te Ching*, attributed to Lao Tzu, who lived in China in about 500 BC. The teachings in the 81 chapters of the *Tao Te Ching* have been one of the major influences on Chinese thought and culture over the last 2,500 years.

LAUD, WILLIAM

Laud (1573–1645) became Archbishop of Canterbury in 1533 and was a bitter opponent of Puritanism. He required strict uniformity in the churches and required obedience to the bishops and the Prayer Book. He became closely associated with **Charles I**'s views and this alliance with the monarchy was not in the long-term interests of the Anglican Church. Hatred of the monarch was easily transferred to hatred of the archbishop. Laud wished to reinstate the surplice, to have the altar separated off in the church, and for heads to bow at the name of Jesus. At his execution in 1645 he said, 'I was born and baptised in the Church of England established by Law. In that profession I have lived, and in that I come now to die'.

Canterbury Cathedral, where William Laud became Archbishop in 1533. ▼

LAUREN, RALPH ✷

Although the mallet-swinging polo player had existed in various guises since 1896, when the American Brooks Brothers produced their first button-down polo shirts it was not a recognised trademark, until Ralph Lauren (b. 1937) used it to launch his womenswear line in 1971. The logo's appeal as a symbol of Ivy-League success was immediate, and it soon appeared on everything from Ralph Lauren menswear (launched in 1967) to diffusion lines like 'Chaps', 'Ralph', 'Double RL' and 'Polo Sport'.

LAWRENCE, D. H. 📖

The novelist D. H. Lawrence (1885–1930) shocked the public by eloping with the wife of a German baron; was prosecuted for indecency for his novel *The Rainbow* (1915); and both *Women in Love* (1920) and *Lady Chatterley's Lover* (1928) were too shocking for British publishers. *Lady Chatterley's Lover* stayed unpublished in the UK until Penguin Books won a famous 1960 court battle. Lawrence lived in Mexico during the early 1920s, but died in France of tuberculosis at the age of only 44.

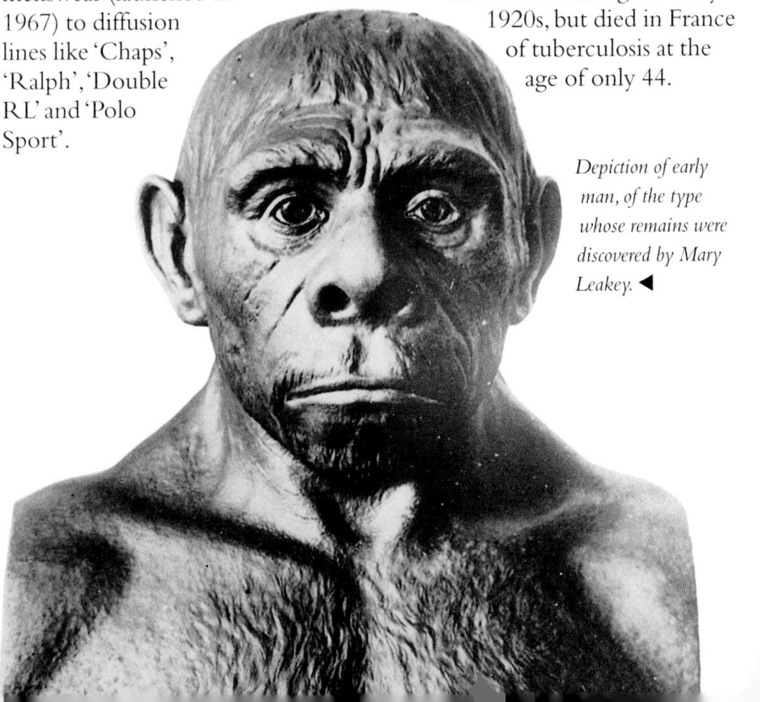

Depiction of early man, of the type whose remains were discovered by Mary Leakey. ◄

Mary Leakey's discoveries enlightened the world about many aspects of man's evolution. ◀

Sulphuric acid and sodium chloride (common salt) were heated to produce hydrogen chloride and sodium sulphate. The latter was then roasted with limestone and coal to make the sodium carbonate, which could be dissolved in water and crystallised. The Leblanc process was a benchmark for chemical processing that influenced many others.

LEAKEY, MARY DOUGLAS

Mary Leakey (1913–96), the wife of Kenyan archeologist, Louis Leakey, was a British anthropologist who discovered fossil footprints in Tanzania in 1976, which prove that our ancestors walked upright 3.6 million years ago. Her finds were probably the most important in piecing together the history of the evolution of man.

LEBLANC, NICOLAS

Nicolas Leblanc (1742–1806) introduced an industrial-scale method for producing washing soda or sodium carbonate, called the Leblanc Process in 1787.

LEE, ROBERT E.

Robert E. Lee (1807–70) was a US military strategist and Confederate general in the American Civil War. He sustained the South far beyond their true capacity, defeating numerous Union generals in decisive and well-managed battles. He failed to defeat the Union army at Gettysburg, and, in 1864, faced **U. S. Grant**, the new Northern commander. Forced on to the defensive, he inflicted heavy losses on Grant at the battles of the Wilderness, Spotsylvania and Cold Harbor. Early in April 1865, he met Grant at Appomattox and surrendered the army of Northern Virginia.

LEIBNIZ, GOTTFRIED WILHELM

Gottfried Wilhelm Leibniz (1646–1716) was a German philosopher and mathematician, who devised the calculating machine in 1671.

LENIN, VLADIMIR

Lenin (1870–1924) and his followers believed that private property was wrong, that all businesses, farms and public services should be owned by the State. Workers should be paid according to the value of the work that they did, and not according to who they were or what they could demand. Not surprisingly, therefore, in the months after the Bolsheviks seized power, all businesses, banks etc. were taken over by the State. Land, houses and money were all confiscated. To enforce his actions, Lenin set up a secret police force, the Cheka, led by Felix Dzerzhinsky, which ruthlessly murdered Lenin's opponents. Russia became a dictatorship far more violent and far more extreme than it had been under the tsars.

LENNON, JOHN

In the 1960s, as a member of The Beatles, John Lennon (1940–80) had made jangly pop an art. Post-Beatles, working with his wife Yoko Ono, he had made music that was more experimental and

Under Lenin's dictatorship, Russia was ruled more violently than it had been under the last monarch Nicolas II (left). ◀

challenging, the pop chords giving way to primal screams. Meanwhile, his political statements and rallying for world peace had made him the voice of a generation. Mark Chapman, although a fan, had decided Lennon was the 'anti-Christ'. He had asked for Lennon's autograph, and later the same day he gunned the star down outside the Dakota building in New York in December 1980. At the time of his death, Lennon was one of the most famous men in the world.

John Lennon. ◀

LEONER, ALEXANDER

Colonel Alexander Leoner of the Soviet Union was the first man to leave his spacecraft and walk in space. Tethered only by a thin cord attached to his craft, the cosmonaut emerged in a bright orange spacesuit and somersaulted against the heavens. Leoner remained outside for about 10 minutes and travelled 4,828 km (3,000 miles) in that short time, 483 km (300 miles) above a small, blue Earth.

LEOPOLD, ALDO

Aldo Leopold (1887–1948) worked as a conservationist for the US Forest Service. His posthumously published work, *A Sand County Almanac* (1949), introduces the concept of the ecosystem as an interacting web of living organisms that has its own natural balance. To manage an ecosystem it is necessary to 'think like a mountain' and obtain an overview of the whole system. His 'Land Ethic' was based on the moral maxim that 'a thing is right when it tends to preserve the integrity, stability and beauty of the biotic community. It is wrong when it tends otherwise'.

LIEH TZU

Lieh Tzu, one of the most important names in Taoism since the fourth century BC, may never have existed. The *Lieh Tzu*, the book attributed to him, appears to be an edited compilation of various works. The contents are similar in style to those of the *Chuang Tzu* and may originally have been by the same author(s), however they are more confused than the philosophical writings of the *Chuang Tzu*, suggesting that they were written or compiled later.

LINCOLN, ABRAHAM

The Republican Abraham Lincoln (1809–65), a congressman from Illinois, was elected as the 16th president of the USA in 1860. An inspired leader during the American Civil War, Lincoln's famous address at Gettysburg in 1863 has become the code of belief for a nation. Lincoln was also responsible for inaugurating the first Thanksgiving Day, a national holiday that is observed to this day. He was assassinated at the end of the war in 1865.

The flag of the United States of America. ▼

Hans Lippershay, inventor of the first telescope. ▶

LINDBERGH, CHARLES

The American aviator Charles Lindbergh (1902–74) first achieved international fame in 1927 as the first person to fly alone across the Atlantic. He made the daring expedition in the *Spirit of St Louis*, his single-engine monoplane, travelling from New York to Paris in 33½ hours. In 1929 he married Anne Spencer Morrow, daughter of the US ambassador to Mexico, and she became his co-pilot and navigator on many subsequent expeditions, including the 1929 flight over the Yucatan peninsula, during which he photographed Mayan ruins. These photographs made an important contribution to the study of the Mayas and to the field of archeology.

LIPPERSHEY, HANS

Hans Lippershey (*c.* 1570–1619) was a Dutch lens-maker, credited with inventing the telescope as a military reconnaissance device in 1608.

LISTER, JOSEPH

The British surgeon Joseph Lister (1827–1912) revolutionised surgery with his antiseptic practices. He began using carbolic acid to destroy germs, and later introduced gauze dressings and sterile catgut ligatures.

LITTLE, MALCOLM

Malcolm Little (1926–1965) became known as Malcolm X during his campaign for black equality in America. Exhorting these civil rights at the same time as **Martin Luther King**, Little's methods marked the opposite end of the scale to King. While King's campaign was characterised by 'peaceful protest', Little preferred violent ways to achieve black equality, suggesting the time for talk was past. Both men were extremely influential in their own ways, and both met the same end. Little was assassinated in 1965.

LIVINGSTONE, DAVID

David Livingstone (1813–73) was a Scottish missionary and explorer who made extensive journeys across Africa in the mid-nineteenth century. In 1849 he crossed the Kalahari Desert and in 1853–56 crossed the entire continent, discovering the Victoria Falls on the way. In 1858 he set off from the Zambezi and discovered Lake Nyasa and in 1866 discovered Lake Tanganyika. By this time his travels had caught the attention of the world and when he failed to emerge from Tanganyika, H. M. Stanley, an American journalist, set out to find him. The two men met in a famous encounter on the shores of Lake Tanganyika in 1871.

LOCKE, JOHN

In England the political philosopher John Locke (1632–1704) gave shape to a new concept of individual natural rights against the state. Locke believed that natural rights should protect from other persons as well as from the state. His book *Essay in Human Understanding* (1687) is his most famous work, and his influence on the philosophy of

Black rights campaigner Malcolm Little, known as Malcolm X. ◀

David Livingstone. ◄

politics has been enormous. His religious views revolved around the requirement to reduce Christianity to the New Testament: it was this plain proposition that constituted Christianity. Moral rules are laid down by God and are in the Bible, he said; men should follow them otherwise they will be punished.

LOOS, ALFRED

Alfred Loos (1870–1933) was one of the first modern architects to react against the decorative trends of Art Nouveau. Following architecture school, he lived in the United States for three years and studied the work of the Chicago School. Returning to Vienna in 1896, he wrote a series of articles condemning ornament in favour of functionalism. Houses he designed were built of concrete and had flat roofs, planar walls and strict symmetry.

LOUIS VII

Louis VII (*c*.1120–80), crowned in 1137, married Eleanor of Aquitaine. His participation in the Third Crusade (1147) led to their divorce and her marriage to Henry II of England.

LOUIS XIII

Louis XIII (1601–43), strongly Catholic in outlook, continued the suppression of the Huguenots. He increasingly fell under the thrall of his *eminence grise*, Cardinal Richelieu.

LOUIS XIV

The Sun King was Louis XIV, King of France (1643–1715). He made France the most powerful country in Europe. Louis was only five when he became king and did not rule in person until 1661. He followed the practice of centralising power into his own hands. Louis also established a dazzling court at his new Palace of Versailles, just outside Paris. The bishops and nobles of France flocked there to pay court to the king. Their days were often spent watching the king get up, the *levée*, or go to bed, the *couchée*. They were also expected to watch him have breakfast, lunch and dinner. This ensured that the French nobility were kept where Louis could keep an eye on them.

LOUIS XV

Louis XV (1710–74), uninterested in politics and administration, became dominated by his mistresses Mme de Pompadour and Mme du Barry. He ceded control of Canada to Britain.

LOUIS XVI

Louis XVI (1754–93) became king of France in 1774. He was totally unsuited for the role that he had to play as an autocratic monarch. In the 1780s Louis relied on a series of ministers, each of whom tried to solve the increasingly grave

Louis XIV. ▶

The execution of Louis XVI. ▲

financial problems in France. The central issue was that the First and Second Estates, the clergy and the nobility, were exempt from all taxes, which meant that the Third Estate had to pay for everything. This not only reduced the potential income of the state, but it also became an increasing source of grievance with the rich bourgeoisie, the lawyers and merchants, who emerged as the leaders of the Third Estate. Louis XVI was not prepared to break this system. If a minister suggested radical change, he was replaced.

LOVELOCK, JAMES

The Gaia hypothesis, as outlined in biochemist James Lovelock's *Gaia* (1979), is a hypothesis that the planet Earth, its soil, oceans, atmosphere and biosphere, constitutes a self-regulating system that can be thought of as living. He has often been accused by scientists of arguing that the Earth is conscious, but this view, common amongst many of his supporters, forms no part of the theory. His studies of atmospheric chemistry, which led him to discover the hole in the ozone layer and the wide distribution of pesticides, have also provided much evidence for the theory.

LUMIÈRE, AUGUSTE AND LOUIS

Auguste (1862–1954) and Louis (1864–1948) Lumière were French brothers who pioneered cinematography. They gave the first film performance in Paris in 1895. The images were so realistic that the audience, seeing a train coming towards them on screen, panicked and ran out of the cinema. Despite this unfortunate beginning, the cinema became the first mass-entertainment medium, and a rival in Britain to the music hall.

LUTHER, MARTIN

Martin Luther (1483–1546) was a German Christian church reformer and one of the founders of Protestantism. While a professor at the University of Wittenberg in 1517, he nailed a list of objections to the sale of indulgences on a church door (the 95 Theses). Indulgences were certificates that supposedly absolved the buyer of sin, and were used by the Pope as a way of raising money. Luther stated that sins could not be absolved by buying an indulgence, but only by true repentance by the individual. This was the start of the Reformation and the beginning of the Lutheran Church, which believed that priests and bishops were unnecessary. Luther defended his views at the Diet of Worms in 1521, but was banned from the Catholic Church.

MACARTHUR, DOUGLAS

Douglas MacArthur (1880–1964) was a US general in the Second World War, commander of the US forces in the Far East and, from March 1942, of the allied forces in the south-west Pacific. After his evacuation of the Philippines, he

Martin Luther (left). ◀

Niccolo Machiavelli. ▲

had vowed that he would return to liberate the country. True to his word, he achieved this and was present at the formal capitulation of the Japanese armed forces in 1945.

MACHIAVELLI, NICCOLO

Niccolo Machiavelli (1467–1527) was responsible for a revolution in political thought as a result of the publication of his *Il Principe* ('The Prince') in 1513. In common with other Renaissance thinkers his views are secular, they centre on man and the world and they are inspired by classical literature. His advice to the Italian city states and their princes was based not upon religious principles, such as the divine right of kings, but simply upon doing whatever worked. This empirical and pragmatic approach can be seen as a precursor to the Scientific Revolution. He looks at past events, such as the lives of Romulus, Theseus and Brutus, as described in Livy's *Histories*, for lessons about the most effective ways for a state to maintain its power.

Harold Macmillan. ▲

MACKINTOSH, CHARLES RENNIE

The designs for the new Glasgow School of Art were begun in 1897, when Mackintosh (1868–1928) won a competition for an extension to existing buildings. At the time, they were condemned for their radical Art Nouveau style, but ironically the school is now revered as the best early modern-movement building in Britain. At the Glasgow School of Art, Mackintosh did not reproduce Art Nouveau wholesale, but adapted it in a unique way, using traditional Gaelic and Celtic patterns. The commission was to build several studios, a lecture theatre, a library and private rooms for the director. In plan, the School of Art is masterful juxtaposing rooms of different shapes and sizes.

MACMILLAN, HAROLD

Harold Macmillan (1894–1986) was a Conservative prime minister between 1957 and 1963, whose premiership oversaw political trends that characterised post-war Britain. Elected in the wake of the Suez disaster he came to power on the back of the slogan 'You've never had it so good', and a national mood reflecting a desire for domestic prosperity. Consumer-led affluence continued to create a feel-good factor following the years of war and post-war austerity. He advanced Britain's retreat from its colonies with his 'wind of change' speech in Africa and set Britain on course to gain entry to the European Economic Community, though this was vetoed by the

French. Macmillan was undermined by illness and a spy scandal involving his war minister, John Profumo. He retired in 1963.

MACMILLAN, KIRKPATRICK

The style and form of the modern bicycle was created in 1840 by the Scot Kirkpatrick Macmillan who attached driving levers and pedals to the basic machine, as well as handlebars for steering.

MADISON, JAMES

James Madison (1751–1836) was the fourth president of the USA, in office 1808–16. He was a Democrat-Republican.

MADONNA

Madonna Louise Veronica Ciccone (b. 1958) stormed on to the pop scene in 1984 with the hit single 'Holiday'. It was to be the beginning of a prolific and successful career. Later the same year she achieved her first number 1 single with 'Like a Virgin', which was followed by a stream of further worldwide hits. Popular on both sides of the Atlantic, Madonna made a name for herself with her outrageous and shocking style, and her success has been maintained by her ability to change with the times.

Macmillan's lever-driven bicycle. ▼

MAGELLAN, FERDINAND

Ferdinand Magellan (*c.* 1480–1521) was a Portuguese navigator, who later transferred his services to Spain. In 1519 he set sail from Seville with the intention of reaching the East Indies by a westerly route. Having explored the east coast of South America, he finally sailed through the Strait of Magellan at the southern tip of the continent, crossed an ocean he named the Pacific, and in 1521 reached the Philippines where he was killed by the indigenous people. The ships continued to India and Africa, thereby making the first circumnavigation of the globe, to prove the world's oceans were linked. Only 18 of the 250 explorers survived the voyage.

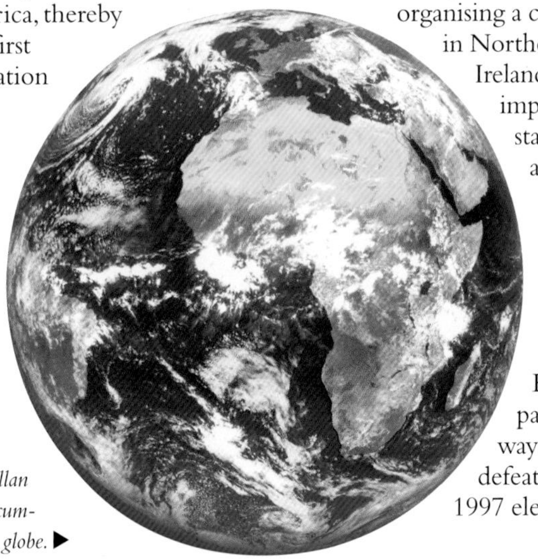

Ferdinand Magellan made the first circumnavigation of the globe. ▶

MAJOR, JOHN

John Major (b. 1943) was foreign secretary (1989) and chancellor of the exchequer (1989–90). Following **Margaret Thatcher**'s resignation in 1990, he became leader of the Conservative party and prime minister. He gained support over his handling of Britain's efforts in the Gulf War (1991) and was re-elected in 1992. Following this, he faced mounting public dissatisfaction over several issues, including Britain's withdrawal from the ERM, drastic pit and hospital closures and past arms sales to Iraq. His success in organising a cease-fire in Northern Ireland (1994) improved his standing, but a number of senior minister scandals and party divisions over Europe paved the way for his defeat in the 1997 elections.

Nelson Mandela. ▲

MALORY, THOMAS

Historians are unsure about the identity of Sir Thomas Malory (*c.* 1416–71), but he may have completed his distillation of the English and French versions of the Arthurian legends while in Newgate Prison on charges of rape and theft. But if, as some sources suggest, he helped the pioneer printer William Caxton (*c.* 1420 –91) with the text of his book before printing in 1485, it must have been somebody else. *Le Morte D'Arthur* was enormously influential, at a time when a Welsh king had taken the throne, naming his son, the Prince of Wales, Arthur.

MANDELA, NELSON

On 11 February, African National Congress leader Nelson Mandela (b. 1918) walked free from Victor Verster prison in South Africa's Cape Province, after 27 years in prison for treason. Celebrations around the world were followed by negotiations between the ANC, of which Mandela was elected deputy president, and president F. W. de Klerk. Mandela became the first black president of South Africa on 10 May 1994. When Mandela was sentenced to life imprisonment in 1964, he came to symbolise black political aspirations. He and de Klerk shared the Nobel Peace Prize for negotiating South Africa's peaceful transition to multi-racial democracy. After the ANC victory in the April 1994 elections, Mandela worked to ease racial tensions, court foreign investment and provide services to the black victims of apartheid.

MAPPLETHORPE, ROBERT

Mapplethorpe (1946–1989) began his career as an independent film-maker and sculptor. He is best known for intense black-and-white compositions in which the subject appears as object, even icon. Mapplethorpe's gallery shows scandalised some viewers and critics with their juxtaposition of straight portraits and elegant still-lifes, such as *Tulip*, with overtly homoerotic, even sadomasochistic, male nudes. Mapplethorpe became successful as a commercial fashion photographer and celebrity portrait artist. Learning in 1986 that he had AIDS, he used a series of self-portraits to help focus attention on the disease.

MARCONI, GUGLIELMO

With the help of **Hertz**'s discoveries using electromagnetic waves, Marconi (1874–1937) made a 'wireless' telegraph, the ancestor of radio. He established wireless communication between England and France in 1899, and across the Atlantic in 1901.

MARIE-ANTOINETTE

At the age of 14, Marie-Antoinette, daughter of the Austrian empress, Marie Theresa, was married to the 15-year-old French dauphin. She became queen of France in 1774 when her husband became Louis XVI. The poverty and starvation in the country, however, led to the French Revolution and in 1791 the king and his family were forced to flee from the revolutionaries. They were captured and returned, and in

Guglielmo Marconi. ◀

Maximilien Robespierre, leader during the French Reign of Terror, in which Marie-Antoinette was executed. ▶

October 1793 Marie-Antoinette was executed, nine months after her husband had met the same fate at the hands of the guillotine.

MARLOWE, CHRISTOPHER

The playwright Christopher Marlowe (1564–93) was only 29 when he met his mysterious and violent death in a Deptford tavern, probably as a secret agent employed by Francis Walsingham. He was also a free-thinker, a homosexual and wildly indiscreet. His writings led to accusations of atheism, blasphemy and subversion. They reached a climax with his play, *Edward II*, the tragedy of a homosexual king undermined by his barons – paving the way towards **Shakespeare**'s sophisticated historical tragedies – and *Doctor Faustus*, the story of a man who makes a pact with the devil. He spent the last months of his life in plague-ridden London, writing the narrative poems *Hero and Leander* and *The Lyrical Shepherd*.

MARSHALL, GEORGE

General George Marshall (1880–1959) was a US general and diplomat. In 1947, as US secretary of state, he announced the European Recovery Programme, to help European reconstruction after the war. Known as the Marshall Plan (1948–53), it was drawn up under the leadership of the USA, Britain and France, and Congress made American funds available, gladly supporting the principle of giving aid to anti-Communist governments; 14 European nations accepted the aid, including Britain.

MARX, KARL

Karl Marx, a middle-class German Jew, studied philosophy at the University of Berlin before editing a radical newspaper. After the failed 1848 revolt in Germany, he fled to England, where he wrote *The Communist Manifesto* and *Das Kapital*. In these, he attempts to provide a scientific foundation for socialism (countering the utopian socialism of Proudhon and Bakunin). Like the English economists, he saw production as based on land, labour and capital, but he pointed out that whoever controlled the mode of production controlled the economics and politics of the country. Control by landowners caused feudalism, control by investors caused capitalism and control by labourers caused socialism. Public ownership of the means of the production was seen as the necessary basis for fair and meaningful work.

MARY I

Mary I (1516–58) became queen of England and Ireland in 1553, following the death of her brother Edward VI, despite his attempts to give the throne to the protestant Lady Jane Grey. The daughter of Catherine of Aragon, she was a devout Catholic. Upon her succession, she set about halting the anti-Catholicism practised by her father **Henry VIII**. Her policies, especially her decision to marry her Spanish cousin **Philip**, proved

Mary I. ▼

Mary II. ▶

unpopular. Still she continued with her policies and officially reconciled England to Rome. Her religious fervour earned her the nickname of 'Bloody Mary'. She is said to have executed over 300 Protestants during her reign. Like her father, though, she was defeated by nature. She died childless in 1558, failing to produce a Catholic heir, and her Protestant half-sister **Elizabeth I** took the throne.

MARY II

Mary II (1689–1694) reigned jointly with her Dutch husband **William of Orange**. It was during their reign that the Bank of England was incorporated in 1694.

MARY, QUEEN OF SCOTS

Mary (1542–87) was the daughter of James V of Scotland and Mary of Guise, his second wife. She became Queen of Scots at just one week old, after her father was killed at the Battle of Solway Moss. To avoid a union with the young Prince Edward of England, she was betrothed straight away to the French dauphin. In 1561, after the death of her husband, Mary returned to Scotland, where she later married Lord Darnley. Mary's reign from this time was beset with intrigue and murder: Darnley murdered the queen's secretary and favourite, Rizzio; he was later murdered by the Earl of Bothwell, who then married Mary. In the ensuing outrage, the queen abdicated, passing the throne to her infant son **James VI**. She was imprisoned for nearly 20 years before being executed.

MASLOW, ABRAHAM

Abraham Maslow (1908–70), and his colleague Carl Rogers, were the founders of humanistic psychology, a school that emerged in the USA in the 1950s. Maslow was a student of **Alfred Adler**. Whereas earlier psychology focused on the study of psychological illness and abnormality, Maslow studied the behaviour of people who were mentally healthier than average. For him the aim of therapy was to remove all the inner obstacles to the open-ended process of 'self-actualisation', of achieving our true potential.

MATILDA

Matilda (1102–67), the only legitimate child of **Henry I**, was queen of England for a few months in 1153 until the throne was seized from her by her cousin, Stephen.

MATISSE, HENRI

Matisse (1869–1954) began his adult life as a lawyer, but after an illness he gave up the law and went to Paris to study art. He now ranks amongst the greatest painters of the twentieth century, also excelling at sculpture, illustration, graphics and set design. He developed a radical new approach to colour, using it in a structural rather than a descriptive way. After flirting with Fauvism, Matisse never again belonged to any identifiable school or movement. His final masterpiece, completed when he was more than 80 years old, was the decoration of the Dominican Chapel of the Rosary in Vence, near Nice in southern France.

MAURICE, F. D.

F. D. Maurice (1805–72), founder of Christian Socialism, was a Tory paternalist with a Christian duty to

The Crucifixion of Christ; F. D. Maurice was the founder of the Christian Socialist movement. ▶

The Diet of Worms. ▶

help the poor. Christian Socialists saw the Christian ideal of co-operation being applied to economic life. Each act of co-operation was a gesture to defy capitalism, but was doomed as a form of nineteenth-century idealism. Maurice's book, *The Kingdom of Christ* (1837), envisaged Christ's kingdom, in which there were no class distinctions, no rich or poor, oppressor or oppressed. The Christian Socialists were overtaken by the un-Christian Socialist thinking of **Karl Marx**.

MAXIMILIAN I

Maximilian I (1459–1519) was emperor of Germany, and convened the Diet of Worms in 1495 to reform the German Constitution. Lack of support from his lieges doomed it to failure.

MAXWELL, ROBERT

Jan Ludvik Hoch (1923–91) was born in Slatina-Selo in Czechoslovakia. He managed to escape the Holocaust and fled to France and then to Britain, where he changed his name to Ian Robert Maxwell. After the war he obtained German academic and scientific papers and published them all over the world. He founded the Pergamon Press in 1951 and by the 1960s he was a major force in publishing. He also served as a Labour MP until 1970. In 1981 he bought the British Printing Corporation, selling it in 1987. He then purchased the Mirror Group, using it as a foundation to create

Maxwell Communications. He secretly siphoned off $1.2 billion to support his shaky empire. Faced with exposure, he died after falling off his yacht in 1991.

McADAM, JOHN

In the late 1820s, John McAdam (1756–1836) devised a new process for making road surfaces, using a mixture of heated bitumen or asphalt and stones, which would set by cooling to provide a smooth durable top layer. The first application was on a road in Vauxhall, London, in 1835. His invention was dubbed 'Macadamising' and has remained a ubiquitous form of road surfacing ever since.

McCARTHY, JOHN

John McCarthy was a journalist working in the Lebanon when he was abducted by fundamentalists. He spent some of his time in captivity with Brian Keenan, and later the two men were also held with Tom Sutherland, Frank Reed and Terry Anderson, all American prisoners. McCarthy was deeply affected by the ordeal, suffering beatings and solitary confinement. He obviously played a great role in helping his fellow captives survive the years of imprisonment. McCarthy was one of the last hostages to be released, in August 1991.

McCARTNEY, PAUL

The Beatles achieved their first number one hit with 'Please Please Me' in 1962, but it had been a long slog since **John Lennon** (1940–80) first met Paul McCartney (b. 1942) in a Liverpool band called The Quarrymen in 1957. They fixed Liverpool as the capital city of the so-called 'beat generation', stamped their mark on the 1960s and became the ultimate international pop success. The Beatles' story culminated in the universal popularity of *Sergeant Pepper's Lonely Hearts' Club Band* in 1967, just in time for the Summer of Love the following year. Legal wrangles over their company, Apple, meant that by 1970 they could no longer bear to be in the same room. Hopes that they might reunite ended when Lennon was shot in New York a decade later.

McENROE, JOHN

New York tennis ace John McEnroe (b. 1959) earned himself a reputation as a bad-tempered, volatile player, but despite his

Paul McCartney. ◀

nickname 'Superbrat', McEnroe was arguably the best of his era. His victory over Bjorn Borg in 1981 was a momentous one, as it ended Borg's undisputed five-year reign as Wimbledon men's singles champion. Many felt that the volatile American's victory was poetic justice after the Swede had beaten him in the 1980 final. In 1981, McEnroe defeated the Swedish master in a riveting match, winning 4–6, 7–6, 7–6, 6–4 in three hours and 22 minutes.

McKINLEY, WILLIAM

William McKinley (1843–1901) was the 25th president of the USA, a Republican elected in 1896. He went to Congress in 1876 and was repeatedly re-elected. In 1892 he was made governor of Ohio, his name being identified with the high protective tariff carried in the McKinley Bill of 1890. His term as president was marked by the USA's adoption of an imperialist policy, as shown by the Spanish-American War in 1898 and the annexation of Cuba and the Philippines. In November 1900, as in 1896, he secured a large majority and was re-elected. He was shot by anarchist Leon Czolgosz in 1901 in Buffalo, New York, and died eight days later.

The massacre of the Huguenots, believed to have been ordered by Catherine de Medici. ▲

MEDICI, CATHERINE DE

Catherine de Medici (1519–89), *de facto* queen of France 1559–74, is held responsible for the bloody massacre of Huguenots in Paris in 1572.

MENCIUS

'Mencius' is the latinised name of Meng Tzu (372–289 BC). He was the most well-known disciple of **Confucius** and his writings are the most important source of Confucian philosophy. He taught that the highest aim of the state is to protect the welfare of the people, that the wise emperor is the one who rules in accord with the Order of Heaven (*T'ien ming*) and that an unjust ruler should be overthrown. He believed that the heart/mind (*hsin*) of man was naturally good and that it should be cultivated to realise its full potential.

MENDEL, GREGOR

The grandfather of genetics was Gregor Mendel (1822–84), who pioneered the study of inheritance with his pea experiments. His work was ignored at the time (1866) but rediscovered in 1900, and provided the foundation for further experiments with genetics that eventually led to man's understanding of this complex science.

MENDELEYEV, DMITRI

The 'Periodic Table', based on atomic mass, was devised by Russian chemist Dmitri Mendeleyev (1834–1907) in 1869. The table grouped similarly massed elements together vertically, and ranked them horizontally according to characteristics. It had to include blank spaces as well, indicating the elements that he knew were as yet undiscovered. Most of these have since been found or have been artificially created by scientists.

MENUHIN, YEHUDI

At the age of 10, violinist Yehudi Menuhin (b. 1916) was already causing a sensation. His effortless performance of *Symphonie Espagnole* was a fantastic technical feat. Despite his youth, he had a mature vision of music that gave depth and understanding to his fresh, spontaneous style. He did not abandon his gift as he grew older. During the Second World War he gave over 500 concerts for American and allied troops in the theatres of war.

Mencius was the best-known disciple of Confucius (left). ◀

Gerardus Mercator. ◀

MERCATOR, GERARDUS

Flemish map-maker Gerardus Mercator (1512–94) was the first man to produce a map of the world as a cylindrical projection. Mercator's projection displayed the lines of longitude and latitude (parallels and meridians) as a grid, which became immediately popular because it meant that courses could be plotted in straight lines with a pair of compasses. All map projections distort reality however they work, though, and the flaw in Mercator's was that exaggerations in width occurred moving away from the equator north and south, until the poles were stretched to equal the length of the equator itself.

MERCURY, FREDDIE

Freddie Mercury died of an AIDS-related illness on 24 November 1991. The flamboyant star had been the lead singer of rock band Queen for nearly 20 years. The band's music – basic hard rock glammed over with lush production values – and their outrageous stage shows won them huge popularity. The single 'Bohemian Rhapsody' became their best-known song, an operatic pop anthem with falsetto backing, and layer upon layer of vocals, which stayed in the charts for nine weeks. Weeks before his death, Freddie Mercury re-released the single and donated all the proceeds to an AIDS charity. The band couldn't continue without him.

MERIWETHER, LEWIS

Lewis Meriwether (1774–1809) was a US explorer, commissioned in 1803 by President Thomas Jefferson to find a land route to the Pacific. He chose fellow explorer William Clark (1770–1838) to accompany him. They followed the Missouri River to its source, crossed the Rocky Mountains and followed the Columbia River to the Pacific, then returned overland to St Louis.

MICHELANGELO

Perhaps the most famous artist and sculptor of the sixteenth century, Michelangelo (Michelagniolo Buonarroti, 1475–1564) spent his life working in Rome and his native Florence. He began his famous statue of *David* in 1501. The pinnacle of his career, however, was his paintings in the Sistine Chapel in Rome. The *Creation of Adam*, on the ceiling, was begun in 1512, and the *Last Judgment* on the altar wall was completed in 1541. This work remains to this day the epitome of Italian Renaissance art.

MILL, JOHN STUART

John Stuart Mill (1806–73) was a Liberal MP and the most significant founder of Liberal philosophy. His *Principles of Political Economy* (1848) outline the principles of a free and just economy. He advocated a free market consisting of workers' co-operatives and pointed out that true human needs are not effectively valued by the economy. For this reason, he argued that in the interests of people and the environment there should be a limit to both economic growth and population growth. In his *Utilitarianism* (1861) he argued that man should act to bring the greatest good to the greatest number, but in his *On Liberty* (1859) he argued that man should never coerce anyone except in self-defence.

Thomas Jefferson, who commissioned Lewis Meriwether to find a land route to the Pacific. ▶

MILLAIS, JOHN EVERETT ✷

When Sir John Millais (1829–1896) painted a little boy blowing soap bubbles, the sentimental painting was enormously popular – but it received a new life of its own as a popular icon when the painting was bought by Pears Soap. The little boy chosen by Millais for the painting grew up to be Admiral Sir William James (1881–1973), known throughout his naval career as 'Bubbles'.

MILLER, GLEN

On 16 December 1944, *en route* to a concert date in France, the aircraft carrying the world-renowned band leader Colonel Miller (1904–44) went missing. There was no sign of the wreckage and the pilot had not signalled that there was a problem. Miller had volunteered for service in 1941, but had been persuaded that the morale value of his music would be of more use to the war effort. From 1941 to 1944 his band played in almost every war zone in the world from the Pacific to Europe. His music dominated broadcasting during the latter part of the war.

MILNE, A. A.

The playwright A. A. Milne (1882–1956) was a former assistant editor of *Punch* magazine who became known for his successful light comedies – and then he published the verses written for his young son, Christopher Robin, starting with *When We Were Very Young* (1924). But it was the stories about Christopher Robin's toys which, to his frustration, made him internationally famous. *Winnie-the-Pooh* (1926) and *The House at Pooh Corner* (1928) were enhanced by the illustrations by E. H. Shepard.

MILTON, JOHN

Arguably the seventeenth century's greatest poet, John Milton (1608–74) – later to write *Paradise Lost* (1667) – came to political prominence as the propagandist for Parliament against the Royalist cause, defending the decision to execute **Charles I**, even drafting letters for **Oliver Cromwell** to send to foreign rulers. His pamphlets about education, and the controversy over his view that a mismatch of minds was a better reason for separation than sexual incompatibility or adultery, were

John Milton drafted letters for Oliver Cromwell (right), during his reign as Lord Protector of England. ▶

overshadowed by his great defence of freedom of speech. *Areopagitica* was a protest against the reimposition of censorship by Parliamentarians.

Almost blind, his life was saved after the Restoration by an enormous fine and the intervention of fellow poet Andrew Marvell.

MIRÒ, JOAN ✷

The Spanish painter Joan Mirò (1893–1983) was a leading exponent of abstract and Surrealist art. Mirò was influenced much more by the Fauves and the primitivism of Henri Rousseau than by the rigours of Cubism. His first paintings in Paris combined extreme realism and geometrical abstraction, often inspired by the austere landscape of his Catalan homeland. In the 1920s, Mirò began to experiment with Surrealism, and from 1924 onwards he was a key figure in the circle of André Breton and other Surrealists. Throughout the late 1920s and 1930s, he experimented with ever-freer compositions based on the interplay of elements rather than on a design imposed by the artist. He was best known for the humour and idiosyncratic vision he brought to Surrealist art.

MONET, CLAUDE OSCAR ✷

Claude Monet (1840–1926) was the most famous of the Impressionist painters. Although not the first to experiment with the Impressionist style, which developed in France in the ninteteenth century, he adopted the ideas and made them his own. Although he struggled to make a living in the early years, he eventually built up a reputation in his native France that would spread to the rest of the world. His works sum up the ideals of the movement, concerning themselves with the immediate feeling of the subject, emphasised in many small brushstrokes in light colours and shades, rather than rigidly following actual form or structure.

Claude Monet in his Floating Studio, by Edouard Manet. ◀

MONROE, JAMES

James Monroe (1758–1831) was the fifth president of the USA, from 1816–24. He was a Democrat-Republican.

MONROE, MARILYN

Marilyn Monroe (stage name for Norma Jean Mortenson or Baker, 1926–62) was a US film actress and the twentieth century's ultimate tragic sex symbol. In many ways a victim of her own success, Marilyn struggled in the limelight. By the time of her best-loved film, *Some Like it Hot* (1959), stardom was beginning to affect her work, and director Billy Wilder took to writing her lines on the furniture in the hope this would get her through the scenes. Eventually Marilyn took her own life at a tragically early age. Amongst her other great films are *Gentlemen Prefer Blondes* and *The Seven Year Itch*.

Marilyn Monroe. ▶

MONTESSORI, MARIA

In the early twentieth century, the Italian physician-educator Maria Montessori (1870–1952) created the Montessori method of self-paced learning for children. The Montessori method has influenced the modern-day development of alternative-education programmes.

MONTEZUMA II

Montezuma II (1466–1520) was emperor of the Aztecs from 1502–20. When the Spanish conquistador **Hernán Cortés** invaded Mexico in 1519, Montezuma was imprisoned and killed during the Aztec attack on Cortés's forces as he tried to leave Tenochtitlán, the Aztec capital city.

MONTFORT, SIMON DE

Simon de Montfort, 1st Earl of Leicester (1208–65), led the baronial opposition to **Henry III**'s misrule during the second Barons' War, and in 1264 he defeated and captured the king at Lewes, Sussex. De Montfort then summoned a 'Parliament' to which he invited both the Barons, or 'Lords' as they came to be called, and also, for the first time, representatives of the Commons. This is regarded as the first real evidence of the existence of Parliament, although the name had been used since the 1240s.

MONTGOLFIER, JOSEPH AND JACQUES

Joseph (1740–1810) and his brother Jacques (1745–99) Montgolfier were the sons of a wealthy French paper manufacturer. After several early experiments, Joseph began to think about an 'air machine', which would be filled with a gas that was lighter than air. Their first public demonstration of a hot-air balloon was given in 1783, at the invitation of the king and queen, **Louis XVI** and **Marie-Antoinette**. As the king believed that air travel was too dangerous for people, the balloon carried as passengers a cockerel, a duck and a sheep.

The Montgolfier balloon in Versailles. ▶

MORE, THOMAS

Sir Thomas More (1478–1535), Lord Chancellor of England, was the principal figure in the English Renaissance. He was a humanist Christian and, like his contemporary **Erasmus**, regarded the happiness and well-being of humanity as the highest Christian ideal. His beliefs and his critique of the political and religious situation of his time are to be found in his *Utopia*, published in 1518. This depicts an imaginary society, inspired partly by **Plato**'s *Republic*, that lives in accord with basic Christian teachings such as the absence of private property, non-violence, the abolition of hunting, religious tolerance, humane penalties for crimes and the rejection of wealth. He was executed for treason against **Henry VIII** in 1535.

Henry VIII (above) had Sir Thomas More executed for treason. ▲

MORO, ALDO

Aldo Moro (1916–78), an Italian Christian Democrat politician, was prime minister in 1963–68 and again, with a coalition government, in 1974–76. After this government fell in January, Moro became premier again between February and July, as head of a caretaker government. In October 1976 he became president of the Christian Democrats, remaining a powerful influence on Italian politics, even though he held no public office. On 16 March 1978, Moro was kidnapped in Rome by Red Brigade terrorists while on his way to attend a special Parliament session. After government officials repeatedly refused to release 13 members of the Red Brigade on trial in Turin, Moro was murdered by the kidnappers.

A William Morris Tapestry. ◀

MORRIS, WILLIAM

William Morris (1834–96) was a famous designer of naturalistic textiles and wallpapers as well as being a visionary poet and writer. In 1883 he created the Socialist League, but he opposed the authoritarianism of state socialism, advocating instead a socialism inspired by the medieval workers' guilds. His poem 'The Earthly Paradise' (1868–70) and his novel *News from Nowhere* both depict a visionary and utopian society – a kind of medieval socialist world with minimal government, founded on co-operative work, craftsmanship and small communities.

MORSE, SAMUEL

The inventor of the Morse code, Samuel Morse (1791–1872), built the first electric telegraph in 1835. Electrical pulses were sent along the telegraph wire using his code; at the receiving end, a series of clicks were heard that had to be deciphered by the operator. This was the first modern form of telecommunication. In 1843, Morse obtained financial support from the US government to build a demonstration telegraph system, 60 km (35 miles) long between Washington and Baltimore. Wires were attached by glass insulators to poles alongside a railroad.

MOSES ☯

Moses was the Jewish leader to whom God revealed his teachings, including the Ten Commandments, which were given to Moses on Mount Sinai around 1200 BC. A key figure in many religious followings, Moses was a great leader, responsible for the exodus from slavery in Egypt, leading his people to the 'Promised Land'.

MOTHER TERESA ☯

Born Agnes Gonxha Bojaxhiu, Mother Theresa (1910–97) took the name by which she is now known after joining the Sisters of Loreto in 1928. In 1948, she came across a woman lying in front of a hospital in Calcutta and stayed with her until she died. From that point, Mother Theresa dedicated her life to helping the poor in India. In 1952, she established a hospital for the dying in Calcutta and here received anyone, suffering from any disease. Her aim was to allow these people to die with dignity, instead of lying on the streets. She won the Nobel Peace Prize in 1979, and continued her work until her death in 1997.

Moses receiving the tablets containing the Ten Commandments from God on Mount Sinai. ▲

MOTT, LUCRETIA COFFIN ☒

Lucretia Coffin Mott (1793–1880), an American reformer, campaigned vigorously for the abolition of slavery and for women's rights. With Elizabeth Cady Stanton, she organised the first women's rights convention in the USA in 1848.

Benito Mussolini, leader of the Facsist regime in Italy up to and during the Second World War. ◀

MOUNTBATTEN, LOUIS

Lord Louis Mountbatten of Burma (1900–79) was born in Windsor. The great-grandson of **Queen Victoria**, he served at sea in the First World War and, during the Second World War, was chief of combined operations in 1942 and commander-in-chief in South-East Asia in 1943. As the last viceroy of India (1947) and first governor-general of India until 1948, he oversaw the country's transition to independence. He returned to service at sea and was 4th Sea Lord (1952–55) and appointed 1st Sea Lord (1955–59). He was killed by an IRA bomb aboard his yacht while sailing near his holiday home in County Sligo in the Republic of Ireland.

MOZART, WOLFGANG AMADEUS

Pushed by his father, Mozart (1756–91) was a musical genius, playing for royalty, from an early age. Not only a brilliant pianist and violinist, Mozart had composed several symphonies and sonatas before he reached adolescence. He was very much a product of his time, his influences including Haydn. During his lifetime he travelled to Vienna and to Paris, where he earned his living as a freelance musician, giving subscription concerts featuring his own compositions. He was responsible largely for the development of the concerto, although all his works now are hailed as some of the greatest pieces of classical music in history.

MUHAMMAD

Muhammad (AD 570–632), he prophet of Allah, was born in Arabia, and married a wealthy widow, Khadijah. In AD 610 he received his first revelations from he Angel Gabriel in a cave during a olitary retreat. To Muslims, he was he Final Prophet, in the line of Abraham and Moses, and his message was to have faith in the One True God. His first converts were Khadijah and his cousin, **Ali**. He was opposed by polytheists in Mecca, who used the Kaaba for idol worship, but eventually he captured Mecca and rapidly spread his faith.

MUNCH, EDVARD

The Norwegian painter and graphic artist Edvard Munch (1863–1944) was one of the great masters of modern European art, and a key figure in the development of Expressionism. His tragic early life left its mark as Munch set out to record the anguished psyche of modern humanity. In several stunning Expressionist paintings, such as *The Scream* (1893), he created stark and terrifying images of alienation and despair. Munch's works of the 1890s heavily influenced the founders of German Expressionism. In 1908, he suffered a severe nervous breakdown, and although he recovered, his later work shows less visible emotion and torment.

MUSSOLINI, BENITO

Benito Mussolini (1883–1945) was the leader of the Fascist Party in Italy. He had fought in the First World War and was very angry at the treatment Italy had received at the Treaty of Versailles. From 1919 to 1922 he organised a propaganda campaign through his paper *Il Popolo d'Italia*. He made himself out to be a strong man who could solve Italy's problems. His supporters, known as the Blackshirts, were organised into *Fascio di Combattimento* and in some parts of Italy they became the main source of law and order. They punished criminals, broke up strikes and attacked Mussolini's opponents. In October 1922 Mussolini organised a 'March on Rome' by his Blackshirts. This was intended to put pressure on the government; in fact it led to Mussolini being appointed prime minister of Italy. He became the first dictator in western Europe, and his 'Evil Empire' matched that of his German counterpart **Hitler**. Mussolini was murdered at the end of the Second World War.

NANAK

The founder of Sikhism was Guru Nanak (1469–1539). Born in the Punjab, Nanak taught that all religions are the way to the same God, and all should be respected.

NANSEN, FRIDTJOF

Norwegian scientist Fridtjof Nansen (1861–1930) was a principal polar explorer who completed the first expedition to the Greenland ice cap (1888–89). He then designed a ship capable of withstanding the pressure exerted by ice and embarked on an expedition across the Arctic basin in 1893, by drifting with the ice instead of ramming it. After realising the ship was not drifting towards the North Pole, he set off with a companion to reach it on specially designed sledges, but was forced to turn back 230 km (370 miles) from their objective.

Fridtjof Nansen. ▲

NAPIER, FREDERICK JOHN

Napier (1868–1933) conducted a study of democracy and government in India. The results of this study, and the recommendations it made, led to the passing of the Government of India Acts in 1919. These Acts saw a slow increase in the number of Indians in government.

NAPOLEON III

Napoleon III (1808–73), a nephew of **Napoleon Bonaparte**, came to power after the 1848 Revolution. He pursued intervention in Mexico, the Crimea and Italy, before abdicating in 1870.

NASSER, ABDEL

Egyptian general, Gamal Abdel Nasser (1918–70), was the driving force behind the Neguib coup in 1952, which ended the Egyptian monarchy. Nasser became prime minister (1954) and then president of Egypt from 1956 (president of the United Arab Republic from 1958). His nationalisation of the Suez Canal in 1956 led to an Anglo-French invasion and the Suez crisis. Nasser had ambitions for an Egyptian-led union of Arab states and this resulted in disquiet in the Middle East. Although a strong advocate of Arab unity towards the end of his presidency, he became increasingly dependent on arms and aid from the USSR.

Abdel Nasser's nationalisation of the Suez Canal bought about an Anglo-French invasion and ignited the Suez Crises of 1956. ▼

NAVRATILOVA, MARTINA

One of the most enduring and popular figures in women's tennis, Martina Navratilova outplayed many young hopefuls as well as many of the sport's stalwarts during her lengthy and successful career. At the age of 33, but with the spring of an enthusiastic teenager in her step, Navratilova overwhelmed Zina Garrison 6–4, 6–1 to realise her dream of a record ninth Wimbledon singles title.

NEBUCHADNEZZAR

King Nebuchadnezzar (*c.* 630–561 BC) revived the waning fortunes of the Babylonian Empire, restoring the city of Babylon and nearly every temple in the land. He built the Hanging Gardens of Babylon, a series of terraces irrigated by a hydraulic system, and now one of the Seven Wonders of the Ancient World.

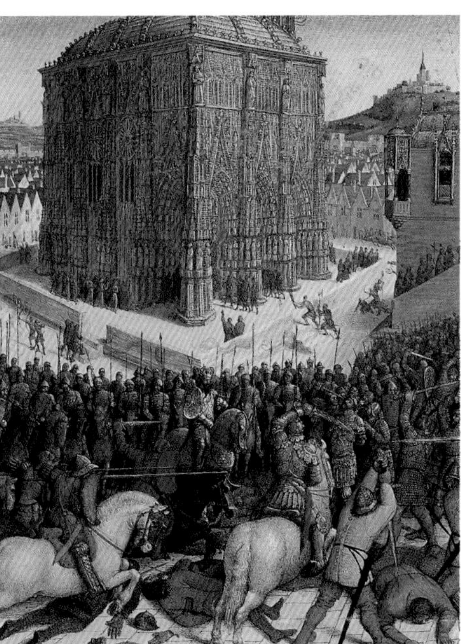

NECHO

One of the earliest expeditions ever ordered by a government, expressly to achieve greater geographical knowledge, was made during the reign of the Pharoah Necho (*c.* 610 –594 BC). Necho instructed a group of Phoenician sailors to voyage around Libya. The Phoenicians sailed south along the East African coast. During the third year, they sailed through the Strait of Gibraltar and back into the Mediterranean.

Nebuchadnezzar of Babylonia attacks Jerusalem. ◀

NEHRU, JAWAHARLAL

Jawaharlal Nehru (1889–1964), an Indian nationalist politician, became prime minister of India in 1947. Prior to the split of British India into India and Pakistan, he had led the socialist wing of the Nationalist Congress Party and he was second only to **Mohandas Gandhi** in his influence. Between 1921 and 1945, he was imprisoned nine times by the British for political activities. As prime minister from the creation of the dominion of India, he conceived the idea of neutrality and peacemaking towards the major powers. He committed India to a policy of industrialisation. He died in 1964 and his daughter Indira Gandhi later became prime minister.

Nelson on deck at the Battle of Trafalgar. ▲

NELSON, HORATIO

The British Royal Navy under Nelson (1758–1805) won a victory over the French at Trafalgar during the Napoleonic Wars. This victory ensured British naval supremacy for the rest of the nineteenth century. Nelson himself was killed at the Battle of Trafalgar in his flagship HMS *Victory*.

NERO

The bloody reign of Nero (AD 37–68) was marked by the murder of his wife and his mother. He persecuted the Christians, blaming them for the fire of Rome in AD 64.

NESTORIUS ☯

The Christians of Jerusalem, following the destruction of the Jewish Temple in AD 70, fled mainly to Syria. Here Nestorius (AD 381–451) created the Syriac, or 'Nestorian' church, which taught (like Arius) that Jesus was not himself God, but was a human made divine by God.

NEWCOMEN, THOMAS

Thomas Newcomen (1663–1729) was an English inventor who, in 1712, invented the 'atmospheric engine', which was designed to pump water from mines, and so reduce the danger of flooding which would otherwise overtake workers underground. The invention drastically improved conditions for miners in England.

NEWMAN, HENRY JOHN ☯

Henry John Newman (1801–90) had fascinated many people with his ideas while an Anglican, and still retained that interest when he became a Roman Catholic. Originally an evangelical, he became vicar of the university church in Oxford where he ceased to be a Calvinist. Newman, a liberal, had submitted to an authoritarian church but it was not until Leo XIII became Pope that the official attitude to him eased. In 1879 he was made a cardinal; for him it was a symbol that he was recognised and accepted by the Church he had joined.

NEWTON, ISAAC

Isaac Newton (1642–1727) was an English physicist who can truly be considered the father of modern science. Amongst the many discoveries that are attributed to him are the laws of gravity and that white light is made up of many colours. He created calculus, developed the three laws of motion that are still used today and invented the reflecting telescope. His careful experiments, and determination to prove his theories beyond doubt put paid to many scientific beliefs that had endured for centuries.

Isaac Newton. ◀

NICHOLAS II

Tsar Nicholas II (1868–1918) was unsuited to being the autocratic ruler of 140 million people. He was easily influenced by others and lacked the determination to carry out serious changes in Russia. He believed that it was his duty to pass on the power that he had inherited to his son, so he tended always to side with his most conservative, even reactionary ministers. Nicholas allowed Russia to be rushed headlong into war in 1914, and when the Russian army was badly beaten by the Germans in the early battles, appointed himself commander-in-chief in August 1915. As a result, and for the first time, Russians came to blame the tsar personally for the country's failures. He was forced to abdicate after the Russian Revolution and was executed with his family in 1918.

Nicholas II. ▲

NIEPCE, JOSEPH-NICEPHORE

French doctor Joseph-Nicephore Niepce (1765–1833) produced the first photograph, from nature on pewter plates, with a camera obscura and an eight-hour exposure in 1826. It was his assistant, **Louis Daguerre**, however, who would develop the idea.

NIETZSCHE, FRIEDRICH

When Friedrich Nietzsche (1844–1900) took as his starting point 'God is Dead', the German philosopher was saying, in effect, that religious conviction was not an option for the intelligent human being. Certainly the elite still challenged traditional belief at this time, while following basic Judaic-Christian moral values. All the Churches, except possibly the Salvation Army, appeared to have inadequate ecclesiastical machines that could not cope with the world of the late nineteenth century onwards. They themselves became secularised, no longer were there absolute values and the individuality of the past. The horror of war, brought close to ordinary people, caused deep reflection on the meaning of God, and if there were a God, what justification was there for such violent behaviour?

NIGHTINGALE, FLORENCE ☒

Florence Nightingale (1820–1910) was an English nurse and the founder of nursing as a profession in Britain. She trained in Kaiserswerth and Paris and, in 1853, became the superintendent of a hospital for invalid women in London. She volunteered for duty in the Crimean War and took 38 nurses to Scutari in 1854. She organised the barracks hospital after the Battle of Inkerman, and her rules of discipline and sanitation reduced the Crimean War hospital death rate from 42 per cent to two per cent. She later founded the Nightingale School and Home for Nurses in London (1856). She also devoted many years to the improvement of nursing and public health in India. In 1907 she was given the Order of Merit, the first woman to receive this honour.

The First World War caused many people to question the existence of God. For Niezsche, faith was not an intelligent response to such atrocities. ▲

NIJINSKI, VASLAV FOMICH ☻

Vaslav Fomich Nijinski (1888–1950) entered the Imperial Ballet School in St Petersburg in 1898. In 1908, he met Serge Diaghilev, who was to become his mentor. Nijinski performed in Europe with the Ballets Russes, achieving success in such productions as *The Pavilion of Armide* (1909), *Sylphides* (1909) and *Scheherazade* (1910). Nijinski created two ballets in 1913, *Games* and *The Rite of Spring*; both were highly innovative, and the latter created a riot due to its heavy, asymmetrical, primeval choreography. Many of his contemporaries considered Nijinski's experiments with style to be an artistic dead end. Today, however, his ideas have won great respect.

NIXON, RICHARD

Trained as a lawyer, Republican Richard Milhous Nixon (1913–94) first entered Congress in 1947 and, in 1948, as a member of the Un-American Activities Committee, pressed for the investigation of Alger Hiss, accused of being a spy. Nixon was senator for California from 1951 until he was elected vice-president under **Eisenhower**. He lost the presidential election in 1960 to **John F. Kennedy**, partly because televised electoral debates put him at a disadvantage. He did not seek presidential election in 1964, but tried again in 1968. His campaign based on 'law and order', defeated vice-president Humphrey in one of the most closely contested elections in US history. He was inaugurated as the 37th president in 1969.

NOBUNGA

Nobunga became shogun of Japan in 1573. He established the Japanese firearms industry and began producing European-style ships. After he was assassinated in 1582, his lieutenant, Hideyoshi, crushed the dissidents and reunited Japan.

Florence Nightingale. ▼

NOSTRADAMUS

Nostradamus is the Latinised name of Michel de Notredame (1503–66), the French physician and astrologer who was consulted by **Catherine de Medici**, and Charles IX of France. His book of prophecies in verse, *Centuries 1555*, makes cryptic predictions about world events up to the year 3797. Differing interpretations of these predictions has led some to believe Nostradamus to have been a true prophet, while others see his predictions as ambiguous and, in retrospect, without truth.

Offa's Dyke. ▼

NUREYEV, RUDOLF ☻

Rudolf Nureyev (1938–93) was a Russian ballet dancer with extraordinary technique and a compelling stage presence, who magnetised audiences with his passion. He trained in Leningrad and was then accepted as a soloist at the Kirov Ballet Company. He was billed as their principal dancer on its European tour in 1961, but he was apolitical, non-conformist and professionally ambitious. In Paris, he gave a superb performance of *Sleeping Beauty*, and then at the airport refused to depart with the rest of the Kirov Company, seeking asylum in France. He danced with several companies until, in 1962, he became 'permanent guest artist' at the Royal Ballet with **Margot Fonteyn** as his partner.

OFFA

One of the most ambitious of the Anglo-Saxon kings was Offa (d. AD 796), who seized power in Mercia in about AD 757, and afterwards made his realm supreme south of the Humber. In about 789, Offa built a huge 160-mile long earthwork, later known as Offa's Dyke to protect his territory from attack. The Dyke was six feet deep, with a 25 foot earth rampart,

Despite Offa's inland fortifications, he could not protect the country from Viking invasions from abroad. ◀

strengthened by timber palisades and a stone wall. However, only four years later, new invaders appeared in the east who were far more dangerous and terrifying than any home-grown enemies: the Vikings from Scandinavia.

OLIVIER, LAURENCE ☻

Baron Olivier (1907–89) was an English actor and director. He was for many years associated with the Old Vic theatre and was director of the National Theatre company from 1962–73. His acting and direction of filmed versions of **Shakespeare**'s plays, in particular *Henry V* and *Hamlet*, received critical acclaim, and made the genius of Shakespeare accessible to the masses for the first time. Olivier was, during his lifetime, touted as the epitome of great English acting.

OPPENHEIMER, JULIUS ROBERT

Julius Robert Oppenheimer (1904–67), a professor of science at the University of California, was chosen to lead the team that developed the first fission atomic bomb, tested in New Mexico in 1945.

ORTON, JOE

The actor Joe Orton (1933–67) was briefly the *enfant terrible* of British theatre, specialising in exuberant black farces, starting with *Entertaining Mr Sloane* (1964). He was influenced by the playwright Harold Pinter and the French writer Jean Genet, but he increasingly developed his own style, which took the plays into the then-forbidden areas of sex, incest and violence; this culminated in *Loot* in 1966. His plays thrived in the permissive period after the end of theatrical censorship. His last play, *What the Butler Saw*, was produced in 1969, two years after Orton had been murdered by his lover, who then committed suicide.

ORWELL, GEORGE

George Orwell (1903–50) was once a policeman in Imperial Burma called Eric Blair, but he became well known as a powerful social prophet – lambasting unemployment in his book *The Road to Wigan Pier* (1937). He became increasingly disillusioned with Soviet-style totalitarianism, which he ridiculed in his novel *Animal Farm*. *Nineteen Eighty-Four* is an ironic commentary on the world in 1948, when he was writing it, where Britain has been transformed into Airstrip One in a superstate called Oceania, ruled by the image of Big Brother. It became one of the most important texts of the Cold War.

OTTO, NIKOLAUS

The German engineer Nikolaus Otto (1832–91) is generally credited with building the first practical internal-combustion engine in 1876.

OWENS, JAMES 'JESSE' CLEVELAND

Jesse Owens (b. 1913) is one of the most famous sportsmen of the twentieth century; a symbol of both supreme athleticism and the struggle against racism and bigotry everywhere. His finest hour was at the 1936 Berlin Olympics, where he won four gold medals, triumphing in the 100 m and 200 m, the 4x100-m relay, and the long jump. Nazi leader **Adolf Hitler**, however, refused to shake Owens' hand or present him with his medals. Hitler's handshake would have been superfluous in any case. His disdain of Owens' achievements makes them stand as one of the greatest sporting stories of the century.

PAINE, THOMAS

Thomas Paine (1737–1809) wrote a pamphlet in support of the American Colonialists in 1776, 'Common Sense'; and at the outbreak of the French Revolution he produced his most influential work in its defence – *The Rights of Man* (1791–92) – written in reply to the conservatism of **Edmund Burke**. So supportive was it of the Revolution that he was forced to flee to France. In the second part of his book he argued that governments should recognise the natural rights of all citizens to receive education, old-age pensions and other benefits of social welfare. He died in New York having alarmed governments and offended the Church by promoting an argument for Deism in *The Age of Reason* (1794–97).

PALAMAS, GREGORY

Gregory Palamas (1296–1359) was a major medieval contributor to the development of Greek Orthodox spirituality. As a monk, he lived in the independent monastic state of Mount Athos and, after a Turkish invasion, fled to Thessalonica, where he was eventually made archbishop. He developed the Hesychasm, a form of contemplative monasticism based upon constant recitation of the Jesus Prayer.

Thomas Paine. ◀

Emmeline and Christobel Pankhurst. ◀

PALME, OLOF

Olof Palme was an active member of the Swedish Social Democrats from the 1950s, and joined the government in 1963 as minister without portfolio. He succeeded Tage Erlander as party secretary and prime minister in 1969. Soon afterwards, his attacks on US war policy in Vietnam and his acceptance of US army deserters who sought refuge in Sweden, strained relations with the US, and he lost the 1976 election. In 1989 he acted as UN special envoy to mediate in the Iran-Iraq War. Elected again in 1982, he tried to reinstate socialist economic policies in Sweden. He was assassinated by a lone gunman in 1986 and his murder remains unsolved.

PANKHURST, EMMELINE

Emmeline Pankhurst (1858–1928) was an English suffragette who sought the vote for women as early as 1880. When she founded the Women's Social and Political Union in 1903, her suffragism became more militant. Suffragettes chained themselves to railings, smashed windows and set fire to pillar boxes. Violence was matched by violence, notably the forcible feeding of suffragettes, which so damaged Mrs Pankhurst that it contributed to her death. Her efforts, however, made such a prominent issue of votes for women that, after they had done men's jobs during the First World War, some were enfranchised in 1918. All adult women in Britain were allowed to vote after 1928.

PARACELSUS

Swiss physician Paracelsus (1493–1541) was the first scientist to make a nonsense of Galen's ideas about humours controlling the body and mind. He refuted the theory on the basis that the results of observation and experimentation should override the preconceptions of traditional lore, and that the results of his own studies had suggested scientifically based processes at work. He consequently established the practice of seeking external agents as explanations for disease and infection, making important progress in this area, even introducing laudanum as a painkiller.

PARE, AMBROISE

Ambroise Pare (*c.* 1509–90) was a French army surgeon, who dressed wounds with soothing balms rather than cauterising, and prevented profuse bleeding in amputations by tying off the blood vessels.

Paracelsus. ◀

PASCAL, BLAISE ✉

Blaise Pascal (1623–62) was a French philosopher and mathematician who invented the adding machine in 1642. He also introduced the first omnibus (Latin, meaning 'for everyone') in Paris in 1660. It was horse-drawn and not successful. The first successful service was also in Paris in 1827.

PASTERNAK, BORIS 📖

Pasternak's (1890–1960) *Doctor Zhivago* is a novel on an epic scale. It sweeps across three decades of Russian history, including the revolutions of 1905 and 1917 and their violent aftermath. It was hailed by Western writers as a work of genius and awarded the Nobel Prize for Literature. Pasternak was overjoyed. Unfortunately, in Pasternak's homeland, *Doctor Zhivago* was not the unmitigated success it had been in the West.

Early horse drawn bus, a descendant of Blaise Pascal's omnibus. ▼

The author was labelled a traitor by the Soviet Writers' Union on account of his hero's thoughts of disillusionment. Within a week of winning the prize, he had been expelled from the Union; as a result, he felt he could not accept the honour.

PASTEUR, LOUIS

Louis Pasteur's (1822–95) research on fermentation led him to develop pasteurisation, a controlled heating process that protected liquids from spoiling. He was also the first to develop and use vaccines against cholera, anthrax and rabies.

PATTON, GEORGE

George Patton (1885–1945), US general in the Second World War, was known as 'Blood and Guts'. After commanding the 7th Army, he led the 3rd Army across France and into Germany.

PEARY, ROBERT

Robert Peary (1856–1920) adopted a spartan approach to polar exploration. Travelling with scant provisions, Inuit guides, dogs and sledges, he managed to cross the treacherous ice fields to the North Pole. His preparation was scientific and meticulous. His travelling companion, Matthew Henson, a Black American, spoke fluent Inuit and was invaluable as a conduit for local knowledge. By 2 April, Peary and Henson, four Inuit and 38 dogs were 246 km (133 nautical miles) away from the Pole and ready to begin the final stage of the journey. By 6 April, he was 5.5 km (3 nautical miles) away, and on 17 April he and Henson finally achieved their goal.

PELAGIUS

Pelagius's (*c.* AD 360–420) name is associated with the heresy of Pelagianism, and it has remained a strong attraction for the British. Pelagius objected to the emphasis put on the complete sinfulness of human beings so their only chance of salvation was through the grace and forgiveness of God. Pelagius had a strong faith in the inherent possibility of each person to reach perfection without the intervention of God's grace. He left Britain as a young man and never returned, but his message was brought to his homeland by **Georg Bauer** ('Agricola'), a follower, early in the fifth century. Pelagius was condemned and excommunicated by the Pope.

PELÉ

Edson Arantes do Nascimento, known as 'Pelé' (b. 1940) was fond of describing football as the beautiful game. He was not referring to football in general, but to the uninhibited, artistic attacking play that has long characterised his national team, Brazil. He began his international footballing career at just 16 years of age, and went on to play in no less that four World Cups. His skill and passion for the game not only made him a hero in his home country, but endeared him to fans of the sport the world over. He remains the greatest footballer in the history of the sport.

PENN, WILLIAM

William Penn (1644–1718) was a London-born Quaker who, in 1670, together with William Mead was charged with riot for preaching his faith in public. The jury system was often abused by judges bullying juries. The judge in Penn's case was intent on a 'guilty' verdict, but the jury disagreed. What was more, they refused to give in, despite threats of imprisonment and fines. Ultimately, the Lord Chief Justice, Sir John Vaughan, ruled that judges could not 'lead (juries)... by the nose'. The 'not guilty' verdict stood, and the case, known as 'Bushell's Case' from the name of the foreman, Edward Bushell, established the right of British juries to independent verdicts.

Quakers were persecuted by members of other faiths. ▲

PEPYS, SAMUEL

The naval administrator Samuel Pepys (1633–1703) is better known as the author of the diary that has provided the model for diarists ever since. The surviving volumes record his everyday life in code, plus the ups and downs of his marriage, with endearing honesty, from 1660–69. They were left to his old college, Magdalene, in Cambridge, but the code was not broken and the diaries published until 1825. They reveal Pepys as an opinionated man of his time, dismissing a production of *Midsummer Night's Dream* as 'the most insipid, ridiculous play that I ever saw in my life'.

William Shakespeare, whose play A Midsummer Night's Dream *was dismissed by Samuel Pepys as being ridiculous.* ▼

PERÓN, EVITA

In 1945 Lieutenant-General Juan Domingo Perón of Argentina married radio actress Evita (Eva Duarte 1919–52). Strengthened by Evita's popularity, Perón created the Peronista party, based on extreme nationalism and social improvement, and became dictator in 1946. After that, Evita virtually ran the health and labour ministries and in 1951 she stood for the post of vice-president, but was opposed by the army and withdrew. During Perón's rule, Evita campaigned for women's suffrage and acquired control of newspapers and business companies. She also founded the Eva Perón Foundation for the promotion of social welfare. She died of cancer in 1952.

PETER THE GREAT

Peter the Great (1682–1725) embarked upon the modernisation of Russia by employing craftsmen and engineers from western Europe, and built St Petersburg, his 'window to the west'.

Peter the Great of Russia studying shipbuilding. ▼

PHILIP II OF MACEDON

Philip II (382–336 BC) became king of Macedonia in 359 BC. He was ambitious, clear-sighted and a great organizer. After installing friendly governments in most cities and garrisons in some, Philip forced the Greeks to join in a Hellenic league. In 336 BC he

successfully launched an invasion of Asia, but dynastic troubles supervened. He divorced Olympias, exiled his son **Alexander the Great**, and remarried. However, Philip was assassinated at his daughter's wedding, and Alexander was at once presented to the army as king.

PHILIP II

Philip II (1527–98) became king of Spain in 1556. He was a hard-working, bureaucratic administrator, who continued his father's policy of centralisation. Under Philip II, Spain became the most powerful country in Europe.

PICASSO, PABLO RUIZ Y

Pablo Ruiz y Picasso (1881–1973) was perhaps the most influential and successful artist of the twentieth century. His Blue Period (1901–04) was stimulated by his exposure to life in Paris, while in his Rose Period (1905–06), Picasso painted harlequins and circus performers in a lighter, warmer colour scheme. After 1908 he joined with Georges Braque and other like-minded artists to explore the representation of three-dimensional objects on a two-dimensional surface by means of overlapping planes. By 1912, Picasso, Braque and Juan Gris were introducing textured materials such as chair caning and wallpaper, in the form of actual materials or painted imitations, into their works. This reconstitution of reality, called Synthetic Cubism, proved to be of fundamental importance to the development of modern art.

PIERCE, FRANKLIN

Democrat Franklin Pierce (1804–69) was the 14th president of the USA from 1852–56.

PITT, WILLIAM

In 1783 William Pitt (1759–1806) became the youngest prime minister of Britain at the age of just 24. He had entered politics as an MP two years previously. Despite his young age his reputation as a shrewd leader became assured over the period he was in power. Son of William Pitt the Elder, his successes included introducing financial reforms and his time in office was, at first, characterised by a commitment to parliamentary reform. Pitt was also the leader who introduced income tax into the British political and economic system. In 1800, he steered the bill promoting the union of Great Britain and Ireland through Parliament. He died aged just 46.

PIUS VI

Pius VI (1775–99) oversaw the completion of St Peter's Church in Rome. He died a prisoner of the French after his vigorous opposition to the French Revolution.

William Pitt the Younger. ▶

PIZARRO, FRANCISCO

Francisco Pizarro (*c.* 1475–1541) was a Spanish conquistador who became governor of present-day Peru in 1531. Pizarro rejected the friendship offered by the courtiers of the Inca king, **Atahualpa**, and massacred them. The Incas, deprived of leadership and terrified by Pizarro's cannon and horses, capitulated to a numerically inferior force in 1534.

PLATO

Plato's (427–347 BC) teacher, **Socrates**, was put to death for his teachings in 399 BC. This event is recorded in Plato's *Dialogues*, which are a form of memorial to Socrates and which contain many discussions ascribed to him. In these, Plato argued that knowledge can only exist if there are eternal things to which knowledge can refer, and as material things change, they must therefore be only expressions of unchanging Forms. He believed in Forms such as the Good, the True and the Beautiful, which all things expressed to greater or lesser degree. In his *Republic* Plato depicts a state based on his ideals and ruled by philosophers.

Plato. ▲

PLOTINUS

Plotinus was probably born in Egypt and in later life lived in Rome. He was the founder of the Neoplatonist movement, which radically restuctured **Plato**'s teachings. He suggested physical Forms derived from archetypal ideas, themselves derived from the Good, the True and the Beautiful. He believed in the One – the ultimate and unchanging source of reality, of which the world is a reflection and the basis for spiritual practice of seeking union with the One by rising above the worlds of Form and ideas through meditation.

POL POT

Pol Pot (d. 1998) was the leader of a bloody regime in Cambodia between 1975 and 1978. His movement, the Khmer Rouge, was responsible for the deaths of hundreds of thousands of people over this period. Pol Pot's ideas were grounded, he claimed, in Marxism, but the radical Communism that came to characterise the Khmer Rouge was based more in extreme Stalinism. The regime appealed to the impoverished members of the social hierarchy, who were to form the basis of the Khmer guerrilla army.

POLK, JAMES K.

Democrat James K. Polk was the 11th president of the USA, in office 1844–48.

Marco Polo setting off on his voyage around the world. ◀

POLO, MARCO

Marco Polo (1254–1324) was a Venetian traveller and writer. His father, Nicolo, and his uncle, Maffeo, had already travelled to China in search of silks and spices – luxury items in Europe at the time. In 1271 they set out once more overland, taking Marco with them, for the empire of the Great Khan. The journey lasted three-and-a-half years, and **Kublai Khan** allowed Marco to remain at his court until 1292, when all three Polos began the three-year journey back to Venice by sea. Marco Polo was captured while fighting for Venice against Genoa, and, while in prison in 1296–98, he wrote an account of his travels. These remained the primary source of information about the Far East until the nineteenth century.

POPPER, KARL

The Viennese philosopher Karl Popper (b. 1902) argued that it is never possible to have certain knowledge. In his *Logic of Scientific Discovery* (1934) he shows that no scientific hypothesis can be proved – it can only be falsified. Indeed, if it could never be falsified it would not be a scientific theory. Therefore, every good scientific theory is simply a model that has yet to be disproven. His opposition to the concept of certainty led him, in his *The Open Society and its Enemies* (1945), to criticise authoritarian models of human society, such as those proposed by **Plato** and **Marx**.

PORSCHE, FERDINAND

Designed by Ferdinand Porsche (b. 1935) in the 1930s as the German people's car – a small motor car that would be inexpensive enough for the average family – the Volkswagen was not put into large-scale production until after the Second World War. Porsche was a leading exponent of streamlining theory and

Karl Marx, whose authoritarian models were criticised by Karl Popper. ▼

practice, and the Beetle's distinctive body became the most widespread example of 1930s streamlined design. Porsche went on to design sports cars with his son, Ferdinand Porsche II.

PRESLEY, ELVIS

Elvis Presley's (1935–77) earliest musical influences were gospel and country. He was heard by the owner of Sun studios while recording a song for his mother's birthday, and immediately signed to the label. His early songs reflected the country influence of his childhood, but his music gradually moved into the style that would become known as rock and roll. Presley was an almost overnight success, his tours attracted thousands of screaming fans, and his semi-erotic dance style caused shock waves in the institution. His move into films proved equally popular amongst the younger generation. His later years were characterised by drug dependency and associated weight gain, and it seemed he could not maintain the exhausting lifestyle he had forged for himself. Presley died of a heart attack in 1977. He was an icon of his generation, however, and for ever changed the face of popular music.

PTOLEMY

Ptolemy (*c.* AD 100–170), a scientist from Alexandria, first devised the astrolabe. This was a device by which the position of the stars could be used to determine a position at sea or on land, by knowing the date, and vice versa. Although it had obvious limitations, it became the most important instrument for navigation for several hundred years.

PUCCINI, GIACOMO

Italian composer Giacomo Puccini (1858–1924) was gifted with a vivid sense of the stage and a talent for beautiful harmonies and fine orchestration. It made him popular in the theatre, where his music seemed as brightly coloured and flowing as the drama taking place before the audience's eyes. In the summer of 1900, Puccini saw David Belasco's one-act play, *Madam Butterfly*. He was immediately drawn to the character of the little geisha and her tale of love and abandonment. He built an opera around it; *Madam Butterfly* premiered at La Scala in February 1904, and revised in May with astounding success.

An astrolabe, a device which aids navigation at sea, invented by Ptolemy. ▶

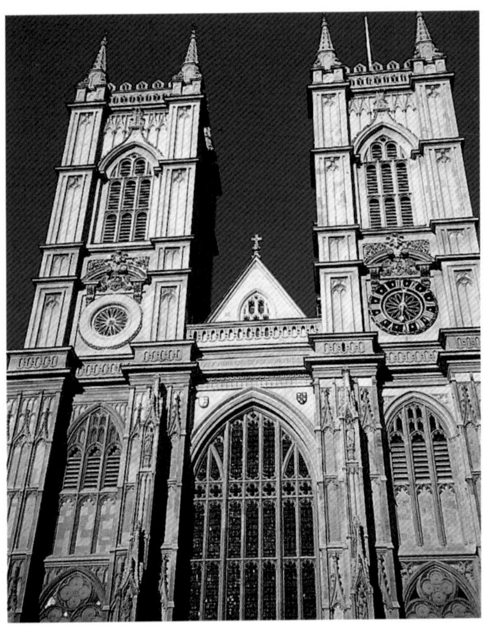

Westminster Abbey, where Henry Purcell was organist and was later buried. ◀

PURCELL, HENRY

Opera did not develop in Britain until 1689, when Henry Purcell (1659–95) was asked to write an entertainment for a young gentlewoman's boarding school in Chelsea. The result was *Dido and Aeneas*, which marked the beginnings of this new art form in Britain. Purcell was also involved in a series of masques, writing melodies around popular historical themes. Purcell had been organist of Westminster Abbey, where he was later buried, and composed music for the coronations of James VII and **William III**, and enormous amounts of chamber music, dance tunes and harpsichord suites.

PYTHAGORAS

Pythagoras (*c.* 580–500 BC), philosopher and mathematician, was the first to elevate mathematics to the realm of a science, and contributed to the development of geometry.

PYTHEAS

One of the most remarkable Greek voyages was made sometime between 320 and 240 BC, by a man named Pytheas, sailing from Marseilles. He wrote a long account of what he had done, which has not survived, but which was used by all the important geographers of the Ancient Greek world.

Pythagorus. ◀

American line, cosmetics, toys, hats, scarves, mugs and even bed linen. In the interim, Quant designed for Alligator rainwear, Kangol and Dupont and continued to exploit and develop London street looks: woolly tights (1958), sleeveless shifts (1959), coloured nail varnish (1966) and vinyl hot pants (1970). In 1966, she was awarded the OBE.

QUANT, MARY ✷

Mary Quant, who began making clothes in her bedsit, went on to open one of Britain's first concept boutiques, Bazaar, in 1955. Here, customers could buy 'a bouillabaisse of clothes and accessories' under one roof. Other shops followed, as well as a mail-order service, an

RAMAKRISHNA ☯

Ramakrishna (1836–86) was a Hindu mystic from Bengal. As a priest he practised *bhakti* (devotional prayer) to the god Kali. He then experimented with prayer, meditation and worship in several of the major religions, including Islam and Christianity, having ecstatic visions as a result of each of these. He is chiefly remembered for teaching that there is one God common to all religions. His life is commemorated in the work of the Ramakrishna Mission, created by his disciple, **Swami Vivekananda**.

RAMESES II

Rameses II was the greatest of the Egyptian pharaohs, reigning for 67 years and fathering, it is reputed, over 100 children. Monuments to this pharaoh can still be seen in Egypt. Rameses was a good soldier and strategist, and was determined to eliminate the new threat from a civilisation called the Hittites, based in Syria. Dividing his army of 20,000 into four divisions, Rameses advanced towards the city of Kadesh with one division. The Hittite general, Mutallu, slipped his force behind Rameses and attacked the supporting division. As the Egyptians fled towards Rameses, the Hittites pursued them and shattered the Egyptian army. With the Hittites more interested in looting the Egyptian camp, Rameses threw his crack Canaanite mercenaries at the Hittites and wiped out the centre of their army. As a fresh Egyptian division threatened, the Hittites fell back into Kadesh. The battle was indecisive and the two civilisations signed a peace pact.

Ronald Reagan. ▼

RASPUTIN, GRIGORI EFIMOVICH

Rasputin (*c.* 1872–1916) has become one of the most notorious figures in Russian history. By the beginning of the First World War, the monk Rasputin's influence in the Russian government was extreme. An adviser of the queen, he was also reputed to be her lover, and his control over court decisions was resented by the Russian people, who saw him as evil and corrupt. This caused a grave loss of faith in the imperial system – the seeds of revolution were sown amongst the working classes.

RAY, MAN

The Philadelphia-born Man Ray (1890–1976) was a pioneering painter and photographer in the Dada, Surrealist and abstract movements of the 1920s and 1930s. After co-founding the Dada movement in New York, he moved to Paris, where he became portrait photographer to the intellectual and artistic *avant-garde*. At the same time, he experimented with cameraless photographic techniques. Man Ray's 'rayographs' were made by placing objects on sensitised paper, which was then exposed to light.

REAGAN, RONALD

Ronald Reagan was born in Illinois in 1911 and became a Hollywood actor in 1937. He appeared in over 50 films, including *Bedtime for Bonzo* in 1951 and *The Killers* in 1964. As president of the Screen Actors Guild 1947–52 he became a conservative. He was critical of bureaucracy that stifled free enterprise, and he named names before the House of Un-American Activities Committee. He joined the Republican party in 1962 and his term as governor of California (1966–74) was marked by battles with students. He lost the Republican presidential nominations in 1968 and 1976 to **Richard Nixon** and **Gerald Ford** respectively. He won it in 1980 and became 40th US president, beating **Jimmy Carter**.

Cecil Rhodes, statesman and entrepreneur. ▶

RHODES, CECIL

Cecil Rhodes (1853–1902) founded the De Beers Mining Corporation in 1880, to dig for diamonds in South Africa. In 1889 he set up the British South Africa Company, which was allowed to explore the area north of the Transvaal. In 1890 he became prime minister of Cape Colony. One of Rhodes's aims was to set up a customs' union between cape Colony, Natal, the Orange Free

State and the South African Republic, but Kruger, the president, refused on behalf of the government in Johannesburg. In December 1895, Rhodes decided to try to force Kruger's hand. Increasing friction between the Boers and British escalated into war after Rhodes attempted to seize the diamond and gold areas of the Boer republics.

RICHARD I (THE LIONHEART)

Henry II died in 1189 and he was succeeded by his son Richard (1157–99). Richard had taken a vow to go on a crusade only a few months before his father's death, and he left England almost immediately. He was away for almost five years. The crusade lasted for two years, but on his way home Richard was taken prisoner by Leopold, duke of Austria, and was held to ransom for 150,000 gold marks, a sum equal to two years' taxes. It was the effort to collect this vast sum that partly gave rise to the legend of Robin Hood and his efforts to help the poor. When Richard finally returned, he left again to fight a series of campaigns in France. He was shot by an archer in 1199.

Cliff Richard. ▲

RICHARD III

Richard III (1452–85) has always been suspected of having murdered his nephews, the Princes in the Tower, but much of the evil myth that surrounds him is perpetuated by **Shakespeare**'s portrayal of the king as a bitter, lonely hunchback – a depiction appropriate to the political climate of Elizabethan England. Richard met his death at the Battle of Bosworth.

RICHARD, CLIFF

Rock took longer to arrive in the UK than the US, where the number one album throughout 1959 was the soundtrack of the film *South Pacific*, but by then Britain had its answer – an 18-year-old called Cliff Richard (b. 1940). He had been born in India as Harry Webb, and produced his first chart success – 'Move It' – in 1958, on his way to being Britain's most successful recording artist. He and his group, the Drifters, met in a London coffee bar called 21s. Their first number one single and gold disc came the following year with 'Livin' Doll', and by 1960 they had

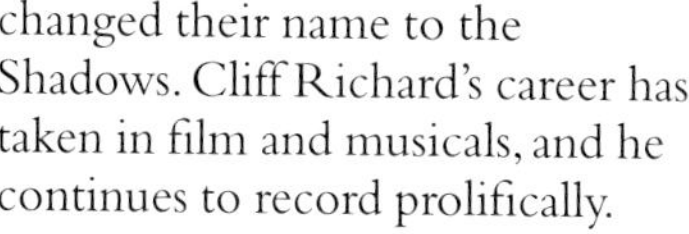

changed their name to the Shadows. Cliff Richard's career has taken in film and musicals, and he continues to record prolifically.

RICHTHOFEN, MANFRED VON

Just months before the end of the First World War, one of the conflict's greatest celebrities, Manfred von Richthofen (1892–1918), became another casualty of the second Battle of the Somme. Even at this late stage of the war, it was a high tide for the Germans. Only the month before, Ludendorff had launched three million men against the Western Allies. The Red Baron and members of his Flying Circus had been giving the ground troops air cover when he was shot down. His red Fokker triplane burst into flames as it hit the rear trenches of the British. In just two years, he had claimed 80 allied kills. He was buried with full military honours at the site of the crash.

The Battle of the Somme, in which Manfred von Richthofen was killed. ▼

ROBERT THE BRUCE

The single most important and famous battle in Scotland's long fight with the English is Bannockburn. Fought in June 1314, Robert the Bruce's (r. 1306–29) forces comprehensively fought off the English armies of Edward II. The consequence of the defeat was far-reaching. Robert was able to move Scottish forces deep into English territory. The Scots, though, were ultimately repelled after their long march south, despite their morale-boosting victories. It was the first major victory for the Scottish during the time of the 'Auld Alliance' with the French, who shared a common hatred of the English. This lasted until the sixteenth century when the Scottish adopted Protestantism. Robert also tried to divert English forces by raising the issue of political rule in Ireland.

Robert the Bruce at Bannockburn. ▼

ROBESPIERRE, MAXIMILIEN

Maximilien Robespierre (1758 –94) was a politician in the French Revolution, who conceived the Reign of Terror between 1793–94. He harboured a typically vicious hatred towards those he considered the enemies of the Revolution, that is, everyone but the common people. Ghastly scenes took place in Paris when Robespierre's victims were brought to the guillotine and beheaded as the crowds roared their approval.

RODIN, AUGUSTE

One of the most prolific sculptors of the late nineteenth and early twentieth centuries, Rodin (1840–1917) was heralded as bringing new life to a dying art. He completed his first masterwork, *The Vanquished* (later called *The Age of Bronze*), in 1876 after a trip to Italy. This sculpture led to the first of many public controversies that were to beset Rodin throughout his career. He received many commissions for public monuments, including the *Burghers of Calais* (1884–95) and the *Monument to Victor Hugo*. Rodin also produced numerous small, intimate sculptures, including *Eternal Spring* (1884).

Maximilien Robespierre. ▲

ROMMEL, ERWIN

Erwin Rommel (1891–1944) was a German field marshal during the Second World War. Nicknamed 'Desert Fox', he was commander of the North African offensive from 1941 until defeated in March 1943. Implicated in the plot against **Hitler** in June 1944, he was forced to kill himself.

Franklin D. Roosevelt. ◀

RONTGEN, WILHELM

X-rays were discovered by Wilhelm Rontgen (1845–1923) in 1895. They are produced when high-energy electrons from a cathode strike a target on a heat-conducting anode, between which a high AC current is running. This discovery gave us the glimpse inside a living organism.

ROOSEVELT, FRANKLIN D.

Franklin D. Roosevelt (1882–1945) was the 32nd president of the USA, from 1933–45. In 1933 he inaugurated a 'New Deal' in response to the depression that afflicted the country. Immediate measures included the provision of employment on public works, government loans to farmers at low rates of interest and restriction of agricultural output to raise prices. The New Deal reduced unemployment from 17 million to eight million.

ROOSEVELT, THEODORE

Theodore Roosevelt (1858–1919) was the 26th president of the USA, from 1901–08. He was awarded the Nobel Peace Prize in December 1906 for his part in ending the Russo-Japanese War. Only a month before, Roosevelt had been the first American leader to leave the USA while still in office. His visit to the site of the Panama Canal construction was seen as a key part of his foreign policy initiatives. The USA was beginning to flex its muscles in world affairs and was already having a great influence on events around the globe. Although wounded by a gunman in 1912, he continued his presidential campaign, losing to **Woodrow Wilson**. Roosevelt, still an influential figure during the war, died in 1919.

Jean Jacques Rousseau. ◀

RUSHDIE, SALMÃN

Salmãn Rushdie (b. 1947) was born in India of a Muslim family, later living in Pakistan before moving to the UK. His novels include *Midnight's Children* (1981), which won him the Booker Prize, and *Shame* (1983), which was a satire and revisionist history of Pakistan. In 1988 he wrote *The Satanic Verses* (the title refers to deleted verses from the Qu'ran), which offended many Muslims with its alleged blasphemy. The book was banned in India in 1988, and in 1989 Iran's Ayatollah Khomeini issued a death threat. Demonstrations followed, in which copies of the book were burnt along with effigies of the author. Rushdie was forced to go into hiding under police protection, and only partially re-emerged in 1998 when the fatwah was lifted.

ROUSSEAU, JEAN JACQUES

Jean Jacques Rousseau (1712–78), one of the great French philosophers of the eighteenth century, emphasised the primacy of individual liberty in such writings as *The Social Contract* (1762) and *Emile* (1762).

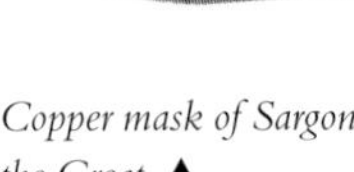

Copper mask of Sargon the Great. ▲

RUSSELL, BERTRAND

Bertrand Russell (1875–1970), the 3rd Earl Russell, was the founder of British analytic philosophy and a major figure in mathematical logic. His most significant work was his *Principia Mathematica* (1910). As well as being a philosopher and historian, he developed a reputation as a pacifist and radical social critic. His analytic philosophy involved reducing philosophical arguments into their constituent parts and linguistically analysing their meaning. In pursuing this path, he was accused of leading philosophy into a dead end.

RUTH, GEORGE HERMAN

George Herman Ruth (1895–1948), universally referred to by his nickname 'Babe', started his pro baseball career in 1915 with the Boston Red Sox. Although he had started out as a left-handed pitcher, by 1919 Ruth had been moved to the outfield because of his awesome talent with the bat. Throughout his tenure, the Red Sox enjoyed enormous success, winning both the league title and the World Series in 1915, 1916 and 1918.

SADAT, ANWAR

Anwar Sadat succeeded **Nasser** as Egyptian president in 1970. He helped to restore Egyptian morale by his handling of the campaign in the 1973 war against Israel. In 1974 his plan for social, economic and political reform in Egypt was unanimously accepted in a referendum. In 1977 he visited Israel at Camp David, to lay plans for a reconciliation between the two countries and he shared the Nobel Peace Prize with Israeli prime minister Menachem Begin in 1978. While reviewing troops in 1981, he was assassinated by Muslim extremists.

SAPPHO

Sappho wrote her graceful lyric poetry on the island of Lesbos in the sixth century BC. Later came the tragedies of Euripedes and the satires of Aristophanes .

SARGON THE GREAT

In Mesopotamia, the most dramatic change occurred during the time of Sargon the Great (2350–2300 BC). Where previous victors had allowed the governments of defeated cities to continue to rule, only demanding payment of tribute, Sargon did away with enemy ruling dynasties and placed his conquests under the control of governors appointed by him. This ensured a loyal subordinate who could administer the internal affairs of a city state with a free hand, while still supplying the dominant ruler with the means to support an army capable of enforcing their authority.

SARTRE, JEAN-PAUL

Renowned as a philosopher, literary figure and social critic, Jean-Paul Sartre (1905–80) was probably most famous as a representative of existentialism.

Jean-Paul Sartre.▶

SCHINDLER, OSKAR ⊠

Oskar Schindler (1908–74) was a German businessman who, during the Second World War, ran an enamelware factory in Krakow, which became a haven for the predominantly Jewish workforce. When the Krakow ghetto was destroyed (1943), he constructed his own for his workers; later, in the face of the Russian advance, he succeeded, by bluff and bribery, in moving both his factory and workers to Czechoslovakia. Schindler's factory, supposedly producing munitions for the war effort, in fact made almost nothing usable. Instead, Schindler bought goods cheaply on the black market, sold them to the Nazis and with the profits maintained his staff.

SCHLIEFFEN, ALFRED VON

Count Alfred von Schlieffen (1833–1913) was the chief of the German general staff and, in 1905, he drew up a military strategy to counter a possible attack on two fronts by France and Russia. He believed that the immediate threat would come from France, but the more serious threat would come from Russia. The Schlieffen Plan involved a sudden attack through Belgium, a neutral country, that would outflank the French Army and surround Paris. This would force the French to surrender; German forces could then be moved east by train to face the Russian armies. Schlieffen believed that the Russians would take six weeks to mobilise. The plan became fundamental to German strategy.

The concentration camp at Buchenwald; Oskar Schindler worked to prevent the mass-extermination of the Jews during the Second World War. ◀

SCHUMACHER, E. F.

E. F. Schumacher's (1911–77) *Small is Beautiful: A Study of Economics as if People Mattered* was published in 1973. He challenged the vast institutions that were emerging in both capitalist and communist countries and called for small communities, decentralisation and technology on a human scale.

SCHWEITZER, ALBERT

The German theologian and missionary Albert Schweitzer was awarded the Nobel Peace Prize for his humanitarian activities. He had founded a hospital in the French colony of Gabon in 1913, and had spent much of his life there tending to the needs of the inhabitants of the area. He managed to raise considerable sums of money to fund his medical work by giving organ recitals and writing books. He was also awarded the Order of Merit in 1955.

Captain Robert Scott. ▲

SCOTT, ROBERT

Captain Robert Scott (1868–1912) led an expedition to Antarctica in 1902. In 1903 he landed on the continent and marched south to 82 degrees, a new record. Scott returned in 1910. Although he was mainly interested in scientific research, he became involved in a race to the true South Pole and set out, with four others, in November 1911. He reached the pole on 16 January 1912, only to find that the Norwegian **Roald Amundsen** had beaten him by exactly one month. Scott's refusal to use dog sledges was one reason for his failure. On the return journey, Scott and his party all died from exhaustion in a blizzard on about 29 March 1912.

SCOTT, WALTER

Sir Walter Scott (1771–1832) was a major cultural influence for well over a century, and his novels were enormously popular. *Rob Roy* (1817) helped rebuild Scottish self-esteem after the defeat of the 1745 Rebellion, and *Ivanhoe* entrenched a fascination for medieval chivalry that was to dominate the nineteenth century, and provide the gentlemanly code of the Victorians.

SCOTUS, JOHN DUNS

John Duns Scotus (1266–1308), philosopher and Scholastic theologian, was named after his birthplace, Duns, in Scotland. As a Franciscan monk he studied and lectured at Oxford and Paris. He taught, like **Thomas Aquinas**, that knowledge had two sources, philosophical reason and divine revelation. These teachings were derived from **Aristotle** and Avicenna, but he rejected their view that man can only know the common essences of things, and stated instead that man can directly know the unique nature of each thing.

SEPTIMIUS SEVERUS

Septimius Severus (AD 146–211) was the first African to become emperor of Rome, when he succeeded in AD 193. This was at a time of considerable unrest and Septimius spent much of his time restoring order. In 205 the Scots had overrun Hadrian's Wall and invaded Britain. Septimius travelled to Britain himself, becoming the first emperor to visit the province since **Claudius**. He re-established imperial power in

The Romans defending Hadrian's Wall. ◀

Britain and authorised the permanent withdrawal from the Antonine Wall. He died at York in 211, the only Roman emperor to be buried in Britain.

Ernest Shackleton. ◀

SHACKLETON, ERNEST

Ernest Shackleton (1874–1922) was a member of **Robert Scott**'s expedition in 1902. He returned on his own in 1907 and reached 88 degrees south, only, 97 miles from the true pole. Food shortages forced the party to turn back, however. Members of his party crossed Antarctica and reached the magnetic South Pole in 1912. In 1914 Shackleton set out on a third expedition planning to cross Antarctica. His ship, the *Endurance,* became trapped in ice and was crushed in November 1915. The crew escaped in boats and reached land on Elephant Island. Shackleton and five others sailed the 800 miles to South Georgia and then returned to rescue the remainder of the crew.

SHAKA

Shaka (1787–1828) became the leader of the Zulu nation and changed southern Africa. From 1818 he created an almost invincible army – based on the 'Impi' – of about 1,000 men. Warriors were strictly disciplined at all times and were not allowed to marry. Shaka changed the tactics of the Zulu army, by ordering his warriors not to throw their assegais. They were to use them only as stabbing weapons. Each warrior was, therefore, only allowed to carry one. To make their hand-to-hand fighting even more effective, the Impis were trained to charge in a closely knit body, which shattered enemy formations. Shaka soon drove other tribes out of Natal, creating the 'Mfecane'.

William Shakespeare. ▼

SHAKESPEARE, WILLIAM

The greatest English playwright, William Shakespeare (1564–1616), also poet and actor, wrote mainly in blank verse. His plays (1589–1613) can broadly be divided into lyric plays, comedies, historical plays and tragedies. His extraordinarily prolific career saw him produce masterpieces such as *Hamlet*, *A Midsummer Night's Dream* and *Romeo and Juliet*. He was also a master of the sonnet form. He was closely associated with the theatres in his native Stratford-upon-Avon and was a member of many theatrical groups throughout his lifetime.

SHAW, GEORGE BERNARD

George Bernard Shaw (1856–1950) became one of the greatest socialist thinkers of his day. Although an outstanding speaker and critic, he is best known for his drama. He used his brilliant, witty plays to show his concern with social and moral issues, such as the English class system, prostitution and slum landlording. He reluctantly accepted the Nobel Prize in 1925 for *Saint Joan*, a work about Joan of Arc. It was his greatest and most successful play, making enough money at the box office for him to decline the prize money, saying it was 'a lifebelt thrown to a swimmer who had already reached the shore in safety'.

SHELLEY, MARY

Apart from being the wife of the great Romantic poet, Percy Bysshe Shelley, Mary Shelley (1797–1851) was also the daughter of two radicals – the pioneer feminist, **Mary Wollstonecraft** and the writer William Godwin (1756–1836). Her important Gothic novel, *Frankenstein, or The Modern Prometheus,* was begun when she was 16, when she, Byron and Shelley were writing ghost stories to pass the time during a summer in Switzerland. She wrote several other novels after her husband's death, and the death of two children and two miscarriages, but none caught the imagination of the public like the first.

Mary Wollstonecraft, mother of Mary Shelley. ▼

SHIH HUANG TI

Shih Huang Ti (259–210 BC) was the first emperor of China. He set up 36 regions, or *chun*, each with civil, military and governing civil servants. Laws, weights and measures were standardised, as were the characters in the written script. To defend the empire, he carried out conquests in the south and linked earlier fortifications to build the Great Wall in 214 BC. He was buried in a tomb complex guarded by 10,000 life-size terracotta warriors (excavated in the 1980s).

The Great Wall of China, built by Shih Huang-Ti. ▼

SHRAPNEL, HENRY

The Shrapnel shell was invented in 1784 by the British lieutenant (later general) Henry Shrapnel (1761–1842). Shrapnel projectiles contained small shot, or spherical bullets, along with an explosive charge to scatter the shot as well as fragments of the shell casing. A time fuse set off the explosive charge in the latter part of the shell's flight, while it was near opposing troops. The resulting hail of high-velocity debris was often lethal.

SINATRA, FRANK

Frank Sinatra (1915–98) was a US singer and film actor, celebrated for his phrasing and emotion, especially on love ballads – in particular *My Way*. His songs have become anthems for our time, and his death in 1998 caused widepread mourning throughout the music industry.

SITTING BULL

Sitting Bull (*c.* 1834–90) was a native American chief, who agreed to Sioux resettlement in 1868. When the treaty was broken by the USA he led the Sioux against Lt-General Custer at the Battle of the Little Bighorn on 25 June 1876. The Sioux victory, however, did not change anything. Fourteen years

later, on 29 December 1890, Sitting Bull was killed during a confrontation with the army at Wounded Knee on the Sioux reservation in South Dakota, where the tribe was now confined.

The Battle of the Little Bighorn, led by the Sioux chief, Sitting Bull. ▲

SITWELL, EDITH

The Sitwell family, Edith (1887–1964), Osbert (1892–1969), and Sacheverell (1897–1988), declared war on philistinism in the name of modern art and writing, and in doing so, they faced reactions ranging from ridicule to outright rage. All had a strong sense of irony and a genius for publicity, and their campaign reached a climax in 1923 with the performance of Edith's cycle of poems known as *Façade* – which she described as 'patterns in sound'. The sounds were delivered to the audience through a megaphone in a painted screen, accompanied by music written by the young composer, William Walton.

Adam Smith. ▲

SMITH, ADAM

Adam Smith (1723–90) was a Scottish economist, and author of *The Wealth of Nations* (1776), in which he advocated the untrammelled workings of free enterprise and the importance of free trade. All these ideas were revolutionary, given the traditional social and economic values they sought to replace.

SMITH, JOSEPH

The Church of Jesus Christ of Latter Day Saints – or Mormons – was founded by an American Christian, Joseph Smith (1805–44), following a vision in 1827, in which he was shown the *Book of Mormon*. Although the original was supposedly written in an American-Indian language on golden plates buried under his parents' farm, he published a translation in 1830, and declared himself the priest of the new church. Opponents drove his supporters out of several states and eventually they moved to Utah under the guidance of **Brigham Young** and founded Salt Lake City. Smith was killed by opponents in 1844.

SOCRATES

Socrates (*c.* 469–399 BC), the great philosopher of classical Athens, reportedly spent his life seeking true knowledge and exposing those who claimed to be wise. He was sentenced to death by poisoning in 399 BC.

SOLOMON

David's son, King Solomon, was renowned for his wealth and his wisdom. He ruled from 967 to 928 BC, during which time he brought considerable wealth to the nation

Mormon Temple in Salt Lake City, Utah, founded by Joseph Smith. ▲

through trade with the Phoenicians. Much money was raised through taxes to build a vast temple in Jerusalem to house the Ark of the Covenant – a project that took 14 years, and employed the services of thousands of Phoenician craftsmen.

SPEKE, JOHN

British explorers Richard Burton and John Speke (1827–64) were the first Europeans to reach Lake Tanganyika (1857) and Speke then went to Lake Victoria, the source of the White Nile (1858). Speke led a further expedition back to the source of the Nile (1860–63) and became the first known European to visit Uganda.

SPIELBERG, STEVEN

Steven Spielberg (b. 1947) is a US film director, writer and producer. His talent for creating not only typical Hollywood box-office hits, but also radical, challenging and adventurous films, has made him one of the greatest success stories of the twentieth century. His credits include such phenomenal box-office successes as *Jaws* 1975, *Close Encounters of the Third Kind* 1977, *Raiders of the Lost Ark* 1981, *ET* 1982 and *Jurassic Park* and *Schindler's List* for which he won seven Academy Awards.

ST BENEDICT ☯

Born in Umbria, Italy, to a noble family, Benedict (AD 480–547) became the founder of the first major monastic order. Shocked by the decadence of Roman society, encountered during his education, he went to live as a monk in a cave near Rome. His growing number of followers invited him to be their abbot and eventually he founded 12 monasteries. Benedict is known mainly for his monastic rule, which was enlightened and humane for its time. This involved simple but comfortable living, abstinence from meat, regular prayer, the shared ownership of possessions and communal consultation on major issues.

Luxurious Roman Villas were the sort of decadence St Benedict was appalled by, causing him to retreat to a cave to live as a monk. ▼

ST FRANCIS OF ASSISI ☯

St Francis (1182–1226), the patron saint of ecology and founder of the Franciscan Order of Friars, has been called the Second Christ. He was born into the family of a wealthy merchant, but following several religious experiences, he abandoned this way of life and gave away all his possessions to become a wandering friar. His reverence for nature is similar to that found in Celtic Christianity. When large numbers began to follow him, he created a simple rule for them to follow. This included complete poverty, abstinence from meat, and service to the poor. Today his order is one of the largest in the Catholic and Anglican Churches.

ST HILDEGARD ☯

St Hildegard (1098–1179), the 10th child of a noble German family, entered a Benedictine convent at the age of eight and became an anchoress – a solitary contemplative – at an early age. In 1141, she had a vision that God asked her to write down all her thoughts and visions. For many years she communicated her visions, distinctive for their ecological and egalitarian content, in the form of many books, paintings and music. In 1150 she

St Francis of Assisi (left) with St Bernard. ▲

moved her convent to Bingen and later created her own convent at Eibingen. Supported in her work by the Pope, she became a spiritual adviser to kings and bishops.

ST IGNATIUS LOYOLA

Ignatius Loyola (1491–1556) was a Spanish theologian and military leader. After sustaining a serious injury, he adopted a religious life and studied spiritual practices. His highly intellectual Jesuit Order, of which he was the general, was organised along military lines, with the objective of rooting out Protestant heresy and restoring the true faith.

ST LAURENT, YVES ✷

The debut collection by St Laurent (b. 1936) for **Christian Dior** was a triumph. Leaving Dior, he went on to create some of the twentieth century's most memorable looks. Like **Coco Chanel**, he used the male wardrobe for inspiration, but he also took ideas from the paintings of Piet Mondrian, the Ballets Russes, De Stijl, the work of **Picasso** and, for his evening wear, the fantasy dresses of women in Marcel Proust's novels. In 1965, St Laurent was the first couturier to launch a cheap ready-to-wear line, 'Rive Gauche', and in the 1970s he became one of Paris's most respected costume designers.

St Patrick. ▲

ST PATRICK ☯

Christianity was brought to Ireland by St Patrick (AD 390–460) in AD 431. Patrick's family, who lived near the sea in Bannavern, were attacked one day and Patrick was taken to Ireland by pirates. He looked after cattle before escaping to Gaul. He received a vision asking him to return to Ireland and in about 430 he was made a bishop for the Irish. He tried to introduce a diocesan form of government, but the rural nature of the country defeated him.

ST PAUL ☯

St Paul (Saul of Tarsus) was a Jewish tent maker, and originally an opponent of Christianity. His sudden conversion experience on the road to Damascus marked the starting point of his promotion of **Jesus**'s teachings. After Jesus himself, St Paul is the most important figure in the history of Christianity in his missionary work, and in his interpretation of Jesus's teachings. He was executed in Rome on the order of **Nero** in AD 62.

The martyrdom of St Peter. ▼

ST PETER

The first Pope, St Peter (AD 42–67), was one of the Twelve Apostles. Tradition holds that he suffered his martyrdom in Rome, possibly by crucifixion.

ST TERESA OF AVILA

St Teresa of Avila (1515–82), the Carmelite mystic, is famous for her ecstatic visions.

STALIN, JOSEPH

When Lenin died in January 1924, he had intended that his successor should be **Leon Trotsky**, who had organised the October Revolution, but, after a power struggle lasting over two years, Joseph Stalin (1879–1953) emerged as the new leader of the Soviet Union, as Russia was now known. Stalin believed that his first priority must be to make Communism safe in the Soviet Union. He was afraid that the countries of western Europe might try to interfere, as they had done during the civil war in 1918. He called his policy 'Socialism in One Country'. From 1928, Stalin set about modernising and strengthening Soviet industry and agriculture as quickly as possible. This meant that the standard of living in the Soviet Union fell and the NKVD, Stalin's secret police, were used even more frequently.

Joseph Stalin. ▲

STEIN, AUREL

Aurel Stein (1862–1943) was a Hungarian-born British archeologist who, in 1899, set out to rediscover the ancient Silk Road across the Gobi Desert and with it, an ancient, but lost, Indian Buddhist civilisation dating from around the second century AD. Stein's quest proved his life's work. He travelled some 25,000 miles across Central Asia and uncovered several tombs, temples and their treasures beneath the sand covering the Silk Road.

STEINEM, GLORIA

Gloria Steinem (b. 1934) is one of the most influential figures of the modern feminist movement. Organizer of the National Women's Political Caucus and the Women's Alliance for Action, she has campaigned for political, economic and sexual liberation of women.

STEPHENSON, GEORGE

George Stephenson (1781–1848) was an English engineer who built the world's first successful railways and the locomotives that operated the trains. Experimenting with the design of **Richard Trevithick**, he built effective locomotives capable of pulling trains. He was asked to build a railway line to carry coal. The resulting Stockton–Darlington line, in northern England, took three years to build. When it opened in 1825, Stephenson himself drove the world's first passenger train, pulled by his locomotive, *Locomotion*. Stephenson and his son, Robert, also built the Liverpool–Manchester railway line (1826–30).

STOPES, MARIE

After studying at University College, London, and taking her PhD in Munich, Marie Stopes (1880–1958) became the first

The Liverpool-Manchester railway built by George Stephenson and his son Robert. ▼

female science lecturer at Manchester in 1904. Initially specialising in fossil plants and coal-mining, she changed direction after the annulment of her first marriage in 1916. She turned her attention to marital unhappiness caused by ignorance, and began a crusade to spread the word about contraception. In 1916 her book, *Married Love*, caused a furore and was banned in the US. She married the aircraft manufacturer Humphrey Roe in 1918 and together they opened the first British birth-control clinic in North London in 1921.

STRAVINSKY, IGOR

Stravinsky (1882–1971) was born in Russia in 1882, the son of a prominent opera singer. As a student at the University of St Petersburg, he learnt orchestration from the great composer Rimsky-Korsakov, and on graduating he decided to pursue composition as his life's work. In 1909 he met Sergei Diaghilev, the ballet impresario, and was commissioned to write his first ballet score, *The Firebird*. This piece of music had much of the sparky originality and rhythmic drive that would come to characterise all Stravinsky's work.

STUART, JOHN MACDOUALL

John Stuart (1815–66) was a Scottish-born surveyor, who made the first south-north crossing of Australia (1860–62) on his third attempt after overcoming water shortages, Aborigine hostility and oppressive heat. During the 1860 trek Stuart found and named the MacDonnall Ranges and came within 240 km (150 miles) of the centre of Australia.

STURT, CHARLES

Charles Sturt (1795–1869) was a British explorer whose charting of the great river basins of the Darling (1828), Murumbidgee and Murray Rivers (1829) led to the development of Victoria and Adelaide. This led to the founding of a new colony, South Australia (1834), which Britain populated by selling land to settlers for 60 pence an acre.

SULEIMAN

Suleiman (*c.* 1494–1566) was an energetic young sultan who became Ottoman emperor in 1520. Suleiman, who was called 'the Magnificent', extended Ottoman

Suleiman the Magnificent. ▶

power deep into Europe and across the Mediterranean. His victories over Hungary in 1526 led to a failed attempt to capture Vienna in 1529. In 1538, an Ottoman expedition even threatened the Portuguese trading post of Diu in India. Suleiman's empire, however, had reached its limits.

SULLIVAN, ARTHUR

No matter how much he strived for recognition as a serious composer, it was light operas that kept Arthur Sullivan (1842–1900) in the public eye. Starting with *Trial by Jury* (1875), his partnership with the light-verse writer W. S. Gilbert produced a string of

successes. Gilbert was also a playwright, but his profoundly cynical view of human nature was more easily swallowed together with Sullivan's jaunty music.

TAFT, WILLIAM H.

William Taft (1857–1930) was the 27th president of the USA from 1908–1912. He was a Republican.

TALBOT, WILLIAM HENRY FOX

William Fox Talbot (1800–77) was an English pioneer of photography who discovered a means of making any number of prints from the same negative.

TALLIS, THOMAS

The so-called 'Father of English Cathedral Music', Thomas Tallis (*c.* 1505–85), was a Gentleman of the Chapel Royal and was able to write church music for Catholic **Mary I** and her Protestant sister **Elizabeth I** alike. In fact in 1575, Elizabeth granted Tallis and collaborator William Byrd a monopoly of music printing and publishing in England. The same year, they produced *Cantiones Sacrae*, which included most of Tallis's choral works and included one piece for eight choirs.

TAYLOR, ZACHARY

Whig Zachery Taylor (1784–1850) was the 12th president of the USA from 1848–50.

TELFORD, THOMAS

Thomas Telford (1757–1834), nicknamed 'the Colossus of roads', was one of the most important civil engineers of the Industrial Revolution. From 1793 he built canals, including the Ellesmere Canal, to carry raw materials and finished goods from Wales to the River Mersey. The 1,400 km (875 miles) of new roads and 11 bridges he built changed the whole way of life in the Highlands. Telford's supreme achievement was the building of a road from London to Holyhead, North Wales, which took 15 years.

TELLER, EDWARD

Edward Teller (b. 1908), a Hungarian-born US physicist, is known as the father of the hydrogen bomb. He worked on the H-bomb after taking part in the atom-bomb project at the Los Alamos research centre in New Mexico between 1946 and 1952. The H-bomb was first tested at Enewetak atoll on 1 November 1952.

Edward Teller is known as the father of the Hydrogen Bomb. ▲

TEMPLE, WILLIAM

The most influential clergyman of the inter-war years was William Temple (1881–1944), Archbishop of York (1929–42) and of Canterbury (1942–44). He tried to reverse the decline in organised religion and to make England an Anglican nation again. He failed, and the Church became a voice of social criticism which caused it to be seen in a much more secular light. He had presided over meetings, written books and formulated statements, yet he was still immensely popular with people who never read his books or heard him preach.

TENNYSON, ALFRED

Occasionally a poet is able to capture the mood of a generation, and Alfred Tennyson (1809–92) managed this in his elegy about his friend, Arthur Hallam, who died in 1833. *In Memoriam* was published in 1850 – the same year he became Poet Laureate – and describes his grief, but also his doubt about faith: 'This I believe but could not prove,' he repeated. Tennyson's greatest poems remained ahead of him, including *The Charge of the Light Brigade* (1854) and *The Idylls of the King* (1859).

THATCHER, MARGARET

In 1979 Britain elected its first woman prime minister – Margaret Thatcher (b. 1925). She became the longest serving and one of the most controversial prime ministers of the century. Mrs Thatcher also won elections in 1983 and 1987, advocating right-wing politics, a monetarist policy, sustained privatisation, and a more vigorous foreign policy, especially in Europe, which earned her the title 'Iron Lady' abroad. Her government's policies were at first deeply unpopular, but she was returned to Number Ten on the back of populist opinion after the Falklands dispute of 1982. Although she commanded large Commons' majorities, which enabled her to pursue her policies, her vote in the country was less impressive. She was driven from office by her own party in November 1990.

THOMPSON, DALEY

Daley Thompson (b. 1958) is one of the finest athletes Britain has ever produced, and one of the best the world has ever seen. The fact that he became famous for winning numerous titles and breaking world records in one of the least glamorous events – the decathlon – demonstrates the extent of his achievements.

Margaret Thatcher. ▲

THOREAU, HENRY DAVID

Thoreau (1817–62), together with essayist Ralph Waldo Emerson, initiated a philosophical and literary movement, known as American Transcendentalism, which drew upon the teachings of the *Bhagavad Gita* and other Eastern texts to provide a basis for experiencing the divine in the natural world. Despite its somewhat exotic origins, the movement's values, such as self-reliance and simple living, fitted well with American society and have since inspired many significant events, from the first World Parliament of Religions in Chicago to the conservation movement and the creation of national parks.

Henry David Thoreau. ▼

THORPE, JIM

Jim Thorpe (1888–1923), undoubtedly one of the greatest athletes of the twentieth century, was probably its most natural sportsman. As well as being an Olympic gold-medal winner in both the pentathlon and the decathlon at the 1912 Olympics in Stockholm, Thorpe was also a fantastic gridiron specialist and solid baseball player, as well as excelling in basketball, boxing, lacrosse, swimming and hockey. Just for good measure, he also won the 1912 intercollegiate ballroom-dancing championship.

TIFFANY, LOUIS COMFORT

Tiffany (1848–1933), the son of a prominent New York jeweller, studied in Paris and, on his return to America in 1878, founded an interior-decorating firm. In 1885, Tiffany founded his glass company and began to produce elaborate and unique stained-glass panels and lampshades, usually employing bold, colourful floral motifs. In 1894, he patented his much-imitated 'Favrile' range of iridescent glass. Tiffany's 'Favrile' punchbowl exhibited at the 1900 Paris Exhibition was probably one of the few works in glass to rival that of the French master glass craftsman, Emile Gallé.

TOLKIEN, J. R. R.

A select group of academics met every Tuesday throughout the war in the Eagle and Child pub in Oxford. The result, among other writings, was the fantasy epic *The Lord of the Rings* by the Anglo-Saxon scholar J. R. R.

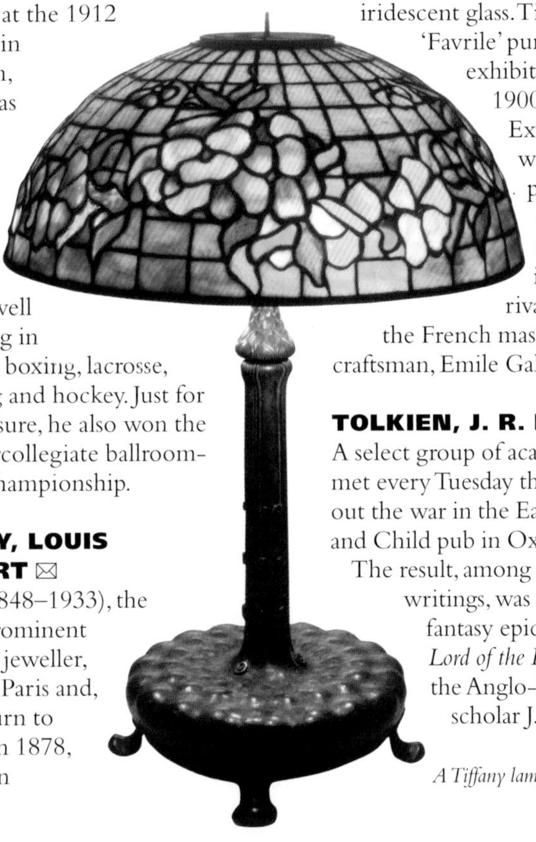

A Tiffany lamp. ◀

Tolkien (1892–1973). Tolkien invented a whole new mythology for his imaginary land 'Middle Earth', and the whole conception of Shire hobbits fighting the evil enemy in the East owes a great deal to the experience of the war. *The Lord of the Rings*, also began a whole new style, and gave birth to a new genre of fantasy and science fantasy.

TOLSTOY, LEO

Count Leo Tolstoy (1828–1910), the Russian novelist and anarchist, was renowned both for his great works of literature – *War and Peace* and *Anna Karenina* – and for his radical Christian pacifism. In 1888 he gave away all his property and emancipated his serfs. In his *The Kingdom of God is Within You* (1893) and *Patriotism and Government* (1900), he argued that Christians have a moral duty to refuse military service.

TRAJAN

Roman Emperor Trajan (AD 98–117) campaigned hard to extend his empire. Throughout Europe he constructed military roads, canals, bridges, harbours and new towns.

TREVITHICK, RICHARD

Trevithick (1771–1833) was the first person to build a steam-powered locomotive, which he ran on the Penydarren railway in Wales in 1804. By the 1820s, locomotives were becoming a familiar sight, and the brittle cast-iron tracks had to be replaced with wrought iron, as they became heavier and more powerful.

Richard Trevithick. ▼

Leon Trotsky. ▲

TROTSKY, LEON

On 24–25 October 1917 the Bolsheviks overthrew the Provisional Government in Russia, in a coup planned and led by Leon Trotsky (1879–1940), **Lenin**'s second-in-command. A month later, the general election was held. This was won by the Socialist-Revolutionary party, but when the Assembly met in January, Lenin dissolved it by force and began to rule as a dictator.

TRUMAN, HARRY S.

On 12 April 1945, Harry S. Truman (1884–1972) became the 33rd president of the USA. While at the Potsdam Conference, he was told that the atomic bomb was ready to be used on Japan. After lengthy discussion, Truman decided to use the bomb. He was told by his chiefs of staff that one million casualties would be caused if Japan were to be invaded. The bomb was dropped on 6 August 1945 on the city of Hiroshima; some 70,000 people were killed. The bomb not only marked the beginning of a new period in the history of mankind, but also increased the hostility between Truman and the Soviet leader, **Joseph Stalin**, who had not been warned about the bomb. It became a factor in the development of the Cold War.

TUBMAN, HARRIET

Harriet Tubman (1820–1913), was a former slave who had escaped along a secret route of hiding places known as the 'underground railroad'. She then resolved to help others and returned countless times to the South, becoming the most famous 'conductor' on the 'railroad'. Between 1850 and 1861 she rescued more than 300 slaves.

During the American Civil War (1861–65), she served as a nurse, laundress and spy for the Union (northern) army.

TULL, JETHRO

Jethro Tull (1674–1741) was a Berkshire farmer who, in 1701, brought a seed-drill from France, which enabled three rows of seeds to be planted at once, and a horse-drawn hoe for destroying weeds.

TURING, ALAN

Alan Turing (1912–54) was a brilliant English mathematician and logician. In 1936 he described a 'universal computing machine' that could theoretically be programed to solve any problem capable of solution. During the Second World War he worked with the Government Code and Cypher School at Bletchley Park, where he helped build a computer with vacuum tubes. It was known as the *Colossus* and was designed to decipher the German 'Enigma' codes, which it did in 1940. After the war, Turing worked in the construction of early computers and the development of programing techniques.

US president Harry S. Truman. ◀

TURNER, J. M. W.

Turner (1775–1851) was at his best painting elemental forces, including the new steam engines in *Rain, Steam and Speed* (1844). The end of a Nelsonian era of wooden ships is celebrated by his famous painting *The Fighting Temeraire*. His revolutionary style moved in and out of favour during his lifetime, and although he left all his paintings to the nation on his death, they did not get a permanent home until 1987.

TYLER, JOHN

The Whig John Tyler (1790–1862) became the 10th president of the USA in 1841 and held office until 1844.

TYLER, WAT

Peasants and artisans in England rebelled against the imposition of the poll tax and the government's decision to collect arrears in the fourteenth century. Most serious of all the uprisings was in Kent, where protesters were led by Wat Tyler (d. 1381). Having seized Rochester Castle, Tyler led a march to London in June. Met eventually by the king – Richard II – the protesters dispersed, but not before the chancellor and Archbishop of Canterbury had been murdered by the rebels. Wat Tyler was also killed.

TYNDALE, WILLIAM

Tyndale (1484–1536) had left Britain in 1524. At the time, Hebrew – the language of the Old Testament – was taught nowhere and Tyndale decided to translate the Bible from Hebrew into the vernacular. Even in his death cell in Brussels in 1535 he requested Hebrew dictionaries and a Hebrew Bible to continue his studies. Printing had revolutionised the spread of knowledge across Europe. Books deemed to be heretical poured into England and after Tyndale's departure, copies of his translations were smuggled into England in bales of wool.

UMBERTO I

Umberto I had been king of Italy since 1878, when he succeeded his father, **Victor-Emmanuel II**, the first king of Italy. He joined the Triple Alliance with Germany and Austria-Hungary in 1882, a pact intended to offset the power of Russia and France. His colonial exploits included the defeat at Aduwa, Abyssinia, in 1896. He was assassinated by an anarchist in July 1900, a month after the defeat of the Pelloux government.

URBAN II

Urban II (1088–99) inspired the First Crusade to the Holy Land, in 1095, by his eloquence and passion at the Council of Clermont, France.

VALENTINO, RUDOLF

The death of Rudolf Valentino (1895–1926) – the 'Great Lover' – caused an unprecedented outpouring of public grief. Thousands wept and mourned; heaving crowds threatened to overwhelm his coffin as he was lying in state. The great male screen idol of his time, Valentino was sleek, graceful and alluringly exotic. He had worked as a gardener in *Central Park* until he became a dancer in New York nightclubs. He played small parts in films but it wasn't until *Four Horsemen of the Apocalypse* that he became a star.

Crusaders, inspired to battle in the Holy Land by Urban II. ◀

VAN GOGH, VINCENT

Van Gogh's (1853–90) early works were characterised by dark portrayals of Dutch peasants, but after moving to Paris in 1888, he fell under the influence of Impressionism, and his works became brighter and bolder. Some of his best-known pieces date from this time. He is known for his bold brush strokes and thick textures. Despite the vibrancy of his paintings, Van Gogh suffered severely from depression, and committed suicide in 1890.

VAUBAN, SEBASTIEN DE

Sebastien de Vauban (1633–1707) was a French marshal and military engineering genius, whose work greatly enhanced the effectiveness of citadels for defence in the seventeenth century. Retaining the basic features of the citadel structure, he devised a means of extending the outer-works so far that no enemy could begin siege operations at close range. Vauban was also a master of offensive siege craft; he developed the concept of using parallel trenches to connect the

Sebastien de Vauban, French military engineer. ▶

zigzag trenches used by besieging troops, and the use of the ricochet shot from cannons plunging over the walls to drop on the defenders beyond the walls.

VESALIUS, ANDREAS

Andreas Vesalius (1514–64) was an Italian physician who investigated the workings of the human body. He revolutionised anatomy by performing post-mortem dissections and making use of illustrations to teach anatomy.

Queen Victoria. ◀

VICTOR-EMMANUEL II

Victor-Emmanuel II (1820–78) was proclaimed first king of a united Italy at Turin in 1861. Following its liberation from French occupation in 1870, he declared Rome his new capital.

VICTORIA, QUEEN

In 1837 Queen Victoria (1819–1901) came to the throne where she remained for 64 years, the longest of any British monarch. She quickly became a symbol of the country in times that were changing fast, and her middle-class sympathies and strong sense of duty made her popular amongst her subjects. She lost popularity after the death of **Prince Albert** in 1861, after which Victoria took to mourning for nearly 10 years. Victoria was renowned for her strict sense of morality, and great advances were made in the areas of democracy and education during this time. She became an icon of imperial Britain, being made Empress of India during her reign. She died in 1901.

VINCI, LEONARDO DA

DaVinci (1452–1519) was the epitome of the Renaissance man; a genius in the true sense of the word, he was centuries before his time in his scientific theories and practical experiments. He is credited with having designed the earliest flying machine as well as an early prototype of a camera – the camera obscura – in 1515. He was also a prolific artist, and it was through him that the art of the early sixteenth century became the High Renaissance, attaining a grandeur that appealed particularly to the popes, who became leading art patrons.

VIVEKANANDA, SWAMI

Swami Vivekananda (1863–1902) was a disciple of **Ramakrishna**, and the most important recent systematiser of Hindu thought. In developing a philosophy that brought together all the main strands of the Hindu tradition from *advaita* (meditation) to *bhakti* (devotion), he virtually created modern Hinduism.

VOLTAIRE

Voltaire (pen-name of François-Marie Arouet, 1694–1778) was a French writer. He was twice imprisoned in the Bastille and exiled from Paris between 1716 and 1726 for libellous political verse.

WAITE, TERRY

Terry Waite (b. 1939) was appointed lay-training adviser to the Bishop of Bristol (1964–68) and the Archbishop of Uganda, Rwanda and Burundi (1968–71). He was consultant with the Roman Catholic Church (1972–79). From 1980 he worked as religious adviser on Anglican Communion affairs to the then-Archbishop of Canterbury, Dr Robert Runcie. Possessing great diplomatic skills, Waite undertook many overseas assignments, and on 20 January 1987 he was seized in Beirut, Lebanon, while seeking to negotiate the release of European hostages. Taken hostage himself, Terry Waite was captive from 1987 until his release on 18 November 1991.

WALLACE, ALFRED RUSSEL

Alfred Wallace (1823–1913) was a Welsh naturalist who collected animal and plant specimens in South America and Southeast Asia,

Charles Darwin (right) and Alfred Russel Wallace independently reached the same conclusions about evolution. ▶

and independently arrived at a theory of evolution by natural selection similar to that proposed by **Charles Darwin**.

WALLACE, WILLIAM

William Wallace (*c.* 1270–1305) was a Scottish warrior who fought against the English dominance of his country in the thirteenth century. He was a key figure in the uprising of 1297, before being caught and accused of treason against the English king. Wallace denied the charge, saying, 'I cannot be a traitor, for I owe him no allegiance. He is not my sovereign; he never received my homage; and

whilst life is in this persecuted body, he shall never receive it'. Wallace was hung, drawn and quartered in 1305.

WALPOLE, ROBERT

Sir Robert Walpole (1676–1745) is recognised as the first-ever prime minister. A Whig, his reputation was made during the collapse of the South Sea Company in 1720. His skills saved King George I from public disgrace as the monarchy was implicated in the scheme, which controlled a large part of the national debt until it collapsed. Walpole became First Lord of the Treasury in 1721, and effectively prime minister. A collector of fine art, Walpole also spent time in prison for corruption in 1712.

WARHOL, ANDY

Andy Warhol (1928–87) was the founder of the artistic style known as Pop Art. In 1960, he produced the first of his paintings, depicting enlarged comic-strip images. He pioneered the development of the process whereby an enlarged photographic image is transferred to a silks creen, which is then placed on a canvas and inked from the rear.

George Washington. ◀

This technique enabled Warhol to produce the series of slightly varied, mass-media images that he began in 1962. Later in the 1960s, Warhol made a series of experimental films. He was obsessed with **Marilyn Monroe**, whom he saw as an icon of popular culture, and used her image repeatedly over the years. In such works, the same image is repeated across the entire surface of the canvas, and the aura of mass production is intensified by Warhol's technique rather than the serial repetition.

WASHINGTON, GEORGE

Federalist George Washington (1732–99) was the first president of the USA, from 1789–96. Born into a planter family in Virginia, he was interested in the military arts, and, with the arrival of the American Revolution he became commander-in-chief of the Continental Army and was responsible, in 1781, for the surrender of the British at Yorktown. With the ratification of the Constitution in 1789, Washington was unanimously voted president. He had a profound influence on the American way of life and was greatly mourned on his death in 1799.

WATSON, JAMES AND CRICK, FRANCIS

Deoxyribonucleic acid (DNA) is the complex giant molecule that contains, in a chemically coded form, all the information required to build, control and maintain a living organism. In 1949 British molecular biologist Francis Crick (b. 1916) and US biologist James Watson (b. 1928) began to research the molecular structure of DNA, trying to crack the code of nucleic acids within that molecule, which enable characteristics to be passed down through generations. During the 1950s they realised that the molecule was two strands wrapped around each other in a spiral or helix, each strand carrying a sequence of bases that carry the code of life. They were awarded the Nobel Prize for Medicine in 1962.

WATT, JAMES

While working at the University of Glasgow, James Watt (1736–1819) was asked to repair a working model of a steam engine used for pumping water that had been invented by **Thomas Newcomen** in 1705. He realised he could build a much better engine using only a quarter of the coal needed by earlier engines, thereby making them cheaper to run and more powerful. In Watt's first steam engine, a coal fire heated water to make steam. In 1782 he built the first rotary steam engine, with cogs and wheels, so that the engine could turn wheels and drive machinery. The watt, the unit of electrical power, is named after James Watt.

WEBBER, ANDREW LLOYD

The 'composer' Andrew Lloyd Webber (b. 1948) achieved his first success with a West End musical in partnership with lyricist Tim Rice with *Jesus Christ Superstar* in 1973. For *Cats*, he used the children's poems of the poet, **T. S. Eliot** and the result was the most successful stage musical of all time; it led to the domination by British musicals of both the West End and Broadway throughout the 1980s. Its success was also due in part to director Trevor Nunn from the Royal Shakespeare Company. The main song 'Memory' was first sung by Lloyd Webber's future wife, Sarah Brightman: within 10 years, it had been recorded more than 150 times around the world.

James Watt's steam engine. ▶

WEBER, MAX

The Protestant Work Ethic and the Spirit of Capitalism, by sociologist Max Weber (1864–1920), has had a significant influence on man's understanding of capitalist attitudes and values. Weber traces the view that maximising profit is the purpose of life, and that leisure is evil.

WEDGWOOD, JOSIAH ⊠

One of the most famous makers of fine porcelain was Josiah Wedgwood (1730–95). His company, near Stoke-on-Trent in England, specialised in making pieces that incorporated white reliefs on a coloured background; Wedgwood blue being the most well known.

WELLESLEY, ARTHUR (DUKE OF WELLINGTON)

Arthur Wellesley, 1st Duke of Wellington (1769–1852), scored an impressive string of victories in the Peninsular Campaign. His military career culminated in the defeat of **Napoleon** at Waterloo.

WESLEY, JOHN ☯

John Wesley (1703–91) was the founder of the Methodist movement, an offshoot of the Church of England. The name derives from the methodical approach he derived from the Bible for developing personal devotion. He promoted his approach through outdoor sermons throughout Britain. His decision to employ lay preachers in support of his mission, then to ordain them, led to a split with the Church of England and, in 1748, he created the Methodist Church.

Scene from the Battle of Waterloo. ▼

Fouder of the Methodist movement John Wesley. ▲

WESTWOOD, VIVIENNE

Westwood (b. 1941) is one of fashion's great innovators. Her 1976 'Bondage' collection was a turning-point in her career. Westwood was prosecuted for her risqué efforts, but her creativity remained undimmed. Westwood shows collections in Paris and London twice-yearly and has been awarded an OBE for her contribution to British fashion.

WHITEHEAD, ROBERT

The cigar-shaped underwater guided missile known as the torpedo was invented by a British engineer, Robert Whitehead, in 1866. His first design was about 4.26 m (14 ft) long and 36 cm (14 in) in diameter. It carried an 8.16 kg (18 lb) warhead of dynamite, was powered by a propeller driven by a compressed-air engine and was held at a set depth by a hydrostatic valve that operated horizontal rudders at the rear.

WILBERFORCE, WILLIAM

William Wilberforce (1759–1833) was an English reformer and one of the most effective public campaigners for the abolition of slavery. In 1788, as a member of the House of Commons, he organised a committee to study the slave trade; this revealed many horrifying statistics about the confined spaces and appalling conditions on the ships in which the slaves were transported across the Atlantic. As a result, and largely through his efforts, the slave trade was abolished in Britain in 1807.

Oscar Wilde. ◀

WILDE, OSCAR

Oscar Wilde (1854–1900) was the best known, and one of the most outrageous, members of the Aesthetic movement, which was busily espousing art for art's sake. The year 1895 was also the most important of his life: not only was his brilliant comedy *The Importance of being Earnest* an enormous success, but he also ended up in Reading Gaol. Although his homosexuality was an open secret, he made the mistake of suing for libel the Marquis of Queensberry – the father of his lover – over a note accusing him of being a 'sodomite'. He lost the case and became the first person prosecuted under the new homosexuality laws. He died in Paris five years later, a tragic and broken figure.

WILLARD, EMMA HART

Emma Hart Willard (1787–1870) was a pioneer in the movement for higher education for women in England; her introduction of mathematics and philosophy in her school for girls was a radical innovation. She was responsible for training hundreds of teachers.

WILLIAM I (THE CONQUEROR)

William the Conqueror (*c.* 1027–87) was the illegitimate son of Duke Robert the Devil, and succeeded his father as duke of Normandy in 1035. Claiming that his relative, **Edward the Confessor**, had bequeathed him the English throne, William invaded the country in 1066. He landed his army at Pevensey on 28 September and moved eastwards along the coast to Hastings. On 13 October **King Harold** took a strong position on a hill near Hastings. Standing close together and protected by great shields, the English wielded their long-handled battle axes. Feigning retreat, William drew the English from their position and annihilated them. After the battle William and his army moved northward to isolate London and was crowned on Christmas Day.

WILLIAM II

William II, Rufus (1087–1100), was the son of **William the Conqueror**, extorted money ruthlessly from his Barons and the church. He was killed by an arrow while hunting in the New Forest.

William I's invasion of England, from the Bayeux Tapestry. ▲

WILLIAM OF ORANGE

In 1688, William of Orange (1650–1702), the Stadtholder of the Netherlands, became king of England when James II fled. French support for James, and William's desire to protect the Netherlands, led to England being drawn into war with France in 1689. William joined the League of Augsburg and landed in the Netherlands with an army. He was defeated in a series of battles from 1692 to 1694.

Ralph Vaughan Williams. ▲

WILLIAMS, RALPH VAUGHAN

'What we want in England is real music,' said the composer Ralph Vaughan Williams (1872–1958), which 'possesses real feeling and real life'. When he first overheard the folk song 'Bushes and Briars' in an Essex village in 1903, he felt he had known it all his life, and went on to weave traditional songs into his music. His 'Fantasia on Greensleeves' in 1934 knits together the traditional song 'Greensleeves' and 'Lovely Joan' – a folk song he discovered in Norfolk in 1908.

WILSON, WOODROW

The League of Nations came into being on 1 January 1920. It was the idea of Woodrow Wilson (1856–1924), the 28th president of the USA. It was intended to have a Council of nine members, five of them permanent, an Assembly, which met once a year and a secretariat headed by a secretary-general. Although it was not appreciated at the time, there were fundamental weaknesses in its organisation and make-up. The USA did not join, as Congress refused to ratify Wilson's actions.

WITTGENSTEIN, LUDWIG

Wittgenstein (1889–1951) is the leading analytical philosopher of the twentieth century, and his influence has moulded philosophy since the 1920s. He spent many years teaching in Cambridge, though born in Vienna and having fought in the Austrian army during the First World War. He revealed that philosophical theories were as open to challenge as religious ones. His agnosticism left the door open to religious faith, which influenced the balance of the debate between religion, science and philosophy.

Ludwig Wittgenstein. ▶

William Wordsworth. ▲

WOLLSTONECRAFT, MARY

The struggle to achieve equal rights for women is often thought to have begun, in the English-speaking world, with the publication of Mary Wollstonecraft's (1759–97) *Vindication of the Rights of Women* (1792).

WOODS, TIGER

On 13 April 1997, Tiger Woods (b. 1975) did not so much win the US Masters as begin a new era in golf. Quite simply, his victory was so breathtaking, so record-breaking, so complete, that he instantly made himself the biggest name in golf and one of the major sporting superstars in the world.

WORDSWORTH, WILLIAM

William Wordsworth (1770–1859), who lived for most of his life in the Lake District, is England's greatest nature poet. His own experiences of nature during his long walks in the Lake District and the Wye Valley, and during his tour of Europe in 1790, are the source of inspiration of most of his poetry. Like his friend and colleague, **Samuel Taylor Coleridge**, his political views, at least in his youth, were radical, and he was an enthusiastic supporter of the French Revolution. In 1799, following a year of highly creative collaboration, he moved with his sister, Dorothy, and Coleridge to Dove Cottage. His major works, *The Prelude* and *The Recluse*, were published in 1805 and 1814 respectively.

WREN, CHRISTOPHER

Christopher Wren was the greatest architect of his time, contributing his expertise to a large number of buildings, many of which still stand as a testimony to his genius. He had worked on many constructions, most notably at Oxford, where he studied, before the Great Fire of London in 1666 left the capital devastated and in need need of large-scale rebuilding. Today, he is best remembered for his work on the new St Paul's Cathedral, which had been completely destroyed in the fire.

The interior of St Paul's Cathedral, designed by Christopher Wren. ▼

WRIGHT, FRANK LLOYD

The Guggenheim Museum, which preoccupied Frank Lloyd Wright (1869–1959) during the last years of his life, eventually opened five months after his death. The design, which was at first extremely controversial, was based on an organic spiral form and was realised in *in-situ* concrete. A metaphor for nature, the spiral is expressed both internally (as a cantilevered ramp) and on the façade as white, outwardly sloping walls. The inspirational space created by the spiral forms makes it equal as a work of art to any of the paintings and sculptures housed within it.

WRIGHT, ORVILLE and WILBUR

The first manned powered flight came in 1903, when Orville Wright (1871–1948) took to the air in the *Flyer*, built by him and his brother Wilbur (1867–1912). They achieved this goal after many experiments with kites and gliders. Together with Charles Taylor, they designed and built a 12–16 horsepower engine that would finally enable them to successfully lift their heavier-than-air craft off the ground successfully.

WYCLIF, JOHN

The radical theologian John Wyclif (*c.* 1330–84) was one of the first Protestants, and in the 1370s found himself questioning the authority of the Pope, the clergy's right to property and much else besides. When his opinions were condemned by Rome in 1377, he responded with a treatise arguing that the word of God revealed in the Bible was the only true authority. This was the beginning of the Lollard movement, the early translations of the bible into English and the spread of literacy among all classes.

XERXES

Xerxes (*c.* 519–465 BC), king of Persia, invaded Greece in 480 BC, by crossing the Hellespont on a bridge of boats. He defeated the Spartans at the pass of Thermopylae.

YEAGER, CHARLES

Throughout 1947 flights were edging ever closer to the sound barrier, until eventually, on 14 October 1947, Captain Charles 'Chuck' Yeager (b. 1923) finally became the first man to fly faster than the speed of sound. His *X1* reached Mach 1.015 or 1078 kph (670 mph) at an altitude of 12,800 m (42,000 ft).

Mormon temple in Salt Lake City. ▶

YOUNG, BRIGHAM

In 1847, Brigham Young (1801–77) led the Mormons to found an 'empire' at Deseret, now Utah; this area was not granted US statehood until 1896.

ZEDONG, MAO

Mao Zedong (1893–1976) was a founder and leader of the Chinese Communist Party. In 1927 their then-allies launched a military campaign against the Communists, who retreated to rural areas, where they gained the support of the peasants. After nationalist forces surrounded them in 1934, the Red Army retreated 6,000 miles to the north-west in the 'Long March'. In 1949 they eventually captured most of China and declared the People's Republic. Chairman Mao promoted rural development, equality and the pursuit of economic self-reliance in the villages, but his government was extremely authoritarian and up to 100 million dissidents may have died in his labour camps.

Mao Zedong. ▲

ZEFFIRELLI, FRANCO

After studying architecture at the University of Florence, Zeffirelli (b. 1923) took up stage design and acting, establishing himself as a scenic designer for Luchino Visconti's operetta productions in the late 1940s. He was assistant director on several Visconti films. In the 1950s, Zeffirelli won acclaim for his own lavish opera and theatre productions, gaining a reputation for his vivid eroticism and opulent sets and costumes. From the late 1960s, he was known primarily as a film director.

ZOROASTER

Zoroastrianism is the religion of the followers of the ancient Persian prophet, Zoroaster (*c.* 628–551 BC), who was born into a settled farming community.

Glossary

ANGLO-SAXONS
Germanic Angle and Saxon tribes settled in England from the fifth century, taking advantage of Roman withdrawal to set up separate kingdoms or provinces.

APARTHEID
Afrikaans word to describe the segregation of races in South Africa, based on a belief in white superiority.

ATHEISM
Unlike agnostics, who are sceptical about God, atheists tend to preclude the existence of a Christian God.

BOERS
Seventeenth century Dutch, Flemish and Huguenot settlers in South Africa, whose descendants call themselves Afrikaners. They introduced racial apartheid.

BUDDHISM
Religion based on the teachings of the sixth-century Buddha; followers believe in the destruction of mortal desires and anguish, and the attainment of happiness by following virtuous paths.

CAPITALISM
Economic system of private rather than state ownership as a means to employ people and produce food and goods.

CATHOLICISM
Division of Christianity, marked by worship of the Virgin Mary, repentance and forgiveness, and the power accorded the Pope.

CHRISTIANITY
World religion derived from the teachings of Christ, the son of God, who came to earth to suffer and die for his people.

CIVIL RIGHTS MOVEMENTS
Post-war political struggles for the right to equality or autonomy: black Americans; native peoples in colonised countries; women; homosexuals.

COLD WAR
Ideological and political tensions in the period 1945–90, between the Soviet Union and the USA, involving nuclear threats, arms races, espionage and destabilising governments.

COLONIALISM
Situation in which one country dominates another for economic gain, and imposes its own language and culture to control the native people.

COMMERCIALISM
Where artists, writers, musicians or painters create something they know will be highly marketable, but may compromise certain artistic principles.

COMMUNISM
A classless economic system of public ownership, where producing goods and food is a communal activity for the general good.

CONFUCIANISM
Chinese beliefs and practices based on the teachings of Confucius, relating to nature gods, imperial ancestors and the balancing of yin and yang.

CUBISM
Early twentieth century movement where painters employed two-dimensional imagery, bright colours and collage to represent the complexity of their subjects.

DEMOCRACY
Political system whereby a country is governed by the people, usually through elected representatives and sometimes through referendums.

ENGLISH CIVIL WAR
War between royalist supporters of Charles I and republicans under Oliver Cromwell. Charles had ruled without Parliament until 1640, and prompted the war in 1642 by attempting to arrest dissenting parliamentarians.

EXISTENTIALISM
Philosophical argument that an individual is sole judge of their actions since their existence is determinable, while no one else's is real to them.

EXPRESSIONISM
Early twentieth century European movement in which natural appearances were distorted in order to express inner emotions through art or narrative.

FASCISM
Authoritarian political movements, particularly powerful in the 1930s and '40s, where democracy and liberalism were opposed in favour of nationalistic ideology.

FEUDALISM

Social and legal system whereby peasant farmers worked a lord's land and served them in battle and in return received protection from them.

FRENCH REVOLUTION

Eighteenth-century popular uprising that saw the overthrow of a decadent monarchy, and French aristocracy stripped of land and power.

GAUL

Area of Europe during Roman times, covering what is now France and stretching to northern Italy and the Netherlands.

HERETIC

Person who held beliefs contrary to the teachings of the established church. Punishment for heresy in medieval times was often burning at the stake for refusal to recant.

HINDUISM

Dominant religion of India; Hinduism's complex system of customs and beliefs include numerous gods, reincarnation and a caste system.

HOLY ROMAN EMPIRE

Denotes from the thirteenth century lands ruled by successive German kings, which at its height covered much of central Europe.

HUGUENOTS

French Calvinist Protestants who fought the French wars of religion (1562–98) against Catholics, endured a period of co-existence, then fled from persecution in 1885.

HUMANISM

Belief from sixteenth-century Renaissance Europe in the individual potential of human beings rather than in religious values; often expressed through art and philosophy.

IMPRESSIONISM

Dominant late-eighteenth-century naturalist form of painting, in which an impression of a moment and the effect of light is captured.

INCA

Ancient Peruvian civilisation which dominated the Andean region from thirteenth to sixteenth centuries, until defeated and enslaved by the Spanish.

INDUSTRIAL REVOLUTION

Process by which Britain and other countries were transformed during the eighteenth and nineteenth centuries into industrial powers. The period saw the creation of many industrial inventions.

ISLAM

Religion founded in the seventh century by the Prophet Muhammad; Islam emphasises Allah's omnipotence and inscrutability.

JESUITS

Roman Catholic order founded in the sixteenth century, aiming to protect the church against the Reformation through missionary work.

MARXISM

Economic ideology framed by nineteenth-century thinker Karl Marx, in which feudalism, capitalism and socialism would be replaced by a classless society.

MAYAS

Central American civilisation which spread to Mexico and Guatemala; powerful from AD 325–925, after which it declined in influence.

MEDIEVAL

Cultures and beliefs of the Middle Ages; after the Roman Empire's fifth-century decline to the fifteenth-century Renaissance.

METAPHYSICS

Philosophy concerned with the ultimate nature of reality, of time and space, the mind and the nature and origin of existence.

METHODISM

Protestant Christian movement founded in 1739 by John Wesley, encouraging non-materialism, hard work, self-reliance and thrift to avoid poverty.

MOGUL EMPIRE

North Indian dynasty 1526–1858, of great artistic, architectural and commercial achievement, until overthrown by the British.

OTTOMAN EMPIRE

Turkish Muslim empire (1300–1920) which stretched to Hungary, southern Russia and North Africa, but crumbled after supporting Germany during the Second World War.

PALEOLITHIC

Covering the period from two million years ago up to the Mesolithic Stone Age, Paleolithic times saw modern man develop from earlier types.

PATRIOTISM

Historically a devotion to, and desire to defend, one's nation and way of life; today patriotism has taken on nationalist connotations.

PHILANTHROPY

Giving to others from kindness or charity, but may perpetuate poverty if means of production are not given to recipients.

POLYTHEISM

The worship of many gods in ancient cultures and modern Hinduism, as opposed to one – as with Christianity or Islam.

PROTESTANTISM

Form of Christianity taking its name from Martin Luther's 1529 protest against corruption in the Roman Catholic church which precipitated major splits in European Christianity.

PSYCHOANALYSIS

Theory founded by Sigmund Freud for treating mental disturbances often caused by unconsciously storing trauma or repressing sexual desires.

PURITANISM

Extreme Protestant group characterised by austerity. Opposition to sexual freedom and the divine right of kings brought persecution by Charles I, civil war and exile.

RASTAFARIANISM

West Indian religion based on Marcus Garvey's call for black people to return to Africa, where Ethiopia is the chosen land.

REFORMATION

Sixteenth century European movement to reform the Catholic Church; used by Henry VIII to separate the Church of England from Rome.

RENAISSANCE

Fourteenth to seventeenth century European intellectual and artistic movement ending the Middle Ages with its emphasis on science and exploration.

REPUBLICANISM
Support for a system in which heads of state are not monarchs; was once realised in England under Oliver Cromwell.

RESTORATION
Period when the English monarchy, under Charles II, was restored after the seventeenth-century civil war and Cromwell's republic.

ROMAN EMPIRE
Roman republic (510 BC–AD 476) which occupied most of Europe, the Middle East and North Africa, introducing its architecture, engineering and art.

ROMANTIC MOVEMENT
Late eighteenth to early nineteenth century classical artistic movement in Europe emphasising individual imagination, inspired by revolution and social changes.

SECULARISM
Belief that rejects religion, particularly in political or civil matters, and embraces worldly and material rather than sacred things.

SEXUALITY
What and whom they desire as distinct from their biological sex and gender identification determine an individual's sexuality.

SOCIALISM
Belief in classless society with equal access to education and employment through state intervention and ownership of major industries and utilities.

SUFFRAGISM
Belief in the extension of suffrage, generally to women and the working classes traditionally denied the right to vote.

SURREALISM
Twentieth-century artistic movement exploring many styles inspired by dreams and visions from the unconscious mind; Dalí is the best-known member of the movement.

TAOISM
Chinese philosophical system from sixth century BC; Ying and Yang balance the universe, the 'way' stresses harmonious existence with the environment.

Acknowledgements

The following authors contributed to this book: David Boyle, Paul Brewer, Alan Brown, Malcolm Chandler, Gerard Cheshire, Ingrid Cranfield, Deborah Gill, Ray Driscoll, David Harding, Brenda Ralph Lewis, James Mackay, Martin Noble, Anthony Shaw, Karen Sullivan, Jon Sutherland, Robert Vint and Rana K. Williamson.

PICTURE CREDITS

Allsport: 28, 44.

The Bridgeman Art Library: 12.

Christie's Images: 15, 49, 69, 75, 102, 104, 165, 168, 177, 204, 214, 239, 264, 271, 273, 282, 292.

Image Select: 5, 18, 25, 45, 53, 55, 59, 78, 89, 126, 135, 150, 83, 170, 181, 184, 200, 202, 208, 244, 248, 261, 269, 270, 283, 297, 306, 307. **Image Select/C. F. C. L.:** 121, 128, 129, 132, 173, 222. **Image Select/ FPG:** 60, 115, 120, 145, 175, 280. **Image Select/Giraudon:** 4, 54, 56, 57, 90, 117, 123, 136, 148, 151, 163, 213, 217, 219, 258, 268, 277. **Image Select/Ann Ronan:** 27, 67, 109, 134, 140, 162, 229, 242. **Image Select/Bibliotheque Nationale, Paris:** 87, 195.

Foundry Arts: 64.

Mary Evans Picture Library: 3, 7, 11, 14, 16, 19, 21, 22, 26, 30, 32, 33, 37, 46, 71, 72, 73, 74, 76, 77, 79, 82, 83, 84, 85, 86 (l), 86(r), 91, 92, 93, 94, 95, 100, 101, 105, 106, 113, 116, 119, 122, 127, 138, 146, 147, 149, 152, 153, 156, 160, 164, 176, 179, 180, 183, 186, 189, 192, 193, 196, 201, 203, 205, 209, 211, 220, 221, 225, 226, 227, 228, 231, 233, 234, 235, 236, 240, 243, 245, 249, 251, 253, 255, 302, 257, 259, 265, 267, 272, 274, 275, 276, 279, 281, 284, 287, 288, 289, 291, 295, 296, 298, 302, 304.

Pictorial Press: 38, 215.

Still Pictures: 23, 41.

Topham Picture Point: 6, 10, 13, 17, 20, 24, 29, 31, 36, 39, 40, 43, 47, 48, 50, 52, 61, 62, 63, 65, 70, 80, 81, 98, 99, 103, 107, 108, 110, 111, 112, 118, 137, 142, 143, 144, 155, 157, 158, 161, 167, 172, 182, 190, 191, 197, 198, 199, 207, 210, 212, 216, 218, 223, 230, 238, 250, 252, 260, 266, 303, 305. **Topham Picture Point/Associated Press:** 66, 125, 139, 178, 185, 187, 188.

Visual Arts Library: 141, 169, 224, 262, 300.

www.aldigital.co.uk: 130.

Every effort has been made to trace the copyright holders of pictures and we apologise in advance for any omissions. We would be pleased to insert the appropriate acknowledgement in any subsequent edition of this publication.

Index